The Economics of
Social Problems

The Economics of Social Problems

Julian Le Grand, Carol Propper and Sarah Smith

Fourth Edition

 macmillan
international
HIGHER EDUCATION

 RED GLOBE
PRESS

First edition 1976
Second edition 1984
Third edition 1992
Fourth edition 2008

Published 2012 by
RED GLOBE PRESS

Red Globe Press in the UK is an imprint of Springer Nature Limited,
registered in England, company number 785998, of 4 Crinan Street,
London, N1 9XW.

Red Globe Press® is a registered trademark in the United States,
the United Kingdom, Europe and other countries.

ISBN 978–0–230–55300–2   ISBN 978–1–349–92210–9 (eBook)

This book is printed on paper suitable for recycling and made from fully
managed and sustained forest sources. Logging, pulping and manufacturing
processes are expected to conform to the environmental regulations
of the country of origin.

A catalogue record for this book is available from the British Library.

A catalog record for this book is available from the Library of Congress.

Contents

Acknowledgements

We are first greatly in debt to Ray Robinson, who, with Julian Le Grand, initiated this book and co-wrote the first three editions. We would also like to thank the many colleagues and students who have commented on earlier editions of the book, helped us to find material and generally stimulated us into thinking about the topics discussed in the book. In particular, we would like to mention Nicholas Barr, Gill Court, John Hills, Damaris Le Grand, Phillipa Marks, Robin Means, Tony O'Sullivan, Randall Smith and Christine Whitehead. We would also like to thank our publishing editor, Jaime Marshall, for encouraging us to write a fourth edition.

Julian Le Grand
Carol Propper
Sarah Smith

Introduction

This book is the fourth edition of *The Economics of Social Problems*. Since the first edition there have been some changes among the editors – Carol Propper joined Ray Robinson and Julian Le Grand for the third edition, Ray left the team after that edition, and Sarah Smith has joined Julian Le Grand and Carol Propper for this fourth edition. While we have taken the opportunity to produce a radical revision and updating of the book, the basic approach to the analysis of social problems remains the same. Indeed, this approach – the systematic analysis of alternative methods of economic organisation within a set of substantive policy areas – is of even more relevance now than when the book first appeared. Since then, proposals to increase the role of the market in health care, housing, education, as well as congestion and climate change – discussed originally as possibilities suggested by academic inquiry – have assumed a central position in the policy portfolio of many governments.

As such, both the approach of the book and the topic areas to which it is applied are of considerable contemporary concern. The basic aim of the book is to introduce students to some key economic concepts and methods of analysis through the study of a range of contemporary social problems. It is our deliberate intention to move away from the more abstract theoretical approach that is a feature of many introductory economics textbooks and instead try to provide a book that emphasises 'learning-by-doing'. This is done through the simultaneous development of the relevant theory and its application to particular social issues. The success of the earlier editions of the book has shown this approach to be both popular and effective.

All the relevant concepts and theories are explained in the text, and so no prior training in economics is required. The book is well-suited to first-year economics undergraduates studying applied economics or public policy. Many of the suggestions for further reading take the analysis to a more technical level than that in this book and can be used to build on the arguments presented here. Our experience has also shown that the book is valuable to students who are studying social policy, sociology and politics, and who want to understand the rationale behind much of the policy intervention in their field, which is often heavily influenced by economic analysis. More broadly, the book should be useful to anyone interested in public policy without economics training, who would like to discover the contribution that the discipline can make towards understanding some of the pressing social problems that confront us today.

The problem areas

We have called the issues discussed in this book 'social' problems, to distinguish them from the more conventional 'economic' problems (such as inflation, unemployment and economic growth) that are usually dealt with in books about introductory principles. This is not a distinction we would seriously defend – all problems faced by a society, including economic ones, are presumably social problems by definition – but we feel that this has support from popular usage.

We would also like to draw a distinction between the social problems presented here and the subject matter of the traditional academic study of social policy. While many of the social problems we investigate form a core part of social policy courses (the chapters on health, education, housing, pensions, poverty and welfare), we also look at road congestion and climate change. These two issues are less often covered in social policy courses and yet are both pressing problems facing society today.

Since the third edition, several chapters, including those on pensions and on climate change, are completely new; and all the remaining 'problem' chapters have been extensively rewritten to reflect current issues, and to respond to developments in the economic analysis of those issues. What has not changed from earlier editions is the adoption of a common structure and analytical approach to all the areas studied. Since this is a crucial feature of the book, it needs to be explained in more detail.

Structure and approach

In the process of teaching the material on which this book is based, we have learnt a great deal about the difficulties that the study of social issues involves when used at the introductory level. In particular, we have found that students often lack a framework that would enable them to introduce some order into their inquiries about particular problems. For this reason, we believe it to be helpful to use a consistent approach for examining a range of problems. This is a key feature of this book: it is not a series of separate essays on individual topics or a discursive examination of 'some economic aspects' of each of the problem areas, but an integrated and systematic framework for studying each problem in a consistent way.

Broadly, each chapter contains three basic sections. First, we ask what society's objectives are in the area concerned. In most cases we decide that these objectives can be summarised conveniently under two main headings: the achievement of *efficiency* and of *equity*. Efficiency considerations refer to the provision of the quantities of housing, hospitals, schools, residential homes and so on that yield the greatest level of aggregate (net) benefit to the community. Equity issues are concerned with the justice or fairness of the way that these goods and services are divided between different members of society. However, while we concentrate on efficiency and equity, there will be other objectives that society will also wish to pursue. The promotion of consumer choice and the fostering of a sense of community or altruism, for example, are two others that figure in some of the areas in this book, and we discuss these where we consider it relevant to do so. Having so specified society's objectives, we can say that a social problem exists whenever the existing system fails to meet the objectives set for it.

The next question to ask is whether the private market – the dominant means of providing the goods and services that we use in our everyday lives – will meet these objectives. In some of the areas we examine, the market is the main means used (housing, for example); but in others, the market has been either replaced or stringently regulated (education and health care, for example). Hence the second main section of each chapter considers the arguments for and against the use of the market system as a means of allocating and distributing the good or service in question.

Then, in the light of certain shortcomings of the market, in the third section we examine the desirability or otherwise of government intervention. Although we consider numerous forms of public policy, ranging from minor adjustments in the market's operation to its complete replacement, we show that they all fall into one or more of three general categories: direct public provision, tax or subsidy policies, and regulation. But each of them is shown to be subject to the same tests of efficiency and equity that were relevant to the private market.

Those familiar with earlier editions of the book will find that there is much greater discussion of the actual use of market solutions – rather than discussion of potential market-based solutions – and much more explicit consideration of 'government failures' in the areas concerned. This reflects changes in economic thought. In recent years, there have been major developments in the economic analysis of government policy, showing how governments, as well as markets, may fail to achieve social objectives such as efficiency and equity. Although the theory of government failure is not yet as well developed as that of market failure, we have tried to give an exposition of the relevant arguments. In addition, there has been much greater reliance on market tools in areas such as education and health, where previously markets were not used. Throughout the book, we have emphasised that the task of the social or economic analyst is not to contrast one perfect system (market or non-market) with another, but rather to compare two or more imperfect ones to discover which is the 'least worst'.

The first and last chapters do not have this structure, since they are not concerned with specific problem areas; but they are none the less an integral part of the whole approach. Before students begin to study a particular problem, we feel it is important that they have at their disposal some general discussion of social objectives and their relationship to the operations of the market system. Chapter 1 is an attempt to provide this. Students will find it useful to look at this chapter before they consult the one dealing with the area in which they are interested. The last chapter, Chapter 10, is an attempt to pull together the links between all the previous chapters. In the context of a general discussion about the merits and demerits of the market and of government policies, it draws attention to the common elements in the discussions of each problem area, and to their wider implications. Again, it differs from the final chapter in earlier editions in that it now incorporates a far more developed theory of government failure: one that, so far as we are aware, has no direct equivalent in other economics texts.

We believe that this format has two advantages. First, it has the unity of approach that, as we emphasised above, is essential for the student to obtain a good understanding of the generality of economic analysis, and indeed of the specific problems themselves. Second, it does, in fact, enable us to cover most of what economic analysis has contributed to these subjects. Much of the debate between economists has been about market versus non-market systems of allocation. But the contributions to this debate are dispersed among countless books and journals. By bringing together the disparate strands of this debate into an integrated study at the introductory level, in the context of social issues of wide concern, we hope to make accessible to the maximum number of readers a systematic critique of market and non-market economic systems.

CHAPTER 1

Social Objectives and the Allocation of Resources

This chapter describes the analytical framework that is used in each of the subsequent chapters for the study of particular social problems. Those readers who have studied economics previously will recognise certain parts of the analysis (such as the theory of demand and supply), but are unlikely to have seen it incorporated within the general framework presented here. This is because we have endeavoured to explain at an introductory level the relationship between social objectives and methods of resource allocation, notably the market system. Explaining this relationship involves dealing with a number of theoretically complex issues and it is for this reason that most economics textbooks delay dealing with it until the intermediate or advanced level. However, the study of social problems is greatly assisted if some appreciation of the subject is acquired at the outset. Moreover, we feel that it is possible to retain an acceptable degree of theoretical precision and at the same time convey key elements of the subject to a more general readership.

Accordingly, this chapter proceeds as follows. After a brief consideration of the concepts of scarcity and choice, we begin by specifying social objectives in relation to economic activity. We suggest that one such objective will be to select the quantity of output for each good and service that results in the highest attainable level of economic welfare. We term this the efficient level of output. Another important objective is to distribute the goods and services produced between the members of society in a way that is generally considered to be fair or just. This we term the equity objective. Finally, we suggest that other objectives within the social policy area are likely to include the desire to preserve individual freedoms, the promotion of a concern for others or altruism, and the related development of a sense of community, citizenship or social solidarity. Having considered these objectives, we go on to explain the way in which a private enterprise or market system of economic organisation will organise economic activity, and to consider the extent to which it can be expected to realise these objectives. We conclude the chapter by describing the forms that government policy may take in its efforts to realise social objectives more fully – efforts that may or may not be successful.

Scarcity and choice

Economics is concerned with the way in which we use scarce resources to produce the goods and services that satisfy our material wants. Because it is through the consumption of various goods and services (commodities) that people satisfy their wants, we can say that these commodities yield economic benefits. Moreover, the amount of benefit enjoyed may be expected to increase as the quantity of goods and services made available for consumption increases. Thus, additional housing, improvements in the quality of education or health care, and increases in the stock of housing will all yield positive benefits. But unfortunately the resources of land, labour and capital that are used to produce these commodities are not available in unlimited supply, and so we cannot hope to produce a sufficient quantity to satisfy all our wants. The scarcity of resources in relation to the demands made on them leads inevitably to the need to make a series of choices about the quantities of different commodities that are to be produced.

Production of a particular commodity will therefore have costs in the form of the other goods that could have been produced with the resources it uses up. For example, labour time or machinery that is devoted to car production is obviously not available to provide hospital facilities or schools. Because it is possible to look at the costs of production in terms of the alternative goods and services that could have been produced, economists have devised the term *opportunity cost*. So the opportunity cost of producing cars is the forgone opportunity of providing other commodities such as hospital facilities.

In many situations, the market price that is paid for the use of a resource reflects its opportunity cost. Thus we may expect the price a hospital has to pay for the services of plumbers or carpenters to be the same as they would receive when employed in the construction of new housing. Therefore the price paid by the hospital measures the value of plumbers' or carpenters' services, not only to the hospital, but also in their alternative use in the house-building industry. But market prices do not always measure opportunity costs. In situations where society's resources are not being utilised fully, the decision to employ an additional resource in, say, the provision of hospital services, will not necessarily imply a reduction in the availability of resources for alternative uses. So if there is unemployment of labour, or if machines are standing idle, the decision to put them to work may incur a zero opportunity cost (as otherwise they would be producing nothing) even though the market price for their services will almost certainly be positive. In any discussion of the costs of resources used in production, the concept of opportunity cost should always be borne in mind.

Efficiency

When deciding on the quantity of a particular commodity that should be produced, we shall need to consider the way that both benefits and costs vary at different levels of output. In general, benefits are desirable and costs are to be avoided, so it would seem logical to try to select that output at which the excess of benefits over costs, the *net benefit,* is largest. When society has selected this level of output and has allocated its resources accordingly, we say that there is an *efficient* allocation of resources or, alternatively, an efficient level of output. In the next two sections we shall investigate a little more closely the level of output that will satisfy this condition, by considering the way that benefits and costs arise through the consumption and production of an everyday commodity – apples. Apples have been chosen because they are a simple commodity familiar to everyone, although this is only for purposes of illustration; as we shall show in the remainder of this book, the arguments can be extended to practically all commodities.

Benefits to consumers

If we look at a typical person, we shall probably find that the *total benefit* (*tb*) s/he derives from eating apples will vary according to how many are eaten. In general, we would expect *tb* to increase as more apples are consumed. However, let us look a little more closely at the way in which benefits increase; specifically, let us consider the benefits that are derived from each separate apple that is consumed. Most probably, this will depend on the quantity of apples that has been consumed already. If the person has had no apples at all, considerable satisfaction is likely to be obtained from the first one. But as the number of apples consumed increases, the person will tend to derive less pleasure from consuming more. By and large, we would expect to find that the benefit derived from each apple becomes less as more immediate needs are satisfied. Hence each additional apple will yield less benefit than the previous one. If we define the last apple consumed at any level of consumption as the *marginal unit,* we can say that the benefit derived from the marginal unit – that is, the *marginal benefit* (*mb*) – declines as the quantity of apples consumed increases. Note that to say that *mb* declines does not mean that the consumer does not derive positive benefit from the marginal unit; it simply means that the benefit is less than was derived from the previous unit.

Now we can extend this analysis beyond the individual consumer to society as a whole. If we define society's benefits as the sum of the benefits received by each consumer of apples, we can add up each person's *tb* to obtain the *total social benefit* (*tsb*). Similarly, we can add up the *mbs* derived by each person to obtain *marginal social benefit* (*msb*) – that is, the increase in *tsb* recorded as we increase society's consumption by a marginal unit. (Note that this process of adding up does require us to actually be able to add the amounts of benefit received by different consumers. Usually this is facilitated by expressing benefits, which are obviously subjective, in terms of a single objective unit of measurement such as money. However, as we shall see later, this procedure can present significant difficulties – especially in the areas considered in this book.)

When we are considering society's consumption of apples, we are more likely to ask what is the *msb* of increasing consumption by tonnes of apples rather than by a single apple; but while the scale of analysis is different from that of the single consumer discussed above, the general principles of the example are unaffected. In particular, just as we would expect *mb* to decline as apple consumption increases, so we expect *msb* to decline. Society will also derive successively less benefit from each marginal unit as the total level of apple consumption increases. This information is depicted in Figure 1.1.

In Figure 1.1(a), *tsb* is measured in £s on the vertical axis and the quantity of apples consumed per week – in thousands of tonnes – is recorded on the horizontal axis. The *tsb* curve shows that as apple consumption increases *tsb* also increases, but that the increases in benefit become less at successively higher levels of consumption. For example, compare the increase in benefit between 40,000 and 60,000 tonnes with that between 120,000 and 140,000 tonnes. These increases in *tsb* are of course the *msb* at each level of consumption; the pattern of *msbs* implied by the *tsb* curve has been extracted and presented separately in Figure 1.1(b). This time, the vertical axis measures *msb* while the horizontal axis continues to measure the quantity of apples consumed. The *msb* curve slopes downwards from left to right, showing that the *msb* declines as the level of apple consumption increases.

Costs of production

Let us now look at the costs incurred in the production of apples; that is, the value of the resources of land, labour and capital that are used up. The actual chain of production of even a reasonably commonplace foodstuff such as apples will be quite complex, extending from the farmer and the equipment and labour used to grow and harvest the apples, through the transport process, to the packaging and marketing in retail shops. It is not our intention to get involved in a detailed examination of all these costs, but instead to draw some broad conclusions about the way we can expect costs to vary as output increases.

If we take the typical firm engaged in the process of apple production we would expect to find that its costs of production increase as its level of output expands, for it will need to employ a greater quantity of resources. Hence *total costs* (*tc*) will increase with output. But how will the costs of producing each additional unit of output – the *marginal cost* (*mc*) – vary as output increases? Numerous studies by economists have shown that when we take a reasonably short period of time, although the *mc* of production may at first decline as output increases, there is a level of production beyond which it becomes increasingly difficult to expand output without incurring heavier costs per unit produced. This phenomenon is commonly known as *diminishing returns*. It is caused by such factors as the need to pay higher wages to induce people to work overtime or to attract new labour to the firm quickly, and to purchase new machines or to bring older, less efficient equipment into service as production increases. Therefore, over an important range of possible outputs, we can expect to find the firm experiencing a rising *mc*.

Now, in the same way that we added up the individual consumers' benefits to obtain social benefits, so we can add up the individual firms' *tcs* to obtain the industry's *tc*. Moreover, if we assume that all the costs of apple production are borne by the industry, its costs will represent the *total social cost* (*tsc*). Similarly the individual *mcs* can be added up to obtain the *marginal social cost* (*msc*) at each level of output. The *tsc* curve of Figure 1.1(a) shows the way that *tsc* is expected to increase with apple output, and the *msc* curve of Figure 1.1(b) shows the corresponding behaviour of *msc*.

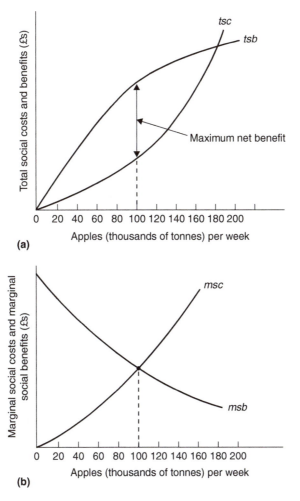

(a)

(b)

Figure 1.1   Benefits and costs of apple consumption.

The efficient level of output

Given this description of the way in which social benefits and social costs vary as apple consumption and production increase, we are now in a position to identify the level of output at which the excess of *tsb* over *tsc* is greatest – that is, where net social benefit is at a maximum. This will be the efficient level of output. This position is identified most easily by again considering Figure 1.1(a). The level of output at which the *tsb* curve is at the greatest distance above the *tsc* curve is 100,000 tonnes per week. At any other level of output the excess of *tsb* over *tsc* will be less. A glance at the corresponding *msb* and *msc* curves in Figure 1.1(b) shows that this point of maximum net benefit will occur where *msb* = *msc*. A moment's thought should confirm why this must be so: as long as the *msb* of a unit of output is greater than its *msc*, society will gain by more being produced, for each unit will add more to benefits than to costs. Conversely, if *msc* is greater than *msb*, society will gain if apple consumption is curtailed, for in this situation the last unit produced is adding more to costs than to benefits. Only where *msb* is equal to *msc* will it be impossible to increase net social benefits by changing the level of output. Hence an equivalent way of defining the efficient level of output is to say that it occurs when *marginal social benefit* equals *marginal social cost*.

As we said earlier, this analysis of the efficient level of apple output is not only relevant to the production of apples but to all goods and services. Hence we can define the socially efficient output of cars, health care, education, housing or any other commodity in exactly the same way. Overall efficiency is achieved when every commodity is being produced in its efficient amount. In such a situation it will be impossible to increase net social benefit by reallocating resources from one area of production to another, because the reallocation of a resource will lead to a reduction in output in the market from which it is taken (and hence a departure from its efficient level) and an increase in the market into which it goes (once again, a departure from the efficient level).

Thus, to say that we have an efficient allocation of resources is a powerful statement, as it means that net social benefit cannot be increased by a reallocation of resources and/or a rearrangement of production. This would indeed seem to be an important aim that any economic system should set itself. However, this will not be the only social objective. It must be stressed that an efficient system does not necessarily imply that it is a fair or equitable one. At first sight this may seem to be a strange thing to say, as we have defined an efficient system as one that produces the maximum net benefit for society. This might be taken to imply that it will be equitable, because a society in which there are gross inequalities of income – where Rolls Royces exist alongside widespread poverty, for example – is hardly likely to produce the maximum benefit for all its members. But such a conclusion would misunderstand the meaning of maximum net benefit. It refers only to the overall level of net benefit for a given distribution of income; it does not concern itself with the way that benefits are distributed between the individual members of society. The notion of equity is not dealt with by the efficiency criterion in the way that the latter is generally used by economists. Let us examine more closely why this is so.

Equity

The distinction between efficiency and equity can probably best be explained by means of an example. Suppose there are just two members of society – Adam and Eve – who produce and consume their own apples. Now assume there is a variety of ways in which Adam and Eve can organise their time and work, but that the amount of apples produced per week for which their total benefit is greatest is ten kilograms (kg). Therefore, following our earlier discussions, we can say that the system of work that produced 10 kg per *week* is an efficient system. Now there are a number of ways in which they could divide these 10 kg between themselves for consumption. For example, they could have 5 kg each, or Eve could have 6 kg and Adam 4 kg, or Adam 10 kg and Eve none. They are all possible combinations, and all could occur at an efficient *level* of output, but we would probably not consider them all to be fair. Questions concerning the distribution of apples between Adam and Eve are matters of equity and need to be considered as being distinct from the question of efficiency.

The distinction is stressed in Figure 1.2. On the vertical axis we measure the quantity of apples consumed by Adam, and on the horizontal axis the amount consumed by Eve. The straight line UU' is called the consumption possibility frontier, as it traces out the maximum combinations of consumption (and hence benefit) open to Adam and Eve. For example, at point A they both receive 5 kg, while at point B Eve receives 8 kg and Adam receives only 2 kg. Now, clearly, any combination, such as C (where both receive 4 kg and there are 2 kg left over), is an inefficient combination, because it would be possible to move to a point on the frontier where both Adam and Eve are better off. The same will be

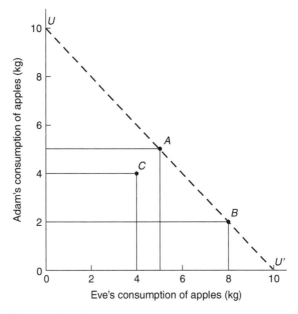

Figure 1.2   Efficiency and equity.

true for any other combination inside the frontier: it will always be possible to make at least one person better off without affecting the other, or to make them both better off. Only when a combination on the frontier is selected do we have an efficient solution.

But the fact that the solution is efficient does not mean that it is equitable. There will be many combinations lying on the frontier, but a number of them will involve quite uneven distributions. The judgement about the equity of these various combinations will depend on one's ethical views about the way that apples, or benefits, should be distributed between Adam and Eve. It is because questions of equity involve personal value judgements about the way in which benefits should be distributed among members of society that many economists claim them to be outside the realm of their professional competence. Economists, it is argued, are no better equipped to supply answers to these questions than are any other citizens. Accordingly, they have confined their attention to the allegedly value-free efficiency condition, claiming that questions involving equity or the distribution of benefits are matters for the political process.

However, one should always be wary of claims about value-free (and hence superior?) social science. Some people who recommend the pursuit of efficiency imply that this is a value-free, technical matter without apparently realising, or revealing, that their prior acceptance of a given income distribution (often the existing one) itself involves a value judgement. In fact, the principal difference between the objectives of efficiency and equity – in terms of their dependence on value judgements – is that there is greater consensus among economists about what constitutes efficiency (as described in the previous section) than there is about what constitutes equity; but this is a difference of degree, not of kind.

Consequently, the view taken in this book is that the economists' methods of analysis may be used to evaluate alternative methods of economic organisation in terms of their success in achieving both efficiency and equity; and, indeed, other objectives such as the promotion of altruism or the fostering of a spirit of community. Furthermore, while we shall always be careful to distinguish between the inevitably value-laden process of specifying an objective (be it efficiency, equity or whatever) and the largely value-free methods of achieving a given objective, it is relevant to note that economic reasoning may also in fact serve to clarify the definition of objectives.

To illustrate this last point, consider the two interpretations of equity often associated with the social policy areas investigated in this book. One of these is the concept of full equality: everyone should have equal treatment for equal health care needs, everyone should receive an equal education subject to their ability and so on. The other interpretation is in terms of minimum standards: no person should fall below a socially specified minimum level of income or consumption. Thus every family should live in a decent house with all the basic amenities, even though some families would still have better-quality housing than others; each person in need of health care should receive at least a minimum level of such care, and so on.

Now both of these objectives can be illustrated in terms of our earlier discussion about Adam and Eve. This is done in Figure 1.3. In the diagram, the line

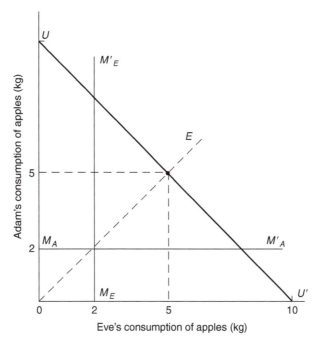

Figure 1.3 Full equality and minimum standard definitions of equity.

$0E$, running from the origin at an angle of 45°, shows how different total amounts of apples could be distributed equally between Adam and Eve, and thus indicates distributions that would satisfy the full equality criterion. With 10 kg of apples available it would obviously indicate that 5 kg each was the preferred combination on both equity and efficiency grounds. On the other hand, suppose that, in this two-person society, agreement has been reached specifying a minimum level of consumption of 2 kg of apples, below which no one should fall. This minimum standard objective is depicted by the two lines $M_A M'_A$ and $M_E M'_E$. They indicate that only combinations of consumption enclosed by the two lines to the north-east of their point of intersection will satisfy the minimum consumption constraint. And, with a consumption possibility frontier UU' defined for 10 kg of apples, they indicate a range of distributions on that frontier that will be considered as both equitable and efficient.

Trade-offs between objectives

There is one final point concerning the relationship between equity and efficiency, and indeed between any set of social objectives, that needs to be stressed. In the example above, we have assumed that the distribution of apples between Adam and Eve was independent of the total amount of apples available; that is, the distribution of the apples did not affect the amount of them that were produced. However, this may not be the case. Suppose that Eve did most of the work involved in producing the apples. If she knew that some or all of the apples she produced were subsequently to be redistributed to Adam, she might not feel inclined to work so hard and, if she followed her inclinations, the total amount of apples produced would fall. The net social benefit from apple production would therefore also fall; and hence efficiency would be less. So the attainment of equity would have reduced efficiency. More generally, in the real world, where the amount people produce may depend on the rewards they receive, there may be a *trade-off* between equity and efficiency; the single-minded pursuit of one may result in the other not being achieved, and vice versa.

The notion that there may be a trade-off between social objectives is one that many people often find difficult to accept. This is partly because such objectives have moral values attached to them, and the idea of trading-off different types of values against one another is one that is not always easy to admit. However, many such trade-offs are an ineluctable fact of economic and social reality, and have to be acknowledged as such. It is unlikely that any society or economy can successfully meet all the possible objectives that the society might have; and hence it is unlikely that any means of organising the economic allocation of resources will be perfect.

Other objectives

Because this book is concerned with the economic analysis of social problems, most of our attention is devoted to the two social objectives most commonly considered by economists: efficiency and equity. However, there are obviously other ends that the members of a society might wish to pursue. One is that of *freedom* or liberty: political freedom, freedom of movement and freedom under the law are all aspects of freedom that relate to some of the issues discussed in this book.

Another objective to which a society may subscribe, and which is of particular importance in the area of social problems, is that of the promotion of altruism, or the linked ideas of 'community', 'citizenship' and what in many continental European countries is referred to as 'social solidarity'. Much of our behaviour is governed by the pursuit of self-interest or the interests of our immediate family and friends. However, within most people there is a strong belief that to act in the interest of others or of the wider community, without any expectation of personal gain, is an honourable activity. Self-sacrifice by war heroes or by lifeboat volunteers, donations of blood to hospitals, or cash to charities all enjoy a prestige deriving from our recognition of the need at times to temper self-interest by displaying consideration for others before ourselves. It has been argued that society should endeavour to develop a system of economic organisation in which opportunities for altruistic or communitarian behaviour of this kind are expanded: a society in which the spirit of 'community' complements the individual pursuit of self-interest.

Again, it is important to recognise that it may not be possible to achieve all these aims simultaneously. A society where individual liberty is paramount is unlikely to be especially communal; it may also not be very equitable. In any social decision concerning the 'best possible' allocation of resources, there is likely to be a trade-off between objectives: no aim will be followed so far that the attainment of other aims is seriously damaged.

The market system

As we stressed earlier, wherever scarcity exists, society is confronted with problems of choice. A variety of ways have been devised, at different times and in different places, to provide particular societies with a set of 'mechanisms' by which these choices can be made. For example, in certain primitive societies, chiefs or councils of elders typically made decisions about what foods should be grown, gathered or hunted. They also decided how their members were to go about these tasks, and who was to receive the food and other goods produced by the community. At a slightly more complex level, feudal societies also operated on a similar system of central direction.

Until the late 1980s, two dominant methods of performing these tasks of allocation could be identified among large-scale societies. On the one hand, there were the so-called 'command' or planned economies of Eastern Europe, the Soviet Union, China, Cuba and North Korea, where primary emphasis was placed on the administrative planning of production by government-appointed decision-makers. Within these societies, the main means of production were in public ownership, and decisions about what and how goods were produced, and to whom they were to be allocated, were made via a government bureaucracy. The particular economic systems of individual countries varied considerably, especially in relation to the amount of decentralisation of power they displayed, but they all – to a greater or lesser extent – shared a common reliance on government decision-making as a means of co-ordinating everyone's activities. However, virtually all these countries have now dismantled their command economies (at the time of writing, just two remain: Cuba and North Korea). Instead, they have adopted the mechanism for resource allocation that dominates the economies of North America, Western Europe, Australasia and Japan, and newly industrialised countries such as Taiwan, Singapore, Thailand and Malaysia: the market or free enterprise system. This is a form of economic organisation in which the majority of allocation decisions are made through the ostensibly uncoordinated actions of large numbers of individuals and private firms. The co-ordination of activities within these countries comes about because each factor of production (land, labour and capital) and each commodity has a price to which diverse groups respond in a way that reconciles their separate actions.

Because of its current dominance as a means of economic organisation throughout the world, a major focus of attention in this book will be on the way in which the market system operates (or could be expected to operate), especially in areas where social problems arise. As a preliminary to those discussions, most of the remainder of this chapter is devoted to an explanation of some of the essential elements of the market system.

Let us continue to use the apple example for illustrative purposes. As in the case of all commodities, we shall distinguish between those people who buy and eat the apples (the consumers), and those who provide the apples for sale (the producers). In general, consumers comprise private households, while the producers are usually organised groups known as firms. Of course, a particular individual will be both a consumer and producer at different times; the categories refer to the actions taking place while performing a particular role rather than to distinct categories of individuals. By looking at each group in turn we can see how their respective, apparently uncoordinated, actions are reconciled by the market system.

Consumer demand

All individuals have a set of tastes or preferences that will determine, among other things, how many apples they would like to consume. However, a general preference for acquiring a commodity only becomes a demand for the commodity when the consumer is willing and able to pay for it. Hence the price of apples and the amount of income individuals possess, as well as their tastes, will also determine how much they demand. Also the prices of other commodities, such as pears, may affect the quantity of apples they demand.

Let us for the moment confine our attention to the way the demand for apples varies as its price varies, with all the other factors remaining unchanged. There is a certain amount of intuitive appeal in the proposition that a consumer's demand will increase as the price falls: that, as apples become cheaper, a person will be induced to buy more of them. If we then add up all the individual demands that would be forthcoming at each price we should be able to see how many apples would be demanded within the economy at each price. This information will be embodied in a market demand curve of the type presented in Figure 1.4(a). In this diagram, the vertical axis measures the price of apples per 250 g and the horizontal axis measures the quantity demanded in thousands of tonnes. The demand curve slopes downwards from left to right, showing that the quantity demanded will increase as the price falls. Thus 100,000 tonnes will be demanded at a price of 70 p per 250 g, while 150,000 tonnes will be demanded at the price of 50 p per 250 g. Later we shall describe how this relationship between demand and the price of apples is affected when the other factors that determine demand – such as income – change, but before then let us look at the conditions under which we would expect apples to be provided for sale.

Producer supply

We said earlier that production takes place within firms. These firms may have a variety of objectives that will determine the terms on which goods are offered for sale. Many economists have looked at the objectives that firms pursue, from both theoretical and empirical points of view. Some claim that firms aim to maximise profits; others maintain that they try to maximise sales; while still others believe that firms do not pursue maximising targets at all but are more interested in a quiet life free from the pressures of extreme competition. These are complex theories and beyond the scope of this book. We shall simply assume

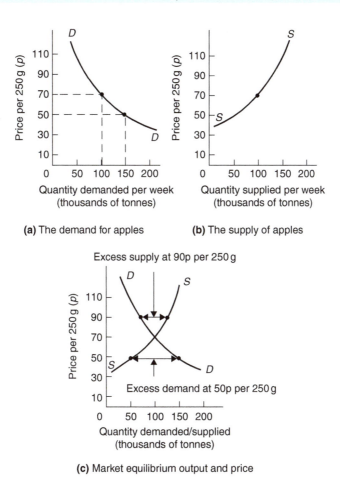

(a) The demand for apples

(b) The supply of apples

(c) Market equilibrium output and price

Figure 1.4   The demand and supply of apples.

that firms are interested in making some profits, and since the profit made on each tonne of apples is the difference between the price at which it is sold and the cost of producing it, the quantities of apples that firms offer for sale will depend on the price per gram they receive and the costs of producing different quantities.

As the price rises – other things remaining equal – the firm initially makes a greater profit on each item it sells, and therefore it is likely to be induced to try to expand production. However, it may be, as we argued earlier, that as production expands it becomes more costly to produce more if output goes beyond the level of production for which the firm had planned (this is likely to be particularly true in the case of agricultural products such as apples, where, for obvious reasons, supply is difficult to increase in the short term; however, it also applies to most other commodities and most other forms of production). So production costs increase because of the need to pay overtime wages and to use older, less efficient equipment to supplement that used in normal times. Hence firms may need higher prices to induce them to supply more.

By adding up the quantities that each firm is willing to supply at different prices, we can see the quantity that the industry will supply at various prices. This information, commonly presented in the form of an industry supply curve, is depicted in Figure 1.4(b). The curve slopes upwards from left to right, showing that a greater quantity of apples will be offered for sale as its price rises.

Market price and output

We have now established a relationship between the quantity of apples that would be demanded and supplied at different price levels. By combining these two figures we can see how much is actually bought and sold, and at what price. This is done in Figure 1.4(c), where both the demand and supply curves are shown on the same diagram. The point where the two curves intersect represents the price and quantity at which both consumers' and producers' requirements are met. In this case, consumers are willing to buy 100,000 tonnes of apples at 70 p per 250 g pack, and firms are willing to supply that quantity at that price. This price–output combination, known as *the point of equilibrium*, is the one that will be established in the market and it will persist until some outside influence disturbs the situation.

We can see why the equilibrium point is the one towards which market price and quantity will move by considering what would happen if the market price were to be above the equilibrium – at 90 p per 250 g, say. At this price, firms are willing to supply 125,000 tonnes of apples but consumers are willing to buy only 75,000 tonnes. If this price persists, firms will over-produce and stocks will begin to accumulate. The only way to rectify this situation is to lower the price. This has two effects: it increases the demand for apples and at the same time reduces the supply coming on to the market. In this way, the discrepancy between demand and supply is reduced until it is eliminated at the equilibrium price.

The same process will also ensure that price cannot remain *below* the equilibrium level. If, for example, the price was 50 p per 250 g, consumers would demand 150,000 tonnes per week while firms were only willing to supply 50,000 tonnes. In this situation, apples would be snapped up as soon as they were offered for sale, and shelves and stockrooms would soon be empty. The more astute firms would soon notice that a lot of demand was remaining unsatisfied at this price and that they could, in the following week, sell all they had to offer at a higher price and thereby make larger profits. Prices would therefore begin to rise. Once again, this would have two effects: it would reduce the demand for apples at the same time as inducing producers to supply more. The tendency for prices to continue to rise would end only when the equilibrium price was reached, as then demand and supply would be equated.

Such are the rudiments of the way the market system operates: the ostensibly uncoordinated actions, and possibly conflicting interests, of consumers and producers are reconciled by the way they both respond to common price 'signals', and in this way market output is determined. For simplicity, we have confined our discussion of the way the market system operates to the case of apples, but obviously the application is far more general. In each commodity market, whether it is apples or bread, health care or housing, decisions regarding the level of output can be decided by the interaction of demand and supply. Furthermore, this process is not only confined to markets for commodities. It also applies to the markets for 'factors of production', such as labour, capital and land. If one looks at the number (that is, the quantity) of construction workers or lawyers who are employed, and the wage or salary (that is, the price) they receive, one can see that demand and supply factors often play a key role.

The discussion thus far of the way in which consumers and producers react to price levels different from the equilibrium price has shown how their respective actions tend to move market price and output to the equilibrium level. These same reactions can also be expected to establish a new equilibrium price–output combination if a change in market circumstances renders the existing one inappropriate. Indeed, one of the most important attributes claimed for the market system as an allocator of both commodities and resources is its ability to respond quickly and smoothly to change. In the next section we look at the way in which it does this.

The market system and change

For the sake of continuity, we shall ask for the reader's tolerance and continue with our apple example. When the demand and supply curves of Figure 1.4 were constructed it was stated that they showed the way in which the demand and supply of apples were likely to vary as the price varied, when all the other factors that might be expected to affect demand (and supply) remained unchanged. We shall now relax this assumption and see what happens when one (or more) of these other factors change. We shall consider one example of a change in the determinants of demand, and one of a change on the supply side of the market.

First, let us look at demand. Suppose that, for some reason, the incomes of a large section of the population increase. We would expect that some of this additional income would be used to buy more apples. In terms of our diagrams, society's increased affluence can be conveyed by constructing a new demand curve to the right of the original one. (This is referred to as *a shift in the demand curve*). Thus in Figure 1.5(a) the curve $D'D'$ shows that a greater quantity of apples will be demanded at each price – at the new higher level of income – than at the previous level. At the original equilibrium price of 70 p per 250 g pack there is a new, higher level of demand – 150,000 tonnes. However, since there has been no change in the conditions under which producers supply apples, the quantity they are offering for sale is shown by the original supply curve (SS). So, at a price of 70 p per 250 g, they are still offering 100,000 tonnes. Thus we have a situation in which demand exceeds supply at the prevailing market price. Then, as we know from our earlier discussion, we can expect some upward movement in the price until a new equilibrium is established. This is shown in Figure 1.5(a) by the point of intersection between $D'D'$ and SS – that is, an output of 125,000 tonnes at a price of 90 p per 250 g. The 20 p rise in

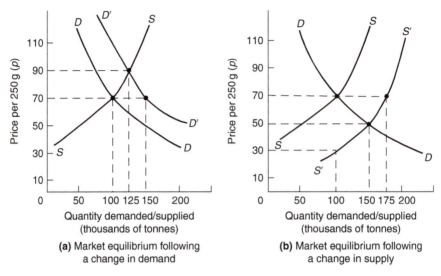

Figure 1.5   Change and market equilibrium.

price has induced producers to supply more and 'choked off' some of the excess demand that existed at the old equilibrium price.

Now let us look at the effects of a change in supply. Consider an improvement in the technology of harvesting apples that enables firms to produce them more cheaply. This may be expected to lead firms to lower their prices and still make the same, or even greater, levels of profit. Thus, at each level of output, firms will charge a lower price. This information is conveyed by the new supply curve $(S'S')$ in Figure 1.5(b). (Verify your understanding by checking to see that each quantity is being offered at a lower price than before. Where would the curve lie if a change in supply conditions led to higher prices being charged?). Now producers are willing to sell the old equilibrium output of 100,000 tonnes at 30 p per 250 g, or to offer 175,000 tonnes for sale at the old market price of 70 p per 250 g. However, neither of these alternatives is compatible with consumers' willingness to buy, as indicated by the unchanged demand curve (DD). At the new lower price of 30 p there would be too much demand, and at the old price of 70 p not enough demand, for the larger amount being offered for sale. Clearly an intermediate price needs to be found. Such a price is given at the point of intersection between the unchanged demand curve DD and the new supply curve $S'S'$ – that is, 150,000 tonnes at 50 p per 250 g. The new equilibrium price is lower than the previous one, but the lower production costs permit firms to produce a larger equilibrium output.

These examples show the way in which changes in the determinants of demand and supply – other than price – can be incorporated into an analysis of the way the market system functions. We have only considered two such changes but, obviously, many are possible. (Again, test your understanding of the way that changes in external factors may be accommodated by considering the effect on the initial price–output equilibrium of the following events: (a) an increase in the price of pears; (b) an increase in the price of fertiliser; and (c) a health education campaign pointing out the link between reducing coronary heart disease and the consumption of apples. After considering the effect of each of these events separately, suppose they happen simultaneously!)

As we mentioned earlier, the way in which the market system reacts to change is often claimed to be one of its main attributes. There is no need for a complex administrative system to make decisions about changes in the composition of output. This is achieved by the supposedly uncoordinated, individual actions of a vast number of consumers and producers, each acting in response to price 'signals'. If apple production becomes more costly, price will reflect this, and demand and output will probably fall while the production of some other good increases. The system is automatic or, in the words of the eighteenth-century economist and moral philosopher, Adam Smith – the father of modern economics – there is 'an invisible hand' at work.

The market system and social objectives

We have now discussed both the concept of an efficient level of output and the level of output that will be established in a market system in terms of our apple example. However, the link between the two approaches is far more fundamental than this choice of an arbitrary example might suggest. The reader will no doubt have noticed that the marginal social benefit and the marginal social cost curves have the same general appearance as the demand and supply curves. This is no coincidence. In fact, an essential part of the theory underlying the market system is that *in certain circumstances* the demand curve is an alternative presentation of the marginal social benefit curve, and the supply curve is an alternative form of the marginal social cost curve. Under these circumstances, the equilibrium output obtained through the market system will be the efficient level of output. Let us look a little more closely to see why this is so.

For any rational individual who wants to maximise the net benefit obtained from consumption, it must be the case that the maximum price that s/he is willing to pay for a commodity is determined by the marginal benefit (mb) derived from it. An individual will not be willing to pay a price greater than the mb received from the marginal unit because this would lead to him/her incurring higher costs than any benefits s/he might obtain from that unit. Similarly a rational consumer will always be willing to pay the market price if it is less than the mb obtained, because net benefit will be increased through each extra unit of the commodity consumed. In such a situation, a person will continue to consume additional quantities of the commodity until the mb derived falls to the level of the price. At this point there is no further possibility for increasing net benefit. Thus the price a consumer is willing to pay for different quantities of a commodity, or the demand curve, is defined by the mb curve. When we discussed the marginal social benefit (msb) curve we said that this was obtained by adding together the individual mb curves of each consumer. Similarly, the market demand curve is obtained by adding together all the individual demand curves.

So, if each individual *mb* curve is identical to the individual's demand curve, the *msb* curve must be identical to the market demand curve. From society's point of view, the price that consumers collectively are willing to pay (or their demand) is determined by the sum of their individual marginal benefits, or the marginal social benefit.

As long as there are many firms in competition with one another, the link between the marginal cost and supply curves can be established in a similar fashion. For each firm, the price at which it will sell a particular quantity of a commodity will equal the costs of production it incurs on the last unit of output as production increases, or the marginal cost (*mc*). If it were to sell a commodity at a price less than the cost of producing the last unit it sells, the firm would lose money on that last unit. If it were to sell the commodity at a price more than the cost of producing the last unit, then other firms could undercut it by reducing their prices to the level of marginal cost. Therefore, under competitive conditions, the marginal cost and supply curves must be the same. Further, if the marginal social cost (*msc*) is the sum of the individual firms' *msc* at each level of output, the result is that the *msc* curve and the market supply curve are also identical.

Thus the interaction of demand and supply can be expected to lead to an efficient level of output. Now this is obviously a very important prediction. We are saying that an unfettered competitive market system in which both consumers and producers are intent on maximising their individual net benefits will lead to the maximisation of society's net benefit. Or, as Adam Smith put it:

> It is not from the benevolence of the butcher, the brewer, or the baker that we expect our dinner but from their regard to their own interest. We address ourselves not to their humanity but to their self-love, and never talk to them of our own necessities but of their advantages.

It is the claim that a market system will produce an efficient allocation of resources that provides the major theoretical basis for preferring it to other methods of economic organisation. But because this claim is often obscured in emotion-laden debates between ideologues of the political left and right, it is important to establish exactly what it asserts.

First, it is necessary to recognise that the prediction that a market system will achieve efficiency rests on certain assumptions about the way in which the market operates. These have not been spelt out in this chapter because an examination of them, and the possibility that they will not be met in specific problem areas, constitutes a major element of the remainder of this book. However, to anticipate our conclusions, the reader will find that we identify a series of important market imperfections that can be expected to prevent it achieving efficiency in the areas discussed. Second, we must emphasise again that, despite its dominance in the economics literature, efficiency is likely to be only one of society's objectives. From among the others, we have selected the aim of equity for special attention. As we have seen, an efficient system is compatible with a number of different distributions of benefits between the members of society, many of which may be highly inequitable.

We have also mentioned other objectives, such as the promotion of individual freedom and a sense of community. Advocates of the market have argued that it is only through a market system that more general freedoms can be preserved. Under a competitive market system, no individual can direct or coerce another in economic matters, as individuals are always free to take their business elsewhere. So competitive markets decentralise economic power. Since the latter is often linked to political power, it is argued that their existence is an essential element in avoiding the centralisation of political power, and hence the erosion of political and other freedoms. On the other hand, the existence of markets may be antithetical to the aim of community. Many of the social reformers who were influential in the establishment of the 'welfare state' viewed the market system, with its apparent dependence on the pursuit of self-interest being the chief motivating force of the actors within it, as inconsistent with the objectives of community, citizenship and altruism they wished to promote. This belief is still held strongly by some present-day supporters of the welfare state, who maintain that government finance and provision of services such as health care and education is more likely to produce a sense of community and common citizenship than are private finance and provision.

So the ability of markets to achieve different kinds of social objectives in the allocation of scarce resources raises fundamental and controversial issues. In the rest of this book, we discuss these issues with respect to specific social problem areas, in a chapter devoted to each area. Finally, we return to the general question of market success and failure in the last chapter.

Government policies

The perceived failure of the market system to realise satisfactorily the objectives our society has set itself has led to various types of government intervention. The precise form of government policy in the areas of health care, education, housing and so on will be the subject of extensive discussion in the individual chapters of this book. However, because it is easy to become immersed in the details of individual policies at the cost of losing sight of the general principles they are meant to embody, it may help the reader if we specify at the outset the general categories into which government policies fall. First, there is government *regulation* of the market system. This involves specifying, via the law, what activities may (or may not) have to be undertaken. Examples of regulation include pollution control standards, rent control restrictions, compulsory schooling, and public health legislation. Second, a government may use *tax or subsidy* policies to deter those activities it wishes to restrict (by taxing them) or to encourage those activities it wishes to expand (by subsidising them). Examples of the use of subsidy policies that are discussed later on in this book are the provision of health care free at the point of use, and the offering of grants or subsidised loans to students in higher education; while examples of the use of tax policies are congestion charges and pollution taxes. Third, the government may seek to achieve the desired allocation of resources through *direct provision* where government or its agents own the providers of the goods and services concerned: public hospitals, public housing and state schools are examples of this policy.

Through the use of regulation, tax/subsidy policies or direct provision the government tries better to achieve the social objectives than the market system can on its own. But it should be stressed that it does not always realise this aim. In subsequent chapters, we shall be discussing not only the potential failings of the market system, but also the failings of government policies designed to rectify market failure in the specific areas concerned.

In the last chapter we return to the general questions of market and government successes and failures. We draw attention to the common elements underlying the discussions of the previous chapters, and show how economics and economic analysis are helpful in obtaining a fundamental understanding of them.

SUMMARY

- Most societies pursue a number of objectives in the allocation and distribution of resources. These may include *efficiency, equity, freedom* and *community*. It may not be possible to achieve all these objectives simultaneously; hence some trade-off between them may be necessary.

- The efficient level of output is the one that yields the maximum net social benefit; that is, where the *marginal social cost* of production equals its *marginal social benefit.*

- Under certain conditions, the interaction of demand and supply within the market system will achieve an efficient level of output. It may also promote freedom, according to some definitions of that term. However, there is less reason to be confident that it will achieve an equitable distribution of resources or promote altruism and a sense of community.

- Given the likelihood that a market system will be able only partially to meet the objectives set for it, if at all, methods of government intervention that may be used in an attempt better to meet these objectives include, for example, *regulation; taxes and subsidies;* and *direct provision.* The ability of these various forms of intervention to meet social objectives, together with that of the market, is examined more thoroughly within the context of specific social problems in the remainder of the book.

FURTHER READING

There are a large number of economics textbooks that develop some of the ideas contained in this chapter at greater length and depth. Individual students and teachers will no doubt have their favourites and so we have just provided some suggestions for the reader who is totally unfamiliar with these texts. Excellent textbooks are Begg, Dornbusch and Fisher (2005), chs 1–3; Lipsey and Chrystal (2004), chs 1–3 and Mankiw (2007); see also Frank (2005). Barr (2004b) provides an immensely useful discussion of the application of economic analysis to the areas to be discussed in this book; however, it requires a basic knowledge of economics.

QUESTIONS FOR DISCUSSION

1. If, as some people argue, 'there is no such thing as society', does it make sense to talk of 'social' objectives such as efficiency or equity?

2. The concepts of social benefit and social cost involve the summation of individual benefits and costs. What problems does this procedure pose?

3. 'The specification of an efficient allocation of resources, unlike the definition of an equitable distribution, does not involve personal value judgements.' Do you agree?

4. The market system is based on consumer demand. How does this differ from consumer need?

5. Will the achievement of an equitable distribution of resources inevitably involve inefficiency and a restriction of personal freedom?

6. Explain how you would expect government regulation in the form of price controls to affect the operation of the market system.

7. Do you think that reliance on the market system precludes the promotion of community spirit or altruism?

8. In what ways would you expect the development of large firms to affect the model of the market system presented in this chapter?

9. Consider the concept of freedom and the extent to which it is promoted by alternative economic systems.

CHAPTER 2
Health Care

Good health is one of the most important factors contributing to individual welfare. It is an essential prerequisite for enjoyment of almost every other aspect of life. A high income or a good education yield little satisfaction to the chronically sick. And, at the extreme, ill-health that leads to death will make all other sources of satisfaction irrelevant.

It is not surprising, therefore, that throughout the world considerable resources have been devoted to the maintenance and preservation of health. In 2007 in Britain, health care expenditure accounted for over 8 per cent of gross national product (GNP). In most other OECD countries, health care absorbed an even higher share of national income; in the United States of America (USA), for example, spending on health care accounted for a sixth of all economic activity (OECD 2007a). Perhaps because of the level of resources involved, health care has become of considerable interest to economists. On the other hand, there is a strong feeling among many non-economists that the role of economics in health is simply to count costs and to stop changes that add to expenditure.

One of the aims of this chapter is to show that this feeling is mistaken. The fundamental problems of resource allocation apply to health just as they do in any other area of life. What proportion of the nation's resources should be devoted to the maintenance of its citizens' health? What is the best method of achieving a given level of health care from limited resources? Should health care be provided privately or publicly? How should it be distributed between rich and poor, men and women, residents of the inner city and the leafy suburb? All these are economic problems in the sense that they are problems of resource allocation, and they are all therefore problems for which the economist's tools can contribute to finding the answers.

Many factors contribute to individuals' states of health. These include diet, working conditions, housing, public health measures (such as sewage disposal and rubbish collection) and the availability and quality of health care. Resource allocation problems arise in each of these areas, and to treat them all adequately would be beyond the scope of this chapter. Therefore, we shall concentrate on the last of them: health care. First, we look at the objectives society might have with respect to the provision of health care. Then we examine the possibility of using the market system to allocate such care: its advantages and disadvantages as a means of achieving the objectives. In the light of certain market shortcomings, we discuss the various ways in which the state can intervene, and the associated advantages and disadvantages of intervention. Finally, we examine recent reforms in health care markets.

Objectives

We saw in Chapter 1 that two important aims that have to be considered in any question of resource allocation are the attainment of efficiency and the promotion of social justice or equity. Let us see how these can be interpreted in the context of health care.

Efficiency

It is sometimes stated that an efficient health care system is one that provides the highest possible standard of care, regardless of cost. As an American doctor has put it:

> It is incumbent on the physician . . . to practice not 'cost effective' medicine but that which is as safe as possible for that patient under the particular circumstances. Optimization of survival and not optimization of cost effectiveness is the only ethical imperative. . . A physician who changes his or her way of practising medicine because of cost rather than purely medical considerations has indeed embarked on the 'slippery slope' of compromised ethics and waffled priorities. (Loewry 1980: 697)

This point of view has a strong influence on the way that medical practitioners actually behave; understandably so, since it is of obvious ethical appeal. Unfortunately, as a policy guide it is a non-starter, as costs cannot be ignored when making policy choices. The building of hospitals, the training of doctors and nurses, the manufacture of drugs and technical equipment, all consume scarce resources. That is, they use up land, labour and capital; resources that could have been put to other uses, such as building schools, training teachers or making cars. The 'best possible' standard of health care could only be achieved by devoting all of the economy's resources to it; hardly a wise course of action, since no other commodities (including those vital to health, such as food) would be produced.

Even within health care itself, the idea that physicians should always provide the best possible treatment regardless of cost makes little sense. Doctors who give their patients 'Rolls-Royce' treatment are likely to be taking resources from other patients. Keeping patients alive as long as possible cannot be a target for the allocation of resources, even within the health sector, for the survival prospects of one patient can only be increased at the expense of the survival prospects of others.

Table 2.1   Social costs and benefits of hospital beds

Number of hospital beds (000s)	Marginal social benefit (£ millions)	Marginal social cost (£ millions)
1	200	100
2	120	120
3	80	160
4	60	220
5	50	300

What is needed is a definition of efficiency that takes into account the costs of, as well as the benefits from, health care. An obvious starting point is the definition suggested in Chapter 1. There, an efficient level of production of a commodity was defined as one where the difference between benefits and costs is greatest: that is, where the marginal social benefit (*msb*) from a production of the commodity equals its marginal social cost (*msc*). A simple example will show how this might be applied in the field of health care.

Suppose we are trying to decide what is the efficient number of hospital beds to provide in a particular town. Imagine that we can measure the benefits and costs of providing hospital beds in terms of money (how this might be done is discussed below). Looking at these benefits and costs, we find that to provide 1,000 hospital beds would yield a social benefit of £200 million and would cost only £100 million. To provide a second 1,000 beds would benefit the town rather less than the first: say, by £120 million; and it would cost slightly more: say, also £120 million. To provide a third 1,000 beds would cost yet more – £160 million – but create benefits of only £80 million. Thus the benefit from providing each extra 1,000 beds, the *msb*, declines, while the cost, the *msc*, increases. This is as would be expected. Once the major needs of an area have been satisfied, the benefits from providing more and more hospital beds are likely to diminish, while with each new hospital built the resources available for building yet another one become increasingly scarce, and therefore more expensive.

These figures, together with their equivalent for the fourth and fifth thousand beds, are summarised in Table 2.1. From this table we can deduce what would be the efficient number of hospital beds to provide. The gain (the *msb*) from providing the first 1,000 beds is £10 million greater than the cost (the *msc*), so those beds are worth providing. The *msb* from the second thousand equals the *msc*; hence they are also (just) worth providing. However, the costs of the third, fourth and fifth thousand beds are greater than the benefits, and so it would not be efficient to provide them. Therefore the efficient number of beds is 2,000, the point at which the marginal social cost of providing more beds begins to exceed the marginal social benefits.

We can make the same point by use of a diagram. In Figure 2.1, the curve running downwards from left to right shows how the *msb* declines as the number of beds provided increases, while the curve running upwards shows how the

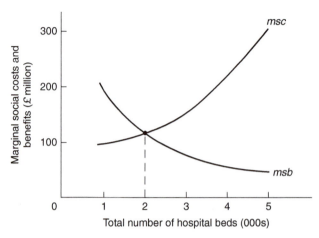

Figure 2.1   Social costs and benefits of hospital beds.

msc increases. The point at which the two curves intersect is the efficient number of hospital beds.

This is an example of how the concept of efficiency outlined in Chapter 1
could be applied in the field of health care. It is, in fact, perfectly general; in
principle, it would be applied to any problem of allocating resources in the area
(such as that of determining the efficient number of doctors to train, or of kidney machines to provide). But to use the concept in practice is not so easy.
Difficulties arise in measuring the quantities involved, particularly the benefits.

The benefits from a course of medical treatment are the value of the improvements in health that result from the treatment. Any attempt to measure these
benefits therefore requires information concerning the value people place on
improvements in their health. But this is not easy to obtain. Ill-health usually
involves a loss of earnings or the potential to earn, and one method of measuring
the benefits from a particular health improvement is to calculate the associated
reduction in lost earnings. However, this does not take into account the value of
any reduction in pain and suffering; moreover, it assumes that individuals with
no earnings or earnings potential place no value on their health. An alternative
is to try to find out how much people would be prepared to pay to reduce the
risk of their health deteriorating; another is to calculate this sum by looking at
the extra amount people are paid to work in industries where their health might
be affected. Yet another is to ask individuals to value different health states.
Somewhat problematically, the different methods tend to come up with different
values. When asked to value states of health, people who are well rate certain
states of ill-health – for example, being in a wheelchair – worse than those who
actually are wheelchair-bound. Yet responses are important, as valuing benefits
is central to establishing the value of particular types of medical intervention.

The fact that measuring the benefits from health care is difficult should not
obscure the essential truth that it is not possible to make reasonable decisions

concerning resource allocation in the health field without taking some view (however crude) of the benefits involved. The hospital administrator who decides to allocate money to heart transplants rather than to kidney machines is making an implicit judgement about the relative benefits to be derived from each. The decision to use labour and capital to build a clinic rather than, say, a school or a mile of motorway, implies that the benefits from the extra clinic are greater than those from an extra school or a greater length of motorway. The difficulties in measuring benefits do not invalidate the definition of an efficient level of health care as one that maximises the difference between benefits and costs, as that definition is simply a formal way of stating a social objective already implicit in most decisions concerning resource allocation. That being the case, it is worth attempting to measure benefits, because the alternative is simply to rely on what may often be ill-informed and arbitrary assessments. Given the range of estimates derived from different methods of valuing bene-fits, governments often set a value based on a range of expert advice. For example, the UK government currently uses the value of around £30,000 for a year of healthy life in deciding whether to buy new pharmaceutical products: it uses the value of £12 m per life saved when assessing the costs and benefits of actions to reduce travel fatalities.

Equity

There is agreement among most people that the health care system should be fair or equitable. Many medical care systems have developed with clear equity considerations, and in the post-Second World War period many countries placed equity, rather than efficiency, goals to the fore in their health care pol-icies. However there are, as always, different interpretations of what is the appropriate definition of fairness or equity. In Chapter 1 we discussed two ways of defining the equitable allocation of a commodity: one in terms of a minimum standard – everyone should have at least a minimum quantity of the commod-ity concerned; the other in terms of full equality – everyone should consume the commodity equally. Both of these have counterparts in discussions concerning the equitable allocation of health care. The first translates into a view that all citi-zens should be entitled to some *minimum level* of treatment if in need. The second translates into a broader objective of full equality, usually phrased in the health care context as *equal treatment for equal need*.

A third interpretation of equity found in discussions concerning the organ-isation of health care is that it should promote *equality of access*. What is meant by this is rarely specified, but one interpretation is to define it in terms of the costs or sacrifices that people have had to make to get medical care. These include any fees or charges that might have been levied, any money lost through having to take time off work, and the costs of travelling to the medical facility concerned. If these differ between people – for example, if some individuals have had further to travel than others – then there would seem to be inequality of access. Hence this interpretation of equality of access implies the equality of the overall personal or private cost of obtaining health care.

The market system and health care

In the United Kingdom (UK), the market system is used to allocate a wide range of basic necessities including clothing and food: it is not employed (by and large) in the allocation of health care. It is apparently believed in the UK – and in many other countries too – that food and clothing will be distributed roughly in accordance with social objectives under the market system, but that health care will not. The purpose of this section is to examine the basis for that belief. Is medical care in some way fundamentally different from food, clothing or any other commodity distributed through the market? Are there special characteristics distinguishing medical care from these other goods? Why should society's objectives be better achieved by non-market provision?

First, consider what the features of a perfectly competitive private market in health care might be. Hospitals would charge their patients a price varying according to the type and length of the treatment. Doctors would operate similarly, charging for consultations and treatment. People in need of medical care could go to the doctor or to the hospital of their choice, provided only that they could pay the appropriate charge or were covered by an insurance policy that would pay the fees. The principal argument for this system is that it would be efficient. Since people would be free to choose, doctors and hospitals who provided inferior treatment at high prices would lose customers to those who provided better and/or cheaper services. For example, a doctor who acquired a reputation for making wrong diagnoses, holding half-hearted consultations and overcrowding the waiting room would lose patients to one known for his/her medical successes and ease of access. A hospital that did not use cost-saving technology would have to charge higher prices than its more efficient competitors and would eventually be driven out of business. Thus medical practitioners of all kinds would have a strong incentive to improve their standards of service and/or reduce their costs.

Furthermore, there would be freedom of choice; people could choose the doctor, hospital and treatment that suited them best. Doctors and hospital staff, knowing that their livelihood depended on it, would be attentive to their patients' desires and preferences. The result would be a system of health care that catered for individuals' wants at the least possible cost – an efficient system.

These arguments are essentially the same as those used in Chapter 1 to demonstrate that the market can allocate apples efficiently. They imply that the *msb* curve in Figure 2.1 coincides with the market demand curve for hospital beds, and the *msc* curve with the market supply curve. Hence the point of intersection of the supply and demand curves – the quantity of hospital beds that would actually be supplied under a market system – will be the efficient quantity. Therefore, the argument goes, if the allocation of health care is determined by the market, the outcome would be efficient.

But will the outcome of market allocation of health care be efficient? Most economists argue that it will not. It is claimed that health care possesses certain characteristics that render market allocation inefficient. In particular, inefficiency in markets in health care arises because of *uncertainty of demand, imperfect consumer information* and *externalities*. Moreover, efficiency is not society's only objective: there are others, such as *equity*, whose requirements are generally violated in the market. Let us look at those arguments in more detail.

Uncertainty of demand

One of the features of health care is that the demand for it is likely to occur unexpectedly. Generally, people cannot predict when they are likely to want health treatment, and it is difficult for them to plan their expenditure and savings to ensure that they could always meet any unexpected medical expenses. This perhaps would matter little if the sums involved were small, but many forms of health care – such as those requiring long stays in a hospital – involve the payment of sums that can be very large indeed.

Within the market system, there is a mechanism for coping with the problem of uncertainty: insurance. In theory – and indeed in practice in several countries – the majority of families could have some kind of insurance plan or policy to help them cope with expenditure for medical care. However, there are two difficulties with private insurance for health care that may reduce its efficiency. These are termed *moral hazard* and *adverse selection:* they are also known as hidden actions and hidden information. In the context of health insurance, both arise because the insured individual knows more about his/her health than does the insurance company. However, both adverse selection and moral hazard arise in many other settings where one party to a transaction has better information than the other. For further examples of adverse selection as it affects decisions in education, pensions, housing and welfare policies, see Chapters 3, 4, 5 and 9; and for examples of moral hazard as it affects pensions and welfare provision, see Chapters 4 and 9.

Moral hazard arises because being insured against an eventuality makes an individual less likely to either prevent that eventuality or, in the context of health care, to try to limit expenditure once that eventuality occurs. In health care, if an individual is fully covered by insurance, his/her incentives to economise on treatment are virtually eliminated. If doctors are also fully reimbursed by the insurer for the treatments given, they also have little incentive to economise on expenditure. This may lead the insured to visit a doctor for frivolous ailments, and the doctor, secure in the knowledge that the patient does not have to pay, may recommend expensive treatment. More specifically, the doctor may recommend unnecessary tests or undertake more expensive surgical procedures rather than more conservative ones that have the same outcomes. The presence of moral hazard will therefore raise utilisation and costs beyond the efficient level.

Adverse selection arises when insurance companies find it difficult to distinguish between good-risk and bad-risk individuals. Bad risks are people who need insurance: in a medical insurance context they are those who are less healthy. Bad risks are more likely, at a given price, to demand insurance than are the good risks. With no way of telling a good risk from a bad risk, insurance companies will set their premiums to reflect the average risk of all the insured. As a consequence, some of the good risks may then not buy insurance, because the price will be above what they would be willing to pay. As a result, the ratio of bad risks to good risks among the insured will rise, claims will increase and the cost of insurance – the premiums – will rise. And more good risks will not buy insurance. The end result will be that there is too little insurance supplied: good-risk people will not have cover. Furthermore, bad-risk people will face expensive cover, which gives rise to an equity problem, as those in high risk of needing health care tend to be those with lower incomes because low income and poor health are often associated.

The existence of moral hazard and adverse selection will mean that the insurance market will be more limited than if the insurance companies had full information about the actions of buyers. So people may not be covered against the costs of medical care. However, it is worth noting that neither of these problems is confined to the health insurance market, and that public funding of health care also may suffer from moral hazard. In addition, there are ways in which governments can intervene to reduce these problems, without abandoning the use of insurance altogether. We discuss some of these later in this chapter.

Imperfect information

For many commodities, consumers have a fair idea of what constitutes quality. Even if they do not, provided that the commodity in question is one that is bought repeatedly, they can acquire knowledge of quality from their use of the good and employ this information to decide whether to purchase it again. For example, if the shoes bought from a particular shop wore out quickly, consumers would acquire this information through several purchases of shoes – and presumably would take their custom elsewhere.

But the situation for health care tends to be somewhat different. At the most extreme, before they have sought treatment, consumers may have little idea of what is wrong with them, of the extent of their illness, of the suitability of various possible treatments, and of the likely effectiveness of any treatment. Therefore they have to rely on their doctors for this information. Furthermore, people often need a particular medical intervention only once, or infrequently, and have limited opportunities for 'learning by doing'. In other words, neither before nor after their treatment can consumers easily acquire information that will enable them to make an informed choice. Instead, the supplier of medical care – the physician – is also the supplier of information. The supplier of care thus acts as the consumer's *agent,* informing the patient both about his/her illness and its treatment.

If the supplier is fully reimbursed for the treatments they give, they may recommend too much care. This is essentially another manifestation of moral hazard on the part of the supplier of health care. On the other hand, if the supplier receives a payment regardless of whether they treat a patient or not, they may recommend too little treatment. Which is the eventual outcome depends on the way the supplier is paid.

This being so, the claim that an unregulated market in health care provides an incentive to doctors and hospitals to provide good service through competition becomes of doubtful validity. If consumers do not know (and cannot find out about) the difference between good treatment and bad treatment, then they are unlikely to shop around for better service. Instead, they will seek to build a long-term relationship with a supplier – to establish a relationship of trust. Given this, consumers will not 'shop around' whenever they become ill, but will seek care from the supplier with whom they have built up the long-term relationship. It will be in the interests of the supplier to develop a good reputation. However, in turn, this gives the supplier monopoly power over the consumer.

The problem as described above stems from the fact that acquiring information is costly for the consumer, but, over time, the costs of acquiring such information may fall. In recent years there has been an explosion of information on health care that is easily accessible to the consumer via the internet. Several countries, following the lead of the USA, now publish detailed information – intended to be available to all – on the quality of health care providers. However, the requirement to publicise information does not mean that the information will necessary be helpful to the consumer. It may still be too complex for consumers to use (Marshall *et al.*, 2003). On top of this, a requirement to publicise information may give providers of health care an incentive to focus effort on activities that contribute positively to how they perform. But in doing so, they may spend less time on activities whose outputs are not measured (Propper and Wilson 2006). However, consumers may also care about these unmeasured outputs.

In sum, because healthcare is a complex product, even a long list of measured outcomes may not provide individual consumers with the information they need. In short, if a supplier can make a gain by providing inaccurate information (say, for example, by selling products for which positive, but inaccurate, claims are made), then the fact that accessing information is cheaper will not in itself remove problems of information asymmetry.

Externalities

A feature of health care that may create problems for market allocation is that it has 'external' benefits, or *externalities*, associated with it. The consumption (or production) of a commodity is said to create an externality when a third party, who is not involved in the decision to consume (or produce) it, is none the less affected by it, but receives no compensation or payment. If the effect is adverse, it is described as an *external cost*, and if it is beneficial, as an *external benefit*.

Certain types of health care, particularly those concerned with communicable diseases, can create external benefits. For example, if some people decide to be vaccinated against whooping cough, then not only do they reduce their probability of getting the disease, but they also reduce the probability of others getting it too. The vaccination has thus benefited the people treated (an *internal* or private benefit); and it has benefited others (an *external* benefit). Similarly, a hospital treatment that cures someone of a particular communicable disease confers external benefits, since it reduces the probability that others will contract the disease.

Since society includes both those who undertake any externality-generating activity and those affected by the externality, the total social benefits (or costs) of an activity are equal to the sum of the private (or internal) benefits (or costs) and the external benefits (or costs). Thus:

private benefits + external benefits = social benefits
(or costs)   (or costs)   (or costs)

The greater the size of the externality, the greater the divergence between social and private costs or benefits.

What are the implications of this for market provision? Simply that, if these externalities exist to any significant extent, the market can no longer be relied on to operate efficiently. Suppose, for example, that charges were levied for vaccination against measles. In deciding whether to be vaccinated, people would take into account the private benefits (the reduction in the probability of their getting the disease) and the private costs involved. Suppose a particular individual decides that it is too expensive, and hence that s/he will not be vaccinated. As a result, not only is the probability of him/her getting measles increased but so is that of everyone with whom s/he comes into contact. If there had been some way of including the benefits to these others in the calculations, the sum of the private and external benefits might have outweighed the private costs. In that case, it would have been more efficient for the individual concerned to have been vaccinated, yet, under the market, this did not occur. Hence, in the presence of externalities, without some government intervention, the market cannot be relied on always to produce the most efficient solution.

This source of market failure is more important where there is communicable disease. It has been argued that the external benefits from much of the health care provided in developed countries are relatively small. So the extent of inefficiency from this source will also be small. Nevertheless, this issue is an important one in countries where communicable disease has not been eliminated; and even in developed countries, communicable diseases can re-emerge (for example, tuberculosis in the USA) or new ones can develop (for example, AIDS in the 1980s). Even in developed countries, vaccination rates may drop because people believe the disease is no longer a problem, or because there is doubt about the side-effects of vaccination against communicable disease. For example, in the UK in the early 2000s, there was public concern over the safety of the MMR (measles, mumps and rubella) vaccination, given to children to protect them from this range of diseases. This led to parents refusing vaccination for their children, and this in turn led to a consequent rise in the incidence of measles.

There is another form of externality that arises because people feel concern when others fall ill, even if they themselves are not directly threatened. If they feel that the sick should always receive the medical care they need, the consumption of health care by the sick affects the utility or the well-being of the non-sick. If this is the case, then treating the sick results in positive externalities. The existence of these *caring externalities* has been used to justify the subsidisation of health care. In practice, it is very difficult to establish either the extent of these externalities or to put a value on them. It is therefore difficult to know how much intervention is justified on the grounds of externalities.

Equity

Earlier we noted that equity concerns in health care are widespread. Will a market allocation of health care be fair or equitable? It seems unlikely. We saw that there were three equity concepts commonly used in the health care context: a minimum standard of treatment for all in need, equal treatment for equal need, and equality of access or cost. In a private market, poor people may not be able to purchase the treatment they need or to afford health insurance. There is no market mechanism to ensure that everyone will be able to obtain at least a minimum of health care. Nor is there a mechanism to bring about equal treatment for equal need. Those with higher incomes are likely to purchase better treatment; and those who are healthier will face lower insurance premiums and so will buy more insurance and be entitled to more treatment if they do become ill. Finally, while the forces of competition might ensure that most people faced the same financial cost or price for each unit of health care, that price would represent a greater sacrifice for the poor than for the better-off (because it would represent a larger proportion of their income). Therefore, it could be argued that inequality of cost or sacrifice, and therefore inequality of access, would persist under market allocation.

The role of giving

A further argument that has been put forward against the use of a market system in health care is that the introduction of commercial considerations would destroy the relationship between patient and doctor – or, more generally, the relationship between the supplier of the service and its recipient. Titmuss (1970), the principal exponent of this view, claimed that to give (and to receive) a service where no financial remuneration is directly involved is a more satisfying form of human relationship than one involving direct payment for services rendered, and because of this is ethically superior.

The basis for the argument is this. To introduce a system linking payment to the quantity and quality of treatment provided is to relate treatment to the supplier's self-interest. This, it is argued, would make the system more efficient. But the Titmuss view states that even if there is an increase in efficiency, the social welfare might none the less be reduced by the use of the price mechanism. This is because its use diminishes the role of altruism and increases the role of self-interest. In a society such as that in the UK, where, ostensibly at least, altruism is valued more highly than self-interest, to decrease the opportunities for the exercise of the former while increasing those for the latter might be a retrograde step.

The Titmuss argument can be linked to a more recent discussion in economics of the roles of intrinsic and extrinsic motivation, advanced, for example, by Frey (1997). This argument recognises that individuals are motivated by both extrinsic rewards (those generally associated with the market, such as being paid more to do a task) and intrinsic or non-pecuniary rewards (for example, the pleasure of giving). Furthermore, these two motivations may be substitutes for one another, so an increased focus on extrinsic rewards may actively decrease intrinsic motivation. Thus paying individuals to do something they previously did for free may back-fire and lead to a decrease in that activity, rather than an increase. In the present context, paying individuals to give blood may have no effect, or even have a negative effect, on the total amount of blood given: it may simply make individuals stop donating blood.

Greater use of extrinsic rewards may also have the effect of changing the type of people willing to provide a service. When extrinsic rewards are used in place of intrinsic ones, they may act as a signal to attract people as service providers who are motivated by such rewards and to deter people who are motivated by intrinsic rewards. This idea is further examined by Le Grand (2006), who argues that the greater use of extrinsic rewards may result in a greater propor-tion of service providers who are 'knaves', motivated by pecuniary rewards, and a lower share of service providers who are 'knights', who are motivated by intrinsic rewards and a desire to 'do good'.

The importance of intrinsic motivation means that in some cases giving may be more efficient. If the good is given for free, suppliers have no incentive not to reveal the truth about the quality of the good they are giving. Thus, in the case of blood, donors will have no incentive to hide infections such as hepatitis or HIV: indeed, if their motive is to help others, they have every incentive to reveal this information. But if they were paid for this blood, they would have an incentive not to reveal such information. In addition, it might be that rather dif-ferent people are attracted to giving blood: not those who want to help others, but rather those who need the money (those with 'knavish' motivations). In this case, the quality of the product given would fall (as indeed it has done in the US market for blood).

Government policies

In the previous section we saw that there are a number of reasons why a market system may fail to achieve an efficient and equitable allocation of health care resources. Faced with these limitations, it should come as no surprise to learn that, in just about every country, governments intervene in the health care mar-ket. But the form of this intervention varies a good deal. In Chapter 1 we clas-sified government policies into three main categories: regulation, direct provision and taxes/subsidies. Examples of all three types of intervention can be found in health care.

Regulation

One strand of regulatory policy in health care is designed to ensure that the quality of such care meets acceptable standards. Doctors have to complete a lengthy period of education and obtain recognised qualifications before they can practise medicine; nurses have to follow specified courses of training and receive registration; post-registration courses are required for specialised nursing such as midwifery; drugs have to satisfy safety standards before they can be marketed, and so on. In the past, governments have felt they lacked the specialised information necessary to carry out these functions effectively, and so the responsibility for regulation has been delegated to professional bodies within the health service itself – so called *self-regulation*. Thus, for example, in the UK, the British Medical Association, the Royal College of Surgeons, the Royal College of General Practitioners and the Royal College of Nursing engage in different forms of regulation for their members. Increasingly, however, governments are making information on the quality of doctors and hospitals available in the public domain, with the aim of giving greater information to buyers of health care, be they insurance companies or the general public.

A second strand of regulatory policy is the control of prices. In health care systems in which patients are charged fees, governments undertake widespread price regulation to control the growth of costs. In the USA, for example, the federally funded medical programme – which meets many of the costs of health care incurred by people over 65 years of age and those who are poor – specifies, in advance, the price it will pay per hospital in-patient case according to the diagnostic group to which the patient is assigned.

Taxes and subsidies

In most advanced industrial countries, governments play a major role in the funding of health care. In OECD countries, government expenditure, on average, accounts for around three-quarters of all health care expenditure. Even in the USA, which is frequently held up as an example of a 'private system', public spending has accounted for over 40 per cent of health care spending for many years. Funds to finance health care spending are raised either from general taxation or from specifically earmarked taxes, often imposed on employers and employees.

In some systems, public taxation is coupled with public provision (see also the next section). The National Health Service (NHS) in the UK is a classic example of such a system. In its simplest form this type of system combines public funding, through general taxes, with direct public provision by public providers. Hospitals and primary care providers (known in the UK as general practitioners) are funded by the government, and services are, for the most part, offered free at the point of use. So because they do not incur user-charges, patients are subsidised at the point of use. In some NHS-type systems, some services that are not viewed as being 'core' health care have lower levels of subsidy. For example, in the UK NHS for opticians, dentistry and drug prescriptions the level of subsidisation has been reduced progressively since the mid-1990s. Nonetheless, over 85 per cent of total health care spending is still financed from taxation.

In other health care systems, subsidies may be targeted at specific groups – such as the elderly, the unemployed and others on low incomes – to decrease the price of health care supplied by private, fee-charging suppliers to these individuals.

The US system, for example, provides cheaper care to certain groups on low incomes through its Medicaid programme. Some countries also subsidise the purchase of private health insurance by making premiums tax deductible (for example, Switzerland).

Provision

The imbalance in information between demanders and suppliers may result in higher prices for medical care, over-provision and an emphasis on 'high-tech' medicine. Direct provision may counteract these tendencies. Several OECD countries run 'NHS'-type systems in which most health care is provided by the state. Examples include Norway, Finland and Sweden, the countries of the UK, Spain, Italy and New Zealand. In the UK, the government owns most of the country's hospitals through the National Health Service (NHS). Within these hospitals, services are provided by salaried doctors and nurses employed by the NHS. Similarly, community health services are provided by NHS midwives, district nurses and health visitors, all of whom are public sector employees. Primary care is delivered by general practitioners who are formally self-employed but, in practice, work under close NHS contracts and have the costs of most of their activities met by the public sector. In addition to these services, the UK government also assumes responsibility for undertaking public health and health promotion activities, such as campaigns about AIDS, drug abuse and heart disease.

   If the government provides health care for a large enough proportion of the population, it becomes the dominant or sole buyer of doctors' services and other inputs. It becomes a *monopsonist*. It can then use this power to counteract the monopoly power of suppliers to reduce the fees paid to staff. In some cases it can also use direct provision to alter the nature and the geographical distribution of the health care produced. In the UK, direct provision, through the operation of cash ceilings, appears to have limited the growth of costs relative to other systems.

Government policies and objectives: an assessment

Each of these forms of government intervention can be viewed as a response to the problems associated with allocation by the market. Thus regulation is an attempt to deal with the problem of monopoly and the problems of excess demand from moral hazard; subsidisation with externalities and equity concerns, and adverse selection; and direct provision with the power of providers. But while market failures exist, the system of incentives created by government intervention may also lead to inefficiencies and inequities. To examine these government failures we look at the effects of intervention in the UK health care market.

Regulation

Self-regulation is very common in the health care sector. However, it may mean that regulatory agencies operate more to serve the interests of the organisations they are supposed to be regulating than to protect the interests of the consumer. For example, it is argued that the medical professions' power over length of training has been used more to restrict the supply of doctors (and hence raise their incomes) than to protect the public against poor-quality treatment.

Price regulation may also set up incentives that reduce efficiency. If prices are regulated to limit monopoly power, prices in health care markets will not act as efficient signals to purchasers and providers. As an example, if prices for new pharmaceutical drugs are set too low, this will discourage innovation and the discovery of new treatments; and if they are set too high, this will discourage consumption of the goods. Price regulation may also set up incentives for inefficient behaviour as providers try to get round the regulation. For example, as many countries have reduced fees paid to doctors, one way that doctors have responded is to see patients more frequently – to have two visits when one might do, to prescribe drugs for a shorter period so that repeat visits are needed and so on. The consequence is that patients may have to wait longer or make more trips, but this cost is not counted by the regulator. Price regulation may also lead medical providers to under-treat certain patients. If a single price is set for a certain type of procedure or operation, providers of services will have incentives to select the least expensive patients and to turn away, or under-treat, the more expensive patients. This is known as 'cream-skimming' and 'patient dumping'. Regulators may try to be more sophisticated and set prices which vary according to patient severity. This will limit incentives to select patients, but as long as the medical provider has better information about the severity of the condition of the patient than the regulator who sets the prices, an incentive to select the less costly patients will still exist. If the less costly patients are also the better-off patients (which is often the case, as poor health is associated with lower incomes), 'cream-skimming' and 'patient dumping' will also have equity consequences.

Provision

When the government provides a good directly, competition is often either prohibited or limited by the size of the public sector. Thus, in the UK, although a small private health care sector has existed since the NHS was founded, it has been dwarfed in any size-based comparison with the NHS. In this case, the state provider becomes a *monopoly*. The lack of competition from other suppliers allows inefficiency to develop in production; because no competing suppliers exist, services will not be produced at their lowest cost. It could be argued that the extent of production inefficiency may be reduced by limiting the funds available to the producer; such as by the imposition of cash limits (as, for example, in the NHS). However, as the state monopolist has no incentive to monitor costs (since it has no competitors) it may be difficult to identify those services that are inefficient. So the imposition of cash limits will not necessarily guarantee that efficient services remain and the inefficient ones are squeezed out. The pattern of services that develops will depend more on the power of individual doctors and bureaucrats than on relative costs and benefits. Direct provision may also limit the extent of innovation as medical technology is generally costly (though it may have huge benefits), and politicians may give rather greater weight to the costs of the service, since they have to raise taxes to pay for these, than the difference between benefits and costs.

In response to the problems arising from a lack of prices in public provision, governments often resort to the use of targets in order to increase the provision of certain services. An example from the NHS is the use of waiting list targets to reduce long waiting times. But targets themselves may have undesired effects. They may increase output of the activity that is being targeted, but they may also lead to a reduction in other activities that are not subject to targets, or to employees putting in effort 'fiddling the figures' in order to appear to meet the target. This phenomenon is not confined to health services; most famously, it arose in centrally planned economies when state-owned firms were given production targets (Smith 1995).

If public provision is viewed as being of low quality, individuals will try to seek ways round the limits. So, for example, as queues for NHS treatment in the UK grew in the late 1990s, individuals increased their purchases of private health insurance, which entitled them to see doctors on a private basis without having to queue. In Italy, another country with an NHS-type health care system, supplementary insurance pays for doctors not employed in the national system. In public systems which are very cash constrained, individuals pay doctors 'under the counter' to increase the quality of the health care they provide.

Subsidies

As subsidies may have considerable distortionary effects, we look separately at their impact on efficiency and equity.

Subsidies and efficiency

Subsidisation reduces the price of a good or service to the buyer or user. This may be an efficient way of dealing with the problem of externalities or of meeting equity goals. However, if the price is reduced too far, subsidisation may result in either *over-consumption* or to *excess demand*. We illustrate this by means of Figure 2.2. In this diagram, the marginal social cost (*msc*) of producing the health care is given by the line marked *msc* (as the line is flat it is assumed the good is produced at constant marginal social cost). The subsidised price, marked by the line *mpc*, is below this cost. The subsidy per unit sold is the distance between the *msc* and *mpc* curves. The marginal social benefit (that is, internal plus external benefits) is as given by the line marked *msb*. It is assumed, as above, that the marginal benefit of each new unit consumed is lower than that of the previous one. If the consumer acts to maximise total benefit, s/he will consume where private marginal cost equals private marginal benefit. This is at Q' units in Figure 2.1. However, because of the subsidy, the true cost per unit produced is higher than the perceived private cost. The socially efficient level of consumption is at Q*. Thus there will be over-consumption of the good.

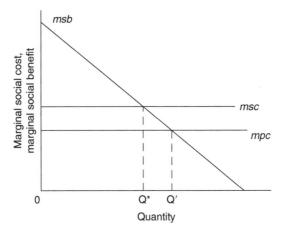

Figure 2.2   The effect of subsidisation on the quantity of care demanded.

The larger the subsidy for any given *msb* schedule, the higher the over-consumption. In the case of a good provided free – for example, health care in the NHS – the consumer will try to expand his/her consumption to the point where the benefit from the last unit of the service consumed is zero (as at this point $mpb = mpc = 0$). In this case, the price mechanism no longer serves as a *rationing* device. Unless the government expands supply up to this point (which would be both inefficient and extremely costly), there is a situation of *excess demand*. More health care is demanded than can be supplied.

In this case, the government must use some other rationing device to determine who gets what. In NHS-type systems, two forms of rationing device are used. The first is the queue (the wait to see a doctor in a surgery or in the outpatient department of a hospital); and the second is the waiting list.

Being in a queue takes up time for the demander of care. Waiting in a queue is least costly to those who have a great deal of free time and most costly to those with little free time. Unless the amount of free time demanders have is in inverse proportion to their willingness to pay, there is no guarantee that those who get the health care first are those who are willing to pay the most. Thus the good is not received by those who value it most highly, so the allocation is not efficient. There are people who would be willing to pay more but cannot get the good. The outcome may also not be desirable on equitable grounds. People who are in lower-paid jobs often cannot take time off work to attend the doctor's surgery. They may also receive sick pay for less time than people in higher-paid jobs. Thus the people who face the highest cost are amongst the poorer segments of the population.

Individuals requiring treatment are referred to a waiting list by their doctor. The problem with delegating the decisions about 'who gets what' to health care professionals is that, in making those decisions, the latter may pursue their own interests as well as those of the patient. It is argued, for example, that doctors may treat 'interesting' cases more rapidly than less interesting ones. In this case, people requiring 'uninteresting' treatment are more likely to be on the waiting list than those whose cases are 'interesting', and it is not necessarily these latter people who want or need treatment most. Another problem is that those people with the right contacts or who know how to 'play the system' may be able to get to the head of the queue first. Again, such allocation is unlikely to be either efficient or just.

In the UK, the government both subsidises and produces health care. As health care services are not sold, the incomes of producers do not depend on meeting consumers' wishes. The outcome that emerges, and its efficiency, depends on the way in which producers are reimbursed. If providers are paid per person using them, they have an incentive to maximise the numbers of people on their register, but to minimise the amount of time spent with each person. In other words, they have an incentive to 'under-doctor'. In contrast, if doctors are paid according to the amount of treatment they provide, and patients pay nothing at point of demand, they have an incentive to 'over-doctor'. (This is exactly the same incentive as given by moral hazard in a private insurance system.) Both systems of reimbursement are thus likely to be inefficient, but, under the first system, there will be under-consumption, and, in the second, over-consumption, of health care.

Subsidies and equity

Subsidies may be used to lower prices of medical care or to increase the rewards from provision of care to achieve equity goals. To improve access by the poor, they may be used to lower the price of care. To promote geographical equity, governments may pay for the medical education of, or pay higher wages to, doctors to work in areas that have too few doctors – for example, remote or rural areas.

Whether such subsidies are an effective way of promoting equity will depend on the type of subsidy and on the definition of equity. Some subsidy schemes, such as Medicaid in the USA, involve a means test; that is, they are confined to people with income ('means') below a certain level. Others, such as the NHS, are universal; that is, all those who need treatment receive it free or at a heavily subsidised price. Both universal and means-tested subsidies can be justified on the grounds that they promote equity defined in terms of minimum standards, as they both reduce the price of medical care to the poor and therefore also encourage its consumption. However, it is often argued that universal subsidies will be the more successful of the two in this respect. Means tests are often regarded by those eligible as stigmatising and socially humiliating; moreover, the procedures involved in decisions over eligibility are often complex and time-consuming. Hence the take-up of the service will not be as large as it would have been had there not been a means test.

On the other hand, means tests are possibly superior to universal subsidies in meeting the other interpretations of equity – equal treatment for equal need and equality of access or cost. Because means tests imply a lower financial cost of health care to the poor, they therefore make the sacrifice involved more in line with that incurred by the rich (thus creating greater equality of access) and perhaps also thereby increase the use by the poor of the service relative to that of the rich (thus promoting greater equality of treatment).

Marrying market incentives with government financing and provision

We have seen that both market provision and government intervention may have efficiency and equity failures. Recognition of this has led to a worldwide search for solutions that draw on the benefits of both market and government allocation mechanisms for health care. The aim of recent reforms has been to introduce *incentive* structures that will counteract some of the failures of either market provision or government intervention. These incentive structures are designed to increase the role for market-based solutions. However, they take different forms depending on the system in place.

One type of reform is to introduce market incentives in the provider community into systems in which government both funds and provides care. The leading example of such reforms is the 'quasi-market reforms' of the UK NHS. Under these reforms, the provider and purchaser functions of the hospital service were separated and a market was created on the supply side. Funding of health care remained public, and providers, both public and private, would compete for the budgets of publicly financed purchasers. Purchasers were to seek out providers, compare prices and quality, and place contracts with the most efficient providers. Some purchasers could keep the surplus from their budgets, thus giving them extra incentives to find good providers. The intention was to reap the efficiency gains of the introduction of competition on the supply side – lower costs and greater responsiveness to patients – without sacrificing the equity goals met through tax-provided finance.

Separating providers from purchasers has had some real effects. Studies have shown that where there was the most competition between providers, prices fell. Purchasers who were able to keep surpluses negotiated lower prices than those who were not. Waiting times for the patients of these purchasers also fell. But the reforms were also limited by the reluctance of purchasers to undertake actions to close inefficient hospitals, and by political concern that the reforms led to better treatment of patients of certain purchasers than others. However, despite a period in which the government backed away from market-based reforms, they were reintroduced in the mid-2000s. This time, they also included the use of regulated prices and the encouragement of entry into the market by non-public providers. Price regulation is intended to ensure that hospitals do not compete by reducing prices and therefore also quality: the entry of private providers is intended to allow more competition between providers.

A second market-based reform is greater cost-sharing by patients at the point of demand. This both makes patients more aware of the costs of the services and reduces government expenditure, because subsidies have fallen and because it reduces the demand for services. Other countries have introduced competition at the level of insurance purchase rather than at the time services are used. Allowing insurers to compete with one another is intended to increase the efficiency of service provision. Insurance market competition has been most prominent in the USA from the 1980s onwards. Prior to the 1980s in the USA, most health care was provided on a *fee-for-service* basis, in which suppliers were reimbursed for each item of care supplied. Generally, finance for this care was provided by insurers who were not the suppliers of health care, and were known as *third-party insurers*. The moral hazard in this system led to rising levels of state subsidy for the aged and the poor, as well as a rapid growth in private expenditure. From the 1980s onwards, lower-priced managed care plans were introduced. These plans offered lower prices but also restricted consumer choice. One example is the *Health Maintenance Organisation* (the HMO). In an HMO, a group of doctors provide care for their patients at a fixed price, paid in advance by an employer or by the patient. Essentially, the insurer and provider roles are merged, thus reducing the moral hazard problem. This form of organisation is not unlike that for GPs in the UK, except that in the UK the government, rather than the patient or private insurer, pays the annual fee.

These reforms did cut costs. But they also brought about equity concerns: that increased use of cost sharing hits the poorest the hardest; aggressive screening of insurance buyers reduces cover available to less healthy groups; and the amount of care may be limited.

Other countries also attempted to increase competition between insurers (for example, Germany, the Netherlands). However, in insurer reforms in Western Europe, concerns over equity – that competition would lead sick people to be denied coverage or discouraged from enrolling in particular plans – limited the extent of competition. For example, in German reforms, plans cannot be contracted selectively with particular providers, and companies are required to pay doctors on the same scale. In the Netherlands, payments to plans were adjusted for the health risk of employees, so limiting the incentives for competition between insurers for individuals who would cost them less. These limits illustrate the trade-off between equity and efficiency: in order to meet equity goals, competition between insurers has to be limited, and so the incentives for efficiency gains are muted.

SUMMARY

▪ There are two principal objectives with respect to health care: *efficiency* and *equity*. An efficient level of health care is one where the *marginal social cost* of further care equals the *marginal social benefit.* Equity can be defined in a number of ways in the context of health care: the most common definitions are a *minimum standard* of treatment; *equal treatment for equal need*; and *equality of access or cost.*

▪ Health care has certain characteristics that in general mean it will not be allocated efficiently by a market system. These include *uncertain demand, asymmetry of information*, and *externalities*. Nor is the market likely to achieve equity under any of its interpretations.

▪ As a result, government intervention in health care is high in all developed countries.

▪ The government may intervene through *regulation, taxes/subsidies* and *provision*. Under a national health service system, such as the UK NHS, all three are used. In the USA, there is both regulation and use of subsidies. Regulation is a way of dealing with imperfect consumer information; subsidies are a way of dealing with lack of insurance markets arising from asymmetry of information, externalities and equity failures; provision is also a way of dealing with lack of equity.

■ Each system has its own problems. Thus provision can create inefficiency because of the absence of competition; regulation often services the interests of the regulated; and unrestricted subsidies can lead to over-use and an inequitable distribution of public expenditure.

■ In response to these failures, recent changes adopted in several health care systems have sought to increase the role of the market in health care while trying also to ensure that equity goals are not affected. In NHS systems, this has led to the introduction of competition between public and, in some cases, private suppliers. In insurance systems, this has led to the promotion of greater competition between insurers.

FURTHER READING

For a reader with some economics background, Barr (2004b) provides a more technical discussion of the issues in the provision of health care raised here, with a focus on the UK. A discussion of the US system for the same audience can be found in Stiglitz (2000).

There are many health economics textbooks. Two texts that assume relatively little prior economics knowledge are Folland et al. (2001) and McPake et al. (2002), the latter of which takes an explicitly international perspective. For a textbook on methods of economic evaluation, aimed at a general audience, see Drummond et al. (2005).

For an overview of a range of topics central to the economics of health care, aimed at those with some (but not graduate level) economics, see Jones (2006). For those with a first degree in economics, an in-depth discussion of key issues in the economics of health is provided by Culyer and Newhouse (2000). For an in-depth discussion of ethical issues aimed at a similar market, see Dolan and Olsen (2002).

Cutler (2002) provides an accessible review of international healthcare concerns and reforms from 1945 onwards. Oliver (2005) provides an overview of the developments in the NHS since its inception, for those with no economics background, with a focus on equity.

Propper et al. (forthcoming) and Le Grand (2007) provide non-technical discussions of the case for greater competition in UK health care. For those with economics knowledge, Ellis (1998) provides an exposition of the incentives given by pricing systems for the differential treatment of patients. Propper and Wilson (2006) provides a non-technical discussion of issues in the use of performance management in health care. For the same audience, Marshall et al. (2003) review the use of public reports on quality.

Up-to-date comparative data on spending on health care systems are regularly published by the OECD (see, for example, www.oecd.org/health/healthataglance).

QUESTIONS FOR DISCUSSION

1. Should blood donors be paid? Should users of donated blood be charged?

2. Should a doctor's aim be 'optimisation of survival' or 'cost-effective medicine'?

3. What is an equitable distribution of health care?

4. 'To place a monetary value on human life is both immoral and impossible.' Discuss.

5. Discuss the various ways in which the benefits from health care can be measured.

6. 'In the market, medical care will tend to be under-supplied relative to the efficient level.' 'Profit-maximising doctors have an incentive to over-supply treatment.' Reconcile these two statements.

7. Are there any reasons, on the grounds of efficiency, for replacing the National Health Service by a system of private health insurance?

8. 'Food is as essential to health as visits to the doctor, yet under the NHS the latter is provided free while the former is not.' Is this an argument against the National Health Service, for a National Food Service, or neither?

9. Will paying doctors by results improve the quality of health care?

10. Why may reducing the price of care to zero not achieve equal access costs for all?

CHAPTER 3

Education

Education matters for many reasons. At its most basic, it provides skills people need in everyday life. At a higher level, education systems are designed to equip people with skills for their adult life, generating both economic and non-economic benefits both to the individual and to society. It is a striking fact that, in all developed and many developing countries, both primary and secondary schooling are compulsory and substantially publicly funded. In almost all developed countries, government funding and provision of higher education is also widespread. In the UK, for example, in 2004, the state funded education to the tune of £63 billion a year, equal to one pound in eight of all public spending, just over 5 per cent of GDP, and second only to health in the scale of public provision. The British state also employed over 1 million people in the provision of education. Spending levels in other OECD countries are comparable or higher. The USA and Denmark top the league table, spending more than 7 per cent of their GDP on education. In Denmark, 96 per cent of this expenditure was public, and in the USA 68 per cent was public (OECD 2007b).

Governments subsidise education systems to raise the level of knowledge and skills in their populations (known as human capital), to enhance economic efficiency. On the equity side, education has long been seen as a potentially powerful force to increase equality and promote social mobility. Access to education has been claimed as a central objective of many policies to advance children from less well-off backgrounds in the hope of breaking generational cycles of deprivation.

However, it is clear that, despite large-scale government intervention, education systems have sometimes failed to deliver. For example, in Britain, where education is state funded and compulsory up to the age of 16 and state funded up to the age of 18, there are large numbers of adults with very low literacy and numeracy levels. In 1999, it was estimated there were as many as one in five adults who were not functionally literate. There is also evidence of inequality in who gains access to higher education. In 2000, a third of young people in England and Wales entered full-time higher education (post-18) – twice as many as in the previous decade and nearly seven times as many as in 1960. Yet those from disadvantaged groups remain under-represented: in 2001, nearly 4 out of 5 students from professional backgrounds studied for a degree, compared with just 1 in 6 from unskilled backgrounds. This inequality has persisted, and in fact widened, since the 1960s, despite the large expansion of higher education (Machin and Stevens 2004).

In this chapter we investigate alternative ways of financing and providing education. We begin by outlining the objectives society has for the education sector. We then examine the case for and against market provision and financing. To do this, we take as our starting point what has become the standard way of thinking about education among economists: what has been called the *human capital framework*. We present this and then use it to examine why a private market may not achieve society's goals. This forms the case for government intervention. In the last part of the chapter we examine methods of using market mechanisms to improve efficiency and equity in the education sector.

Objectives

As in the case of health care, we can discuss the objectives of the education system in terms of two main categories: namely, those concerned with efficiency, and those concerned with equity.

Efficiency

Stated in general terms, the efficiency objective is to try to specify the amount of education (that is, the size of the education system) that will maximise aggregate net social benefit. To translate this into a working definition we need to be able to identify both the costs and the benefits of providing education. While the costs are relatively easy to specify and include the costs of teachers' salaries, books and materials, school and college buildings and so on, the benefits are less tangible. Basically, however, it is possible to distinguish two categories of education benefit that any system will be expected to produce. We may call these *production benefits* and *social benefits*.

Production benefits accrue because one of the main functions of any education system is training the future workforce. Through education, individuals acquire knowledge and develop skills that will increase their productivity when they enter employment. Thus expenditure on education is an investment that yields benefits in the form of additional production in the future. Of course, the link between education and production benefits is more pronounced in some forms of education than in others. Clearly, it is stronger for skills-based further education courses than for general primary education; or for an engineering or accountancy degree course compared with one in English literature or art history. But practically all forms of education will lead to the acquisition of some skills that will prove useful in the workplace. For example, consider the benefits that derive from basic literacy and numeracy, learnt as part of a general primary school education. When basic communication through reading and writing becomes possible, there is scope for the use of more efficient techniques in a whole range of economic activities. Similarly, basic numeracy makes access to an increasing range of computer-based production techniques possible. Furthermore, an increase in the number of people with the elementary qualifications that are a necessary prerequisite for more advanced training will lead eventually to a larger number of highly trained workers. Economists refer to this as the 'option value' of elementary education; that is, it provides the option of further education or training.

In most cases, it is not possible to identify the social benefits of an education system with the same degree of precision as the production benefits, as they tend to assume far more diffuse and less tangible forms. But this should not be allowed to diminish the importance attached to them. For example, most forms of education perform an important socialisation function; that is, they seek to provide pupils or students with a set of values and range of skills that will enable them to function effectively in the wider society outside the school or college. These might range from the consideration of major ethical and moral questions, to understanding how to be a better parent and how to complete a job application form. The precise form of socialisation will vary between different parts of the education system and may vary across institutions at the same level – for example, faith-based schools will stress the importance of religious belief in everyday life; schools that emphasise art and creativity will stress the importance of these in daily life; and yet others will emphasise the attributes of punctuality, reliability and discipline.

In addition to this socialisation function, many people would argue that the transmission of knowledge through education is a good thing in itself, irrespective of whether it serves any ulterior objective. Thus an appreciation of literature and the arts, an awareness of the discoveries of science and technology and so on are seen as desirable ends in themselves.

Equity

Given the importance attached to education, it is hardly surprising that society should be concerned that it is distributed equitably. But there is much less consensus about what is an equitable distribution. Again, as in the case of health care (see Chapter 2), equity is not usually taken to mean that everyone should receive exactly the same amount of education, because their needs and capabilities may vary.

One definition is that everyone is entitled to a certain *minimum level* of education. In developed countries, education is compulsory for all up to a minimum age, usually 16. For children younger than this age, it is accepted that all should have the same amount of education. In countries with fewer resources, equity concepts might be the right of all children to have equal access to primary education. However, while compulsory education might allow access for all, there is an additional equity issue around the quality of education to which individuals have access.

In developed countries, discussion of equity has extended to post-compulsory education, where there is a recognition that not all individuals want, or would benefit from, post-compulsory education. The definition of equity that is often applied to this further education is *equality of opportunity*. That is, all students who are willing and able to benefit from a particular course of post-compulsory education should face the same cost of doing so; put another way, costs should not differ because of irrelevant or discriminatory criteria, such as parental income, race, sex or religion. Increasingly, equality of opportunity in education is seen as a basic right. This view is based on the recognition that education is not just another consumer service, but a process that has a fundamental effect on the recipients' lives. For many people, it is not only a major determinant of their lifetime income (and hence their access to market goods and services), but also the quality of their lives.

The market system and education

As noted above, education can be regarded as an investment in human capital. Undertaking education involves costs and produces future returns, just as investing in a piece of equipment (physical capital) requires an outlay today for the benefit of future production.

What are these benefits and costs? Most education can be expected to increase students' future productivity. Thus potential students (or their families) know that, through education, they can acquire knowledge and learn skills that will widen their future employment choices and, in most societies, increase their future earnings. These benefits will vary with the age of the person being educated: for children, the benefits come in the form of basic literacy and numeracy and the socialisation benefits discussed above; for those considering an investment in university-level education, the benefits are those from entering the graduate labour market rather than the post-compulsory school labour market, plus the range of non-economic benefits that a university-level education may bring.

What are the costs? These are both the direct costs – for example, any tuition fees, the costs of study materials, such as books, and possible additional costs incurred through living away from home (if the individual would otherwise have remained at home). But the major cost will be income forgone through undertaking education instead of going directly to work. This is an opportunity cost of the type discussed in Chapter 1: the opportunity of working has been forgone. Again, these costs will vary depending on the age of the individual being educated. While child labour does bring income into households, in developed countries the amount of income that can be earned by children is small compared to that earned by adults, so the opportunity costs of compulsory schooling may be low. In developing countries, child labour may be relatively better paid, so that the opportunity cost is higher.

When considering whether to undertake education, individuals (or their parents) are effectively faced with an investment decision; should they incur costs in the present in the expectation of receiving additional income in the future? We illustrate this in the case of an individual considering whether to invest in a university-level education, but exactly the same framework can be used to analyse investment in schooling at younger ages.

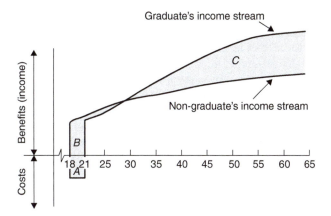

Figure 3.1   Investment in education.

Consider a student who has obtained the necessary entrance qualifications for a three-year degree course and wants to decide whether to accept the offer of a university place or to enter a firm directly. Confronted with this choice, the student will want to know the relative costs and benefits of each option.

A plausible time profile of the flow of costs and benefits is shown in Figure 3.1. In the chart, the potential graduate's annual costs and benefits are compared with those s/he would expect to receive as a non-graduate. The shaded areas $A + B$ represent the costs to the student of a three-year degree course. Area A is the additional cost of attending university compared with working. This will cover the costs of books, living expenses, fees and so on. Area B is the opportunity cost of forgone income; that is, the non-graduate's net income minus any income earned as a student between the ages of 18 and 21 years, and thereafter, the lower income received initially by the graduate compared with the non-graduate who is already established in the workforce. Area C represents the benefit of a degree course. It indicates that from his/her late 20s until retirement the graduate can expect a higher annual income than his/her non-graduate counterpart. By comparing the amount represented by area C with areas $A + B$ the student can estimate the likely rate of return on an investment of $A + B$ in education. This is the investment in 'human capital'.

While students deciding whether or not to go to university, or parents in less-developed countries deciding whether or not to send their child to secondary school may not consciously make these calculations before choosing an education course, what this framework shows is that there are current costs to investing in education that must be weighed against future benefits. As an example of the size of the benefits in terms of higher wages the additional benefit of going into tertiary education for men in the year 2000 in ten OECD countries compared to entering the labour market at the age of 18 have been estimated to range between 7.5 per cent in Italy to 18.5 per cent in the UK (Machin and Stevens 2004).

What are the implications of this for a private market in education? Simply that if returns of this magnitude can be obtained from investment in education, we would expect students to be willing and able to borrow money to finance their studies, and to repay these loans from their subsequent increased earnings. In particular, there should be no need for government financial assistance to students in further or higher education, as lenders would recognise the returns available from investment in human capital.

More generally, the advantages claimed for the market system are as follows. First, in a market system, consumers are able to express their preferences when they make decisions about the type and quantity of education they purchase, and through the expression of these choices the socially efficient quantity of each type of education will be indicated. Second, the market will ensure that the required education is in fact made available. Educational institutions will be in competition for students as they will be the source of the institutions' income, and the educational establishments will need to respond by offering the types of education that are in demand. Moreover, as students will be deterred by unnecessarily high fees, providers will need to ensure that they employ cost-effective methods in running their schools, colleges and universities. In this way, an efficient system responsive to consumer needs will be established.

But can we be confident that the market will operate in this way? In practice, very few systems of education are market-dominated. In fact, in many OECD countries, governments provide more than 90 per cent of the funding for education (OECD 2007b). This suggests that pure market provision and financing suffer from failings that prevent the market in education from operating either efficiently or equitably. These are broadly two sources of inefficiency: imperfect information and externalities.

Imperfect information

The investment framework implies that if the net present benefit of investment in education is positive, parents or students can borrow to finance this investment, and that the capital market (banks or other lending institutions) would be willing to offer loans on these terms. But in practice these conditions do not tend to be met. We can contrast the case of borrowing to finance university education with borrowing to buy a house. In the case of the latter loan, it will have a fixed duration (say, 25 years) and an interest rate. The monthly payment will be fixed, though it may alter to reflect changes in the interest rate. Buying a house is a relatively low-risk activity: the buyer usually knows what s/he is buying, the house is unlikely to fall down, and if the buyer's income falls, s/he has the option to sell the house and end the loan, and because the house acts as a security for the loan, the terms for the loan will not be expensive.

The contrast with borrowing to finance higher education is sharp. On the supply side, lenders do not have the collateral of a house when they lend to someone thinking of investing in education, and financial institutions tend to be cautious about lending to low-income borrowers with little collateral. This means that lenders will charge a high-risk premium, so the loan will be expensive. This will restrict loans to those with more resources, which basically means those with more parental resources. This problem will be compounded if the lenders cannot distinguish between high-risk (those students who are less likely to succeed) and low-risk students. This problem is known as an *adverse selection* problem (also seen in health and in housing, and discussed in Chapters 2 and 4), which arises because the lenders do not have full information about the riskiness of the recipients of their loans. Lenders have incentives to find ways of only lending to the best risks. An obvious way to do this is only to lend to students who can provide security – for example, a home-owning parent or applicants from schools whose students do well at university. The result of this adverse selection is that lending will be inefficiently low. In addition, as lenders will want security for their loans, it will also be biased towards children from wealthier homes.

There are also problems of information on the demand side. It is a basic assumption in economics that consumers know their own interests better than anyone else does. However, in most cases, consumers of education are not mature adults. Consequently, most people would be a little wary about ascribing to them all the usual attributes of sound judgement and rationality that consumers are usually assumed to possess. Generally, however, this problem is overcome because decisions regarding education are made by, or in close consultation with, parents. But in some cases the need for an adult to act on behalf of a child does present problems of its own, as adults may not always act in their children's best interests. This may be particularly important in the case of education, which has been described as a process that sometimes protects children from their families. Failure to act in their children's best interests may result from neglect on the parents' part, but it is more likely to arise because parents cannot always be expected to possess all the information necessary to make wise decisions. Education is a complex process, with many facets that are not readily apparent to those viewing it from the outside. Collecting information on courses, teachers, facilities, out-of-school activities and so on – which are necessary in order to make wise choices – can be very time-consuming. The benefits of education are not always clear to those parents who have not experienced it: in developed countries this may well be an issue in higher education, while in developing countries it might also arise for primary and secondary schooling. These parents – and their children – are likely to under-estimate the value of education and over-estimate the costs.

The result of this complexity is that many students – and disproportionately those from low-income households – may be unwilling to enter into debt to fund education: this has been termed 'debt aversion' (for a discussion, see Barr 2004a). This is not necessarily irrational: it arises from misperception of the costs and benefits of the debt. In addition, banks will be less willing to lend to students from poorer homes, for the reasons discussed above. The net effect of these supply and demand problems is that the level of borrowing will be inefficiently low, and that equity goals of equality of access and opportunity will not be met.

It is sometimes argued that the complexity of choice is just a matter of degree. Further, it is pointed out that, if educational institutions are competing for students, there is an incentive for these institutions to disseminate information more effectively. It is also argued that only by giving parents the responsibility for making choices can they be expected to have sufficient interest to develop the expertise necessary to make wise decisions. However, if we accept that education is very important in determining subsequent job opportunities and the quality of a person's life, we may well feel that the scope for individual mistakes of judgment should be minimised beyond those considered permissible in the case of purchasing other goods. There are other complex goods for which similar arguments have been made (see, for example, the case of pensions in Chapter 4). It is worth recognising that this view involves an element of paternalism; a restriction is being placed on consumer choice on the grounds that consumers may not always act in their own best interests.

Externalities

As we saw in the case of health care, wherever external costs or benefits exist, a private market cannot be relied on to produce an efficient allocation of resources. This is because the existence of externalities will cause private and social costs and benefits to diverge. Neither producers nor consumers will normally take these externalities into account. However, from society's point of view, they will have an effect on the level of welfare enjoyed by each member. If they are positive, this is a case for government intervention to increase the amount of education consumed. If they are negative, then government must act to decrease consumption.

In the case of education, it has been argued that there is a range of external benefits that do not accrue directly to the student, but are passed on to others in the community. We can divide these benefits into two main categories: economic and non-economic.

Economic benefits include those from employment. Employment benefits arise because modern production techniques require high levels of co-operation between workers. People who have been educated, as well as increasing their own productivity, will be able to increase the productivity of their fellow workers through contact with them. Educated workers may achieve this by the use of more efficient methods of supervision and management, thus permitting their less-educated colleagues to use their own time more productively. Similarly, education may increase a person's flexibility and adaptability. Hence an educated person is likely to be more able to respond to changes that arise through rapid technological progress. Flexibility is likely to prevent breakdowns or 'bottlenecks' in the production process. These benefits may then lead to greater growth.

Against this view, some economists argue that while these benefits result from education, they are not externalities. According to this argument, these benefits will be reflected in the earnings of the people who have received the education. Thus the benefit will accrue to them as a private benefit and not to others.

The second category is of non-economic benefits. The socialisation function of education may provide a benefit to society at large. By contributing towards a common standard of citizenship, education will tend to produce a degree of social cohesion that is in most people's interests. For example, crime may fall and child-rearing may improve. Of course, education does not always produce this effect. It also leads to the questioning of accepted practices, sometimes resulting in social unrest and even the unseating of governments. Those politicians who clamp down on universities in times of trouble clearly believe that they impose external costs rather than benefits.

It is difficult to resolve whether externalities in education exist. In the case of production externalities, separating those that are attributable to the education of others from those attributable to the worker's own efforts, his/her own education, and other factors affecting the individual's productivity is no easy matter. Even more so than in the case of employment externalities, the measurement of social externalities such as a reduction in crime or an improvement in child-rearing poses enormous problems. Few estimates exist of the magnitude of external benefits, and of those that do, one leading scholar of education has gone so far as to argue that externalities are 'noticeably elusive' (Hanushek 2002). Of those that do exist, only the growth and production externalities are clearly relevant beyond compulsory levels of education.

Signalling

Most of the above arguments have supported the case for government intervention to increase the uptake of education. There is, however, one view of education – particularly higher education – that, if correct, will reduce the case for government intervention. This is an argument asserting that higher education is simply 'screening'. The key problem is information failure in the employment market, where employers cannot easily distinguish between more and less productive employees when making employment decisions. They therefore have to use a proxy. According to screening theory, higher education is merely a proxy, or signal, for a set of largely intrinsic qualities – including intelligence, good work habits and appropriate social skills – that are sought by employers, but are difficult or expensive for them to test directly. These skills are not learnt in higher education but are innate or acquired from schools and/or parents before entering university-level education. Therefore higher education does not improve the individual's productivity: it merely signals ability. In this strong version of the screening hypothesis, higher education has no impact on an individual's productivity but merely signals to the employer that the individual is productive.

There is a weaker version positing that individuals who have skills will invest in education to make themselves attractive to potential employers. The impact of education is to raise the productivity of the individual, but the social returns are higher than these private returns because of screening (Machin and Stevens 2004).

In both the strong and the weak cases, there will be too much investment in education. So, to the extent that education is merely screening, this decreases the case for government intervention in educational markets, particularly higher education markets.

Equity

From the discussion above, there is nothing in a free market that will guarantee society's equity goals in education will be met. As 'getting an education' means forgoing earnings today for potential gain later, individuals who have less money, who are more credit-constrained, are less knowledgeable about the future benefits that education may bring, and have less ability to borrow will all rationally invest less today. These individuals will generally be those from poorer families. Furthermore, the failure of the market to meet equity goals will be perpetuated across generations. Lack of access to education for poor children leads to these children having (on average) lower incomes during adulthood, which is then likely to result in less education for their children.

Government policies

Signalling apart, the market failures identified here have pointed to a strong case for government intervention in education on the grounds of both efficiency and equity. But while it is clear that governments the world over intervene in education markets, market failure does not establish the form that this intervention should take. Debates on this subject have covered much ground. At the time of writing, much reform in education has sought to increase the role played by market mechanisms. Advocates have stressed the efficiency gains; while critics have argued that these are limited, and that these policies reduce equity. In the remainder of this chapter we shall examine the use and evidence for the impact of such policies. We shall examine pre- and post-compulsory education separately. When presenting empirical examples, we focus to a large extent on the way in which the government has chosen to deal with the problem in Britain, as Britain has been at the forefront of policy innovation in many areas, but we shall also use evidence from elsewhere.

Compulsory education

The traditional form of compulsory education is for the state to both finance and provide local schools. Finance is from either local taxation (as in the USA, where school districts raise money to fund their local schools) or from general taxation (as in the UK, New Zealand and Australia). Children attend their local school. Private education is generally allowed, but is usually limited.

Successive OECD governments' aims have been to ensure there has not been under-provision of education; and they have also attached considerable emphasis to the equity aim – namely, the establishment of equality of access. By controlling the provision of education, and making it available free of charge, governments have sought to ensure that no one is denied access because of income limitations.

The UK had such a system during the years between 1945 and 1990. Over 90 per cent of children attended local state schools. In these schools, education was provided free: the 7 per cent of children who attended private schools were from more affluent homes. Funding for schools was not dependent on school performance, and school performance was not made public.

In recent years, however, there has been an increasing body of criticism that has questioned whether existing methods of direct provision and subsidisation represent the most effective way of achieving these aims. In particular, claims have been directed at the alleged lack of responsiveness of the monopoly government system to the demands of students, parents and employers. This dissatisfaction has resulted in reforms designed to increase consumer choice, and, through this, provider responsiveness to users' preferences. All these reforms involve increasing the use of the price mechanism to give providers greater incentives for economic efficiency (Le Grand 2007). The basic building blocks are to maintain free (or almost free) education, while introducing mechanisms that allow greater parental choice, rewards to schools for greater student numbers, and more publicly available information.

One form is the 'quasi-markets' adopted in England and Wales. The 1988 Education Reform Act introduced a system of open enrolment (Glennerster 1991). Under this system, parents can in theory enrol their children at any school of their choice. Schools, in their turn, receive funding based on the numbers of pupils enrolled (funding 'following the pupil'). Schools are required to make public their performance, including performance in nationally set exams taken at the ages of 7, 11, 14 and 16, with particular emphasis on those taken at age 16 (known as GCSEs). Schools that are undersubscribed can be closed down. These provisions are designed to increase the amount of choice parents have, and to encourage schools to respond to parents' preferences by making funding dependent on each school's success in attracting pupils. It is argued that the competition between schools, in their quest to attract pupils, will increase their efficiency. New Zealand adopted a similar system in the 1990s.

A more extreme version of this choice scheme is an education voucher. Education vouchers are allocated to families, who can use them to 'buy' education services for their children at schools of their choice. Each voucher entitles a student to a given quantity of education services and is presented to a school as payment for the services it provides. The schools – which can be state-run or privately owned – then redeem the vouchers from the government for a cash sum. There are a number of variants of the basic voucher scheme. In a flat-rate scheme, every family receives a standard voucher for each child of school age, equal in value to the average cost of a year's schooling. Income-related schemes link the value of the voucher to the family's income. Another variant allows a family to supplement the standard voucher allocation and thereby purchase more education than the government-specified minimum if it so chooses. Schools might charge more than the voucher: in this case parents would fund the difference between the total cost and that covered by the voucher. In this way, a voucher scheme could combine the guarantee of a minimum amount of education for everyone with the freedom for some to obtain more if they wish.

The voucher system is the predominant system of choice in the USA, where the vouchers take a variety of forms. In many cases, vouchers are targeted at low-income families: they allow a choice of private schools but may or may not cover the full costs.

The assessment of these increased choice reforms has drawn attention to three issues (Wilson, Burgess and Propper 2007). The first issue is the grounds on which parents make their choices, and the impact of these on school behaviour. In both England and Wales and the USA, the most accessible information is on examination performance. Schools are generally required to publish examination scores. In the UK these are quickly converted by the national media into school 'league tables'. Publication of examination scores is not necessarily because educators and schools believe that examination performance is the only purpose of schooling, but because this is easier to measure. Critics argue that this encourages schools to put undue weight on examination performance and to divert effort away from broader educational goals. Schools are also given incentives to (and may attempt to) 'massage the figures'. From the USA there is indeed some evidence of 'teaching to the test', and the systematic exclusion of children who will pull down average school scores, as a response to the publication of performance measures from systems in which schools are assessed on their performance.

In response, policy-makers try to prevent schools from this kind of behaviour, known as 'gaming the system'. So, for example, in England and Wales, the performance measures used in 2006 controlled for initial pupil ability and took into account other aspects of school composition (for example, the number of children from poor homes) to try to provide a more accurate measure of school performance and limit schools' attempts to 'game the system'. These measures were known as 'contextual value added'.

The second issue is the extent to which school choice increases efficiency. At least two elements are required for schools to improve their efficiency: first, there needs to be flexibility on the supply side, and second, there need to be financial implications from both expansion and contraction of numbers. The quasi-market in England and Wales, which at the time of writing has operated since 1990, appears to lack the former (Glennerster 2002). As a consequence, popular schools are heavily oversubscribed, leading to a restriction of applicants to students who live ever nearer to the school. This then leads to an increase in house prices, as parents try to move closer to popular schools (Gibbons and Machin 2003). This system appears to have had negative equity consequences, with richer parents able to buy homes near better schools, and poorer children travelling further to attend less good schools.

A lottery scheme for all children wanting to attend a popular school would remove this house price premium, but the consequence would be that the children of more affluent parents would have to attend poorer schools and the value of houses near good schools would fall, affecting those who had bought such houses. Lotteries to allocate places in state schools have been used widely in the USA. To date, they have been resisted vigorously in the UK through more affluent parents exerting political pressure. Increasing capacity would alleviate this problem (Wilson et al., 2007).

In general, assessments of the efficiency of school choice schemes are mixed. Most of the evidence comes from the USA (Hoxby 2003a). The strongest evidence for an increase in efficiency is from reforms where there was a realistic probability that at least 5 per cent of children could go to choice schools, that non-choice schools will lose money when a student goes to a choice school, and that the reforms have been in place for a number of years. Other studies have concluded that better performance of children in choice systems is not due to the choice, but to the higher motivation of students who chose to forsake their local schools (Wilson et al., 2007).

The third issue is the impact on equity. In the English and Welsh choice system, with limited capacity and no lotteries, it does not appear that choice has increased equity (Le Grand 2007). It is difficult to assess this, partly because the choice system was introduced everywhere at the same time, limiting the scope for comparing a choice system with one where parents and children cannot express a choice. However, it is worth noting that the previous non-choice English and Welsh system was also criticised for lack of equity: children at schools located in middle- and higher-income catchment areas have historically also tended to be educated in better schools and stay at school longer (and hence receive more education) than children from lower-income homes.

Higher education

Higher education matters. No longer a consumption good enjoyed by the elite, it is viewed as being an important element in national performance (though robust support for the link between growth and education is fairly sparse). It definitely has large private returns. So it is no accident that the numbers in higher education have increased in all advanced countries. However, high-quality mass education is expensive and, as we saw, the case for intervention is less on either equity or efficiency grounds than in primary and secondary education. The extent of government funding and provision in higher education is much more variable than in primary and secondary education. Government expenditure on tertiary education in the OECD in the year 2000 ranged from 0.6 per cent of GDP (Korea) to 1.7 per cent (Finland); government expenditure as a share of total expenditure ranged from around 50 per cent (the USA, Australia) to 100 per cent (Finland, Iceland, Norway, Denmark).

The traditional model of state provision and state funding is still adopted in many European countries, particularly in Scandinavia. In this model, students receive grants to attend universities, often their local ones, access is permitted for all students who pass the university entrance exam, no fees are charged, and the universities are in the public sector. However, in many other countries (notable examples being Australia, New Zealand and the UK) there has been a drive towards greater cost-sharing between the individual and the state (while retaining state provision). This has been in recognition of the importance of private returns and the rise in the cost of maintaining high-quality provision. In addition, there has been a greater emphasis on market incentives for providers, linking their funding to their performance.

In this section we assess the case for a greater reliance on market mechanisms. We focus on financing, and consider the case for grants and income-related loans. However, we also discuss changes with regard to provision. We illustrate this mainly with respect to UK policy change.

Financing higher education: grants, graduate taxes and loans

In Britain, attendance in higher education (HE) is lower than many other European countries, but has been rising rapidly. In 1960, one in twenty students went on to tertiary education, and the number in the year 2000 was one in three. However, the rise in HE has not been distributed equally. In fact, contrary to many people's expectations, the expansion of the HE sector has benefited disproportionately people from better-off families. In 1981, around 20 per cent of children from the richest 20 per cent of homes completed a degree; the figure two decades later was 46 per cent. The comparable proportion for children from the poorest 20 per cent of homes was 6 per cent and 9 per cent, respectively (Machin and Stevens 2004). In 2004, the government had a target of getting 50 per cent of young people to participate in higher education by 2010. It is clear that, to meet this target, there will need to be considerable policy effort.

For much of the period of HE expansion, the vast majority of students received education free of charge in government-financed colleges and universities. In addition, most students also received non-repayable maintenance grants from the government which contributed towards their living expenses while studying. Although they are not usually described in such terms, these grants are a form of education voucher: they are allocated to students to enable them to buy education services at approved institutions. Unlike the voucher schemes described in the previous section, however, they are not available to every potential student but only to those who obtain the educational qualifications necessary to gain admission to a college or university.

The grant system was frequently defended because of the need to equalise access to further and higher education by ensuring that students from poorer families were not discriminated against as a result of their limited ability to pay tuition fees and finance a period of study. But it is clear from the figures above that this aim was not achieved in the UK. This means that a policy designed ostensibly to assist those students who would otherwise be denied access to higher education on financial grounds was, in fact, allocating a large proportion of its budget to the sons and daughters of the relatively well-off. Other features of the grants were that they were also unrelated to the cost of the course of study. Grants were also unrelated to potential income after the completion of the higher education. A final criticism in the British context is that if the aim of the policy was really to provide equality of access, then financial assistance was being given at the wrong stage of the education process. Most students from lower-income backgrounds drop out of education before the point of entry into higher education. This suggests that grants, if paid at all, should be paid to students to stay on in education after the compulsory school-leaving age. In recognition of this last point, the UK government has introduced a grant targeted at low-income students to encourage them to stay on at school – the Educational Maintenance Allowance (EMA).

One alternative to grants is a loans system. Under a loans system, a student borrows while at university and pays back the loan over time once university studies are completed. Unlike a grants system, which redistributes the costs of education from taxpayers (who do not necessarily receive higher education) to students, a loans system requires the recipients of education to bear its costs but allows them to redistribute the burden over time. As we have seen, expenditure on education is an investment that can be expected to yield returns in the form of increased future earnings, and a loan scheme requires that some of these earnings are used to repay the costs of education.

Supporters of loans schemes make the claim that they are both more equitable and more efficient than grants (see, for example, Barr 2004a). Greater equity could be achieved because repayable loans would reduce lifetime income inequality: students who receive higher future incomes as a result of education would be required to bear its costs. Loans would not discriminate against students from low-income backgrounds because they – in common with all students – would earn extra income in the future with which they could repay their debts. Moreover, increases in efficiency would result, so supporters of loans schemes claim, from encouraging a more responsible attitude among students: it is expected that they would make better use of their time if they were incurring private costs. Finally, by freeing higher education from constraints arising from dependence on general government revenues, the whole system could expand.

Opponents of loans schemes have argued that loans would deter people from entering relatively low-paid, but nevertheless socially useful jobs, including leaving the workforce for child-rearing purposes. Proponents respond that this concern could be mitigated by making the loans contingent on income. Repayments would be calculated as a proportion of the borrower's subsequent earnings, collected with other taxes until the borrower had repaid the full sum. Income-contingent loans would mean that low earners would make low (or no) repayments. People with low life-time earnings would not fully repay their loan. A larger loan has no effect on monthly repayments, which depend only on the person's income. Instead, a person with a larger loan would repay over a longer period. In efficiency terms, income-contingent loans are designed explicitly to protect borrowers from excessive risk; as we saw earlier, borrowing against human capital investments is inherently more risky than borrowing against a certain asset. Income-contingent loans also assist in access terms as they have built-in insurance against inability to pay.

Several loan schemes currently in operation, such as those in Australia and the UK, charge a subsidised or zero interest rate. The aim of this interest subsidy is to promote access by preventing excessive debt. However, blanket subsidies will not achieve this end. First, interest rate subsidies are costly to the government, partly because they are charging less for the loan than it costs them to raise the money, and partly because subsidised interest loans allow arbitrage; students who do not need the loan accept it and put it into a savings account that pays a higher interest rate. Second, they are regressive, as they do not help students (who do not repay while students) but help graduates. The most efficient rate of interest would be the government's cost of borrowing. This would mean that the loan system would be self-financing after a period of years.

Second, opponents argue that loans would exacerbate existing inequalities of access because they would deter students from low-income backgrounds whereas, in higher-income families, parents would tend to look upon education as a consumption expenditure that they would finance, thereby releasing their children from the burden of debt repayments. Supporters of loan-based schemes also recognise this problem. They argue that making loans income contingent may partially overcome this. But they also tend to agree that other policies targeted towards children from low-income families need to be introduced alongside the loans. One is to make grants available to low-income students alongside loans.

This would compensate them for not having the same parental support as children from richer families. The second is to write off the loans of individuals in specific types of employment (those that are low-paid but deemed to be socially useful, such as nursing). The third is that individuals caring for children or elderly dependents could be granted loan remission.

Third, critics have argued that loans would fail to release government expenditure for other uses for many years, because student loans, like mortgage loans on housing, would only be repaid in the distant future. This is correct. However, compared to grants, loans earn at least some revenue for the government.

Loans schemes are not free from distortions. A loan scheme offered by the government suffers from the same problem as a private insurance loan scheme. Individuals who are considered to be a higher risk will be more willing to take out a loan than those who are considered a lower risk. If low-risk types drop out, rates will rise further, undermining the scheme and, in a private market, leading to credit rationing. However, the government can finance expected losses from the loan scheme by raising taxes, so a loan scheme will redistribute resources from taxpayers to high-risk individuals.

Graduate taxes have been suggested – and used – as an alternative to loans (Barr 2004a). A graduate tax is an extra tax paid by those who complete university. Usually a graduate tax is paid for the entire individual's working life. A graduate tax will only be paid by those who complete university, so compared to grants they redistribute from all taxpayers to just those taxpayers who have received a university education. They share this advantage with loans, but they are cheaper to administer than a loans system. In terms of economic efficiency, loans are probably a better tool. Graduate taxes are not related to the cost of study, but to the income that an individual receives post-university. So the cost to the potential student will not be related to the cost of study, meaning that the individual pays the same regardless of whether their course was expensive or cheap. If courses are priced to reflect their marginal cost, revenues from a graduate tax will not reflect this pricing, so cannot influence economic efficiency in the choice of courses. Finally, for high earners, graduate tax payments are ongoing, and this may lead to greater work disincentives.

Providing higher education: introducing market mechanisms

In all European countries, the prices that HE institutions can charge are regulated by the government. (This is in strong contrast with the USA, where variable fees are taken for granted.) In the UK, HE institutions were not able to charge fees before 1998; and for the following five years they were required to charge the same fee for all subjects at all universities. This was to promote equality of access and, at least in the UK, was built on a maintained fiction that all universities were of the same quality. However, such a policy gives no incentives to universities to improve standards: if they increase expenditure to do so they will not be rewarded in terms of greater budgets. Proponents of greater market principles argue that universities should be free to set their own fees.

The efficiency case is based on the assumption that price signals are useful in higher education. The ensuing competition between institutions will make the system more responsive to both students and employers. On the demand side, resources are misallocated if students face no price signals between subjects; too much will be spent on expensive and/or lower-return courses and universities. On the supply side, price ceilings erode incentives to improve quality as the costs cannot be covered by price increases: price floors erode the incentive to increase efficiency as the benefits cannot be appropriated through lower prices and higher demand. Flat fees, including zero fees, are both a floor and a ceiling.

There is also a political case for variable fees. With flat fees or tax funding, the volume of resources going into the HE sector is fixed by the government, so that prestigious universities compete for the same pot of government money as local institutions. In addition, the government can easily reduce tax payments to the sector to match any across-the-board fee increases. Variable fees allow prestigious universities to reap the benefit from their prestige: they also make it more difficult for governments to reduce tax funding automatically.

Variable fees also make it clear that universities provide different products – and that students will attend universities of differing quality. While this is widely accepted in the USA, in most European debates it raises equity concerns. One way of alleviating this equity concern is to mandate that universities operate schemes to give scholarships to students from low-income families who gain entry into elite institutions. To be effective, especially given higher levels of debt aversion among students from low- income families, such schemes have to be sufficiently widespread and sufficiently generous to ensure that barriers to attending university are genuinely lowered for these students. The schemes operating in England and Wales at the time of writing may be insufficiently generous and will not achieve this aim.

In summary, from the above discussion, greater reliance on price signals and other market-type mechanisms offer the possibility of improving efficiency in the delivery of education. An associated danger is that increasing reliance on the market will reduce equity. Thus to achieve the strong equity goals in education, there is a need for careful design of mechanisms and a balance between liberalisation and regulation.

SUMMARY

- The education system has objectives of both *efficiency* and *equity*. Efficiency requires the adoption of a system that maximises net social benefits; that is, the greatest possible excess of benefits over costs. These benefits take two main forms: production benefits resulting from training of the future workforce, and a more diffuse range of social benefits. The equity objective requires the establishment of equality of access or the guarantee of a minimum standard in education.

- Although a market system in education allows the expression of consumer freedom of choice and has certain other advantages, there are strong reasons for believing that it will not achieve either of these objectives. The attainment of efficiency is likely to be impeded because of capital market imperfections, imperfect information and externalities. At the same time, equity is unlikely to be achieved when access to education is determined by ability to pay and income is distributed unequally.

- For these reasons, some form of state intervention in education is necessary. But this does not establish the form it should take. All developed countries make education compulsory up to early adulthood. The standard method of financing such schools is from taxation, and provision is generally within the public sector. Intervention in post-compulsory education takes a wider range of forms, with some countries funding university education for all who pass the necessary entrance examinations, and providing it in state-run institutions. Other countries have more limited public funding and allow greater private provision.

- Dissatisfaction with existing forms of direct provision and subsidy has led to policy changes in many education systems. Most of these introduce greater market-type elements into education while trying to introduce safeguards to maintain equity goals. In compulsory education, these elements include lotteries and student vouchers; while in post-compulsory education they include student loans and targeted grants.

FURTHER READING

The economics of education has attracted considerable interest since the mid-1990s. For those having some undergraduate economics training, Barr (2004b) provides a clear discussion of the economics of education, with a focus on the UK. Stiglitz (2000) is aimed at the same audience, but with a focus on the USA. A text book for the same audience, covering recent theoretical and empirical developments, is Belfield (2002).

An overview of (some of the current) issues in the economics of education, which can be read by economists and non-economists alike, is provided by various articles in the *Oxford Review of Economic Policy*, vol. 20, no. 2 (2004): a general introduction is provided by Machin and Stevens (2004); Barr (2004a) discusses higher education funding and presents the case for income contingent loans; while Blanden and Gregg (2004) and Feinstein (2004) focus on the relationship between family income and educational attainment.

For those with some economics background, Hoxby (2003a) puts forward strongly the case for school choice. For a similar audience, arguments against school choice are made by Ladd (2002, 2003). A whole volume devoted to the economics of school choice, with a North American focus, is Hoxby (2003b).

For non-economists and economists alike, recent evidence on the impact of school choice is discussed in Wilson *et al.* (2007) and in Le Grand (2007). Quasi-market reforms in England post-1991 are discussed in Glennerster (1991). Post-1997 policy in education in England is discussed in Glennerster (2002).

For both economists and non-economists, a general overview of the impact of performance measures in schooling (and other sectors) is provided in Propper and Wilson (2003). Kane and Staiger (2002) discuss issues in the construction of school output measures for those with more technical training.

Cross-country statistics on education are provided for the OECD (OECD 2007b) and for a large range of countries by the World Bank at http://www.worldbank.org/education/edstats.

QUESTIONS FOR DISCUSSION

1. 'The private rates of return on investment in higher education are sufficiently large for students from both poor and rich households to suggest that the introduction of student loans will not affect the social composition of students entering colleges and universities.' Discuss this claim.

2. Do you think that the education system would be more equitable if grants to 16–18-year-olds replaced grants to students in higher education?

3. Examine the case for using different levels of student grants to encourage students to follow courses that the government deems to be socially desirable.

4. 'As the production benefits of education are more tangible than the social benefits, the latter tend to be undervalued in discussions of education planning.' Discuss.

5. Explain how you would estimate the social rate of return on investment in medical education.

6. Discuss the case for and against greater school choice.

7. 'Private market provision of education emphasises private benefits, whereas state provision is concerned with social benefits.' Discuss this claim.

8. Discuss what is meant by 'equality of opportunity' within the education sector.

9. Do you think that education is a means of promoting social mobility or a means of preparing certain social groups for a predetermined place in the socio-economic system?

CHAPTER 4

Pensions

Pensions constitute a major area of government provision. On average, across the OECD countries, spending on pensions represents 7.4 per cent of gross domestic product (GDP), and for the EU15 countries, the figure is 8.2 per cent. In the UK, total resources spent by the state on the provision of income for pensioners are slightly below this level, at just over 6 per cent of GDP.

In many developed countries, pension systems are under strain as a result of population ageing (and in particular, a growing number of pensioners relative to the working population). A key driver of population ageing is increasing individual longevity. In the UK, average male life expectancy at age 65 has grown from 12.0 years in 1950 to an estimated 19.0 today, and is projected to rise to 21.0 by 2030 and to 21.7 by 2050. Female life expectancy is higher and also increasing, though at a slightly slower rate. Future increases in life expectancy could be even greater than these figures suggest. Projecting future improvements in life expectancy is extremely uncertain, since it depends on the effects of medical advances and behavioural changes (including diet and smoking). In the past, official projections have often significantly understated subsequent improvements. In 1981, the UK Government Actuary's Department projected that by 2004 male life expectancy at 65 would be 14.8 years, a considerable underestimate on the figure given above.

Another demographic driver of the ageing of the population is the ageing of the 'baby boomers', the term used to refer to unusually large birth cohorts. The UK had two baby booms during the twentieth century. The first, smaller boom, occurred immediately after the Second World War, in the mid-1940s, and the second in the early 1960s. Until now, these cohorts have increased the size of the working-age population, but as they age they will temporarily drive up the number of pensioners.

A final factor contributing to ageing populations in a number of countries is low and falling birth rates. Across all European countries, birth rates are below the so-called 'replacement rate' of 2.1 children per woman considered necessary to keep the overall size of the population stable. The highest rates are in Ireland

(1.99) and France (1.90). The lowest are in Germany (1.37), Spain (1.33), Italy (1.32) and Greece (1.27). In the UK, the rate is 1.74.

Together, these factors will increase the proportion of older people in the population. For the EU15 countries, the 65+ age group is expected to double from its current level of 15 per cent of the population to 30 per cent in 2050. For the UK, the increase is slightly smaller – from 15 per cent at the time of writing to 25 per cent in 2050. Without changes to existing pension systems, this rise in the number of older people will drive up the cost of pensions. In the UK, the government appointed an independent Pensions Commission in 2004 to assess existing pension provision and to make proposals for reform. Their assessment was clear: Doing nothing is not an option. With people living longer, there are some hard choices to be made between saving more, paying more in taxes, working longer, or facing lower incomes in retirement.

Against this background, this chapter considers the objectives that the government may have for pension provision, focusing on the important role that pensions play in allowing individuals to smooth spending over their lifetimes. This is discussed in the next section. We then consider whether the market system is likely to achieve the government's objectives, before discussing alternative forms of government intervention.

Objectives

As with other areas of provision, the government is concerned with achieving an efficient level of pension provision and in addressing equity concerns. We discuss what each of these might entail.

Efficiency

Pensions are often seen solely in terms of their role in giving an income to current pensioners. This is clearly an important objective in pension provision and is often the one that dominates policy discussion about pensions. However, in order to think about what an efficient level of pension provision might look like, it is more helpful to think about pensions as fulfilling the role of enabling individuals to maintain their level of spending when their income falls. Typically, this will involve them saving some of their income when they are working. This process is referred to as *consumption smoothing*. This encompasses more than just providing an income in retirement, however; it also takes into account how people accumulate the resources needed to finance spending in retirement, and the relationship between the resources that people have during their retirement compared to their working life.

All individuals face a basic problem of deciding how to allocate their total lifetime resources over different periods of their life. These total resources comprise all the money they earn during periods of employment, together with any inherited wealth and windfall gains (such as a win on the lottery). For the moment, we assume that there is no income from the government. Typically, these resources do not arrive in a perfectly smooth way over an individual's lifetime. There will be periods of employment when individuals are earning money, but also, towards the end of their life, periods when they are in retirement and are no longer earning. There may also be periods of temporarily low income as a result of spells of unemployment, or periods out of the labour market caring for children. However, this chapter is not going to consider the issues raised by such temporary fluctuations in income. Instead, we are going to focus on the problem of allocating resources between periods of employment and retirement. Typically, retirement is anticipated. Most people do not expect to carry on working until they drop dead at their desk. Therefore, individuals will expect to find themselves facing a period in their lives when they are not working and not earning, although the length of this period of retirement may be less certain.

To make matters clearer, consider the following example. This is obviously heavily stylised, but the same arguments apply to more realistic levels of income. Individuals' lifetimes are assumed to have two periods. In period one, they work and earn £10. In period two, they retire and earn nothing. With no inherited wealth, no windfalls and no income from the government, their total lifetime resources are equal to £10. The problem they face is how to allocate the £10 over the two periods. They could spend all their resources in period one, and then be left with nothing in retirement. Or they could choose to spend nothing now and save the full £10 until period two. Or they could do something between these two extremes.

Their objective in allocating their resources is to maximise total lifetime welfare. Critics of the economic approach to analysing behaviour often object to categorising individuals as *homo economicus* (rational, maximising agents). However, it is enough to assume that people are unlikely deliberately to choose an outcome that would make them less well-off than they could be. Individuals are assumed to derive benefit from spending money on goods and services, and their total lifetime welfare is equal to the sum of benefits in both periods.

They are unlikely to achieve their objective in the extreme case in which they spend their total resources in period one. While they might derive a high level of benefit in period one from spending large amounts of money on exotic holidays and high-tech gadgets, in period two they would be unable to afford even a loaf of bread. If they transferred £1 from period one to period two, the increase in benefit they would get from raising their consumption from zero to £1 in period two is likely to be greater than the loss of benefit they would suffer from reducing their consumption from £10 to £9 pounds in period one. Similarly, if they transferred another pound, while it might yield less of an increase in benefit than the first pound, the extra benefit they would get in period two is likely to more than compensate for the loss of benefit in period one.

Underlying this trade-off between the two periods is an important concept referred to as the *diminishing marginal benefit (or utility) of consumption*. This says that, starting from a zero level of consumption, each additional unit of consumption will result in a slightly smaller increase in total benefit. This is illustrated in Table 4.1. The first column shows successive units of consumption (in pounds). The second column shows the total benefit associated with each level of consumption. It says, for example, that consuming £3 yields a level of total benefit equal to 27. The third column shows the increase in total benefit that is

Table 4.1 Consumption and the marginal benefit of consumption

Units of consumption (£)	Total benefit from consumption	Increase in benefit from last unit of consumption = marginal benefit
1	10	10
2	19	9
3	27	8
4	34	7
5	40	6
6	45	5
7	49	4
8	52	3
9	54	2
10	55	1

derived from the last unit consumed – this is known as marginal benefit. It says that consuming the third unit added eight to the total benefit. So, as the level of consumption rises, the marginal benefit from each additional unit of consumption falls.

The numbers in this table can be used to solve the individuals' intertemporal allocation problem. If they consumed their total resources in period one (or in period two), they would derive total benefit equal to 55. If they deferred one pound to period two, they could increase their total benefit to 64 (54 in the first period and 10 in the second). Transferring exactly half their resources to the second period and consuming five pounds in each period yields the maximum possible level of total benefit, equal to 80. This is the efficient outcome. It involves individuals spending half their total lifetime resources when they are working and saving half to be consumed during retirement.

This example is highly stylised, but it serves to illustrate the essence of the lifetime allocation problem, and how to think about an efficient level of saving for retirement. In practice, there are a number of important modifications to the basic framework, including varying consumption needs, discounting of future consumption and returns to saving. We discuss each of these in turn.

First, consumption needs are likely to vary over an individual's lifetime. For example, in the first period, there will be work-related costs (commuting and smart clothes) and for many, the costs associated with children (nappies and school books). Both of these will tend to increase consumption in the first period. In the second period, individuals will also enjoy more leisure time as a result of no longer working and this may either tend to lower their need for spending to derive benefit, or to raise it, since they need to spend additional money on leisure activities, such as bowling or bingo. In extreme old age, spending needs may rise as a result of health and basic care requirements, although these may be met by the government. The efficient level of consumption-smoothing over an individual's lifetime is unlikely to result in a completely flat profile, but one that varies according to changing needs at different life stages.

Table 4.2 Consumption and benefit under discounting

Period One Consumption	Period One benefit	Period Two consumption	Period Two expected benefit
1	10	1	5.0
2	19	2	9.5
3	27	3	13.5
4	34	4	17.0
5	40	5	20.0
6	45	6	22.5
7	49	7	24.5
8	52	8	26.0
9	54	9	27.0
10	55	10	27.5

Second, we have so far assumed that individuals place equal weight on consumption in both periods. In practice, this is unlikely to be the case, since people typically discount the future. This means that they put relatively more weight on costs and benefits occurring today, and less weight on those occurring in the future. This discounting of the future matters hugely, because individuals have to decide in period one how much of their resources to spend now and how much to save until period two in order to finance spending tomorrow. In making the calculation, it is highly unlikely that they will place as much value on £1 spent in period two as on the same amount spent in period one, and this will result in more of their spending taking place in period one. There are several reasons why people discount the future. It may reflect pure impatience – that is, a desire to have things now, rather than waiting for them. Or, more rationally, it may reflect the fact that there is a chance of dying before reaching period two, in which case it makes sense to derive benefit today. The issue of discounting is central to the debate about the economics of climate change, and we return to it in Chapter 8.

To see the effect of discounting, let us go back to our example and assume that individuals place a weight of half on consumption in period two, compared to consumption in period one. This discounting of the future matters at the point at which they make their decision in period one about how much to spend today and how much to save for tomorrow. Table 4.2 shows the values they place on consumption in both periods at this point. The benefit in period two is referred to as *expected benefit*, since it is the benefit they expect to get from different levels of consumption in the future.

With discounting, the total amount of benefit the individuals expect to get from allocating their resources equally between periods one and two is 60. They could increase this total by consuming more today, since this would yield a higher level of expected benefit. In practice, the allocation that yields the highest combined benefit (a total of 62.5) is consumption of £7 in period one and £3 in period two. The more heavily that someone discounts the future (that is, the less weight they place on consumption tomorrow relative to consumption today), the less they will save for tomorrow.

A final, important, consideration is that savings attract a rate of return. If someone chooses to forgo consumption in period one, the money saved can be invested and will typically increase in value by period two. This means that they can increase total consumption (and hence benefit) by postponing some of their resources until the future. Even if the rate of return is very high, they are unlikely to save all their resources for retirement, for the reasons already discussed – that is, diminishing marginal benefit of consumption and discounting of the future. But the return to saving should in principle be high enough to persuade some people to forgo consumption today and save for tomorrow.

Our discussion has considered the efficient allocation of resources over the lifetime, between periods of employment and retirement. The resources that people defer from their working lives and draw on in their retirement constitute a pension, but the discussion so far has not had anything to say about in what form the resources should be accumulated during the working life, and how they should be drawn down in retirement. When we think about pensions, we typically have more in mind than simply another form of saving (on a par with, say, a bank account). While people do often save for their retirement in many different forms (through equity investment, their house or their business, for example), there are several distinct features that come to mind when we talk about saving in the form of pensions. As well as the particular tax treatment of pensions, this typically includes a lock-in, such that people are unable to access their funds until a certain age (or face penalties for early access). More importantly, pensions often require individuals to draw down all or most of the accumulated wealth in the form of a steady stream of income from retirement until time of death. This income stream is known as an *annuity*. If someone saves their money in a bank account, they can choose to take out all of it and blow it on a brand new Ferrari if they wish. The same is typically not true of pensions. If someone saves his/her money in a personal pension scheme in the UK, some of the money can be taken as a lump sum, but the majority must be used to purchase an annuity that will provide them with an income up to their death.

The government has a strong reason for wanting people to annuitise at least some of their wealth, since it stops people blowing their accumulated wealth and falling back on the state to provide them with an income. However, it is also the case that annuitisation will be an efficient outcome for individuals facing uncertainty over when they are going to die. The arguments are very similar to those in the case of lifetime resource allocation. Once they reach retirement, individuals face the issue of how to allocate their accumulated wealth over the remaining years of their life. If they knew exactly when they were going to die, they could allocate their resources to ensure a smooth profile of consumption (subject to varying consumption needs). The problem is that people do not know how exactly long they are going to live for. They do not want to outlive their resources, since they would be faced with periods at the very end of their lives with zero consumption. One possibility might be to plan on the basis of an extreme assumption, such as living to 130. However, this creates another potential problem. If in fact they die at 75, they will leave a lot of unspent resources. Unless they derive a lot of pleasure from bequeathing the money to others, they could have spent this money when they were alive and increased their total welfare. In fact, if individuals are risk averse, they will usually be prepared to purchase an annuity which, at a small cost, offers them a guaranteed level of income until they die. This effectively insures them against the possibility of outliving their resources and they are willing to trade a small amount of their income to avoid the probability of a far greater loss.

Pensions therefore typically perform two roles:

- they act as a form of saving, allowing individuals to smooth their consumption over their lifetimes; and

- they act as a form of insurance, allowing individuals to insure themselves against mortality risk and, in particular, the possibility of outliving their resources.

Of course, the two roles do not necessarily have to be provided by the same instrument. Individuals can choose to save in one form (a bank account or a house) and then use their accumulated wealth to purchase an annuity. And, in many countries, individuals can accumulate savings in a designated pension product without any requirement to annuitise their wealth on retirement. In the UK, however, the various different types of pension (provided by the state, by employers and by individuals themselves) all perform both functions.

Equity

Equity considerations are very important in driving pension policy in practice. These considerations relate almost exclusively in practice to the pensions currently being paid to those in retirement. In the UK, for example, the government has an explicit objective to reduce pensioner poverty. This is defined in terms of reducing the number of pensioner households whose incomes fall below a specified poverty line, currently set at 60 per cent of median household income. The median level of income is defined by the household in the middle of the income distribution when all households (including both retired and working-age households) are ranked in terms of their income. The median is better at capturing the income of an average or typical household, rather than the mathematical mean (or average),which will be affected by the relatively small number of very high incomes at the top of the distribution.

One thing to note is that this is a *relative* concept of poverty, since the threshold level of income below which people are considered to be poor is set relative to the incomes of households in society at the time. This contrasts with an absolute definition of poverty which would apply at all times in all societies, such as, for example, the level of income necessary for bare subsistence. We discuss issues surrounding the definition and measurement of poverty in more detail in Chapter 9. Here we focus on a couple of points relating specifically to pensioner poverty.

The current approach of the UK government treats pensioners exactly the same as other (working-age) households when defining and measuring poverty.

Both a pensioner household and a working-age household are considered to be poor if their income falls below the same threshold level. Moreover, this threshold level (60 per cent of the median) is defined relative to the incomes of everyone in society (both young and old).

This approach implicitly embodies a view that there should be a degree of equality between young and old in society. If pensioner poverty was defined relative to the incomes only of pensioners, then it is possible that pensioners as a whole might fall behind the working-age population. By setting a common standard, there is a presumption that the living standards of pensioners should not be left behind compared to those of the working-age population. Given growth in productivity and wages over time, one implication is that there may be some pensioners who were relatively well-off when they were younger, but who now find themselves to be poor, compared to the average standard of living – and may receive some benefits from the government as a result. Introducing policies to address pensioner poverty then implies a redistribution of resources between generations as well as the more standard redistribution within generations between those with relatively high and low lifetime incomes.

One reason for having a separate pensioner poverty measure might be that pensioners have different spending needs from those of the rest of the population. Typically, poverty measures take into account spending needs associated with additional household members – thus a two-person household is assumed to require a higher level of income than a one-person household to achieve the same standard of living (but not double the level of income, because of economies of scale within the household). Similarly, households with children are assumed to require more income than households without in order to achieve the same standard of living. However, no adjustment is made for other factors that might affect how much income someone needs in order to achieve a given standard of living that might be related to pensioner status, such as work-related costs or health-related expense. If pensioners' spending needs are lower than those of the working-age population – because, for example, they do not have to spend money on travelling to work or buying smart suits – then they will achieve a higher standard of living with a given level of income. Conversely, if they have to spend more on out-of-pocket health expenditure, their standard of living will be lower.

The issue of how pensioners spend their income relative to the rest of the population is also of importance for the annual up-rating of pensions. In the UK, pensions are increased in line with inflation – measured by the rise in the cost of a basket of goods that reflects the spending of the general population. But if pensioners spend a relatively higher proportion of their incomes on particular goods (such as gas and electricity to heat their homes) and if the cost of those items rises a lot, then pensioners' living standards will fall if their pensions are increased only by the rate of inflation. This issue has led some to call for a separate pensioner price index.

One implication of a common income poverty measure is that pensioner poverty is likely to vary over the business cycle. Pensioners' incomes are typically fixed in nominal or real terms, whereas the incomes of working-age households vary over the business cycle because of unemployment and pro-cyclical variation in wage levels. One implication of this is that pensioner poverty is likely to rise during periods of economic boom and to fall during periods of recession, even though there is no underlying change in pensioner incomes. The mechanism is simply changes in median household income. In part, this variation is valid, since we may care about how pensioners are doing compared to the rest of society. However, if pensioners are objectively no worse off, it may make little sense to worry too much about cyclical fluctuations, or at least to adjust for the cyclical element in order to understand the underlying trends.

The market system and pensions

This section looks at whether a pure market system will achieve the desired efficiency and equity objectives. We start with equity, since this is often the main driver of intervention in the area of pension provision.

Equity

The previous section showed that it was optimal for individuals to smooth their consumption over their lifetimes, saving some of the money they earn when they are working in order to finance consumption in retirement. But, there may be some people – those with very low lifetime incomes – who simply cannot afford to save enough when they are working. Suppose that there is a minimum level of consumption (including spending on food, basic accommodation and clothing) below which it is not possible to exist. Going back to our earlier example, if the minimum level necessary for survival is £6, individuals will only have £4 left over to transfer to period two. They will therefore not have enough money to live on in retirement.

One possibility is that they could work for longer. We have so far assumed that the periods are fixed, but in practice, individuals have some flexibility over how long they continue to work. Delaying retirement would be one way of increasing lifetime resources (as well as reducing the amount of money needed to finance consumption in retirement). However, in practice, carrying on working may not be an option if, for example, low lifetime earnings are linked to health problems.

The government will want to intervene in order to provide some help to people who were genuinely unable to save enough when they were working in order to finance an adequate level of consumption in retirement. But, looking simply at someone's income in retirement, the government is unable to distinguish between this group and another group of people who had sufficiently high lifetime earnings to allow them to save for retirement, but who chose to spend it all. It might be viewed as unfair that the government provides financial help to people who are poor in retirement purely as a result of the spending choices they made when they were younger, while those who earned the same amount, but chose to save their money, receive nothing. In principle, the government could attempt to separate these two cases through some sort of lifetime earnings test, but this would be extremely complex and burdensome in practice. Moreover, it would not solve the problem entirely, missing out, for example, people who squandered large amounts of inherited wealth. This discussion highlights a possible tension between trying to achieve an equitable outcome that redistributes to the poor defined in terms of their current income, and one that treats people fairly according to their total lifetime incomes.

Efficiency

If it is optimal for individuals to smooth their consumption over their lifetime by saving to finance spending in retirement, then what role is there for the government in pension provision, other than to help those whose lifetime earnings are too low to allow them to save for themselves? In practice, there are a number of potential market failures that may justify government intervention. First, there may be problems of information that prevent individuals from making optimal savings decisions. Second, there are some risks that the markets may be unwilling or unable to offer adequate insurance against. We discuss each of these in turn.

Information problems

In practice, solving the intertemporal allocation problem is far from straightforward. One of the biggest problems is the lack of information needed to make the right decisions. It is useful to distinguish between several different kinds of information failure. One is genuine uncertainty involving, for example, future earnings or the timing of death. Individuals do not know what these will be, because no one knows. The other is that individuals may not possess all the relevant information, or may lack the ability to process the relevant information, regarding options for pension investment. Many economic models posit a rational, well-informed agent who is well-equipped to solve the intertemporal allocation. However, there is a growing body of evidence showing that the reality may be quite different.

The evidence suggests that individuals find pensions to be hugely complicated. If someone wants to take out an individual personal pension, there are thousands of different products to choose from, and all will entail making difficult decisions about how much to invest and in which assets to invest, essentially a decision about how much investment risk is involved. Of course, consumers make big, complex decisions in relation to other products (such as cars or computers). However, pensions are fundamentally different. They are usually a one-off purchase, so that consumers cannot learn by trial and error. In any case, it is hard for the consumer to judge whether they have made the right decision, since the outcome is inherently variable. Someone who buys a car does not need to understand how it works – they can judge whether it works by driving it; but it is far harder for someone to assess their pension in the same way. In addition, many pension products seem designed to confuse rather than clarify, with, for example, complicated and opaque charging structures.

One response to these information problems has been to require financial providers to give consumers standardized information to try to help them make the right decisions. However, another issue is low levels of financial literacy, which may mean that individuals are unable to make sense of the information, even when it is available to them. Research on adult numeracy suggests that half the adult population in the UK cannot go beyond simple addition and subtraction, and are unable to understand percentages, compound interest and other concepts fundamental to making sensible use of any information provided.

Rather than buying financial products directly, many consumers choose to buy through a financial adviser, who does have the relevant information and the knowledge to process it. However, many of the underlying issues that prompt consumers to seek advice in the first place may create similar problems in the advice market. If consumers cannot properly judge the product, then they cannot necessarily assess the advice they have been given. If someone goes to the hairdresser to have a haircut, they will pretty soon be able to tell whether the hairdresser has done a good job or not. But if they go to an adviser for financial advice, it will be far longer before they know whether the advice they received was sound. If advisers are remunerated through commission on the products they sell (as is often the case) then they have strong incentives to recommend specific products – and not necessarily the ones that are in the consumer's best interests.

The concern is that these information problems act as a barrier to individuals saving for their retirement. Barr and Diamond (2006) point out that the problem may have equity as well as efficiency implications, since the people who are worst-informed are also disproportionately the least well-off. There is certainly plenty of evidence that people with lower incomes do not save very much. However, it is much harder to be certain that they do not save 'enough'. Making this judgement requires a lot of information about people's current wealth as well as a number of assumptions about their future earnings, age of retirement, saving behaviour, and so on. For many on low incomes, the presence of means-tested benefits means that it may be optimal not to save, as we discuss further below.

There is some evidence that people's consumption falls at retirement (see Banks et al., 1998), which is consistent with people not saving enough, although this has been shown to be mainly a result of early retirement through ill-health, rather than systematic under-saving (see Smith 2006). However, from a number of recent studies showing that the way pension choices are framed can have an important effect on saving behaviour, there is convincing evidence that information problems represent a genuine barrier to saving. For example, automatic enrolment (that is, individuals have to choose to opt out of a pension scheme) boosts participation in company schemes compared to conscious enrolment (that is, individuals have to opt in). Simplifying pension options, such as by reducing the number of funds, also increases participation. Choi et al. (2004a, 2004b) and Thaler and Benartzi (2004, 2007) provide further discussion of the findings of this new behavioural economics. These findings are probably not surprising to most people, but they would not happen in a world in which rational individuals were already making well-informed pension choices, and they suggest that problems of information – as well as problems of inertia and procrastination – have a real effect in preventing people from making optimal decisions. Policies to promote pension saving need to be designed to take into account these behavioural problems.

Aggregate risks

In retirement, an annuity provided by a pension acts as a form of insurance against outliving one's resources, or of dying with a lot of money unspent. Insurance works by pooling risks across individuals. The insurer (the annuity provider) knows the average mortality risk for a cohort of individuals, although it does not know exactly when the different individuals will die. It relies on the fact that some people will die fairly soon after retirement, whereas others will live to a ripe old age. There will be losers (those who die sooner), who will get less than they paid to buy the annuity; and winners (those who die later), who get more. On average, however, the two groups should balance each other out.

But, what happens if everyone lives longer than the insurers expected? In this case, there are more winners than losers, the insurers lose money and, in the worst case, go bust. This is a problem of aggregate, or social risk. All the insured customers face the same risk, and the private insurance market fails because it cannot pool risks. Technically, the risks are not independent events. Unlike private companies, the government can deal with social risks because it can spread them between generations by, for example, taxing the current working population to pay for the pensions of the current retired population. The risk of unexpected increases in life expectancy is a very real one, as we saw earlier in the chapter. The government therefore has an important role to play in providing insurance against such risks, either through providing compensation in case insurers default on annuity payouts, or through providing pensions directly.

Inflation is another social risk. Consumers can purchase annuities that offer indexation against inflation – in other words the value of the annuity rises in line with increases in prices (measured by the consumer price index). However, in the event of inflation, the insurers face an increase in payouts on all their policies and, if inflation is sufficiently high, might find themselves unable to meet all their commitments. Most real annuities are therefore index-linked up to a maximum inflation rate of 5 per cent. Again, unlike private insurers, the government can spread the risk by raising taxes on the working population. Through price-indexation of the basic state pension, therefore, the government offers some insurance against aggregate inflation risk.

Government policies

We have seen that there are a number of reasons why the market outcome is likely to be inefficient or inequitable, and this may justify some form of government intervention. In this section we discuss the different ways in which the government might intervene, including direct provision of pensions, regulation (including compelling people to save) and subsidies for pension saving. Box 4.1 provides brief summaries of pension provision in three countries which have opted for very different systems.

BOX 4.1   Alternative pension systems – the UK, Germany and Australia

The UK

The first tier of the UK pension system is the Basic State Pension, a flat-rate, fairly minimal pension paid to men from age 65 and women from age 60 (which will rise to 65 by 2020) if they have made sufficient years of contributions. This has changed little since it was introduced by Sir William Beveridge in 1948. It operates on a Pay-As-You-Go (PAYG) basis, with pensions being paid out of current contributions. Since the early 1980s, the Basic State Pension has been uprated annually in line with inflation (rather than wage growth) and its value has fallen relative to earnings. At the time of writing it is less than the level of means-tested benefits available for those aged 60+ , and in practice, these benefits also form part of the first tier of pension provision for those with no (or little) additional pension income.

Since 1978, people have also been compelled to contribute to a second tier of pension provision. The default is membership of the state scheme (formerly the state earnings-related pension scheme (SERPS), now the state second pension (S2P)), but individuals can choose to 'opt out' into a private pension. When it was introduced, SERPS was intended to pay a pension worth one-quarter of an individual's best twenty years' earnings (up to a specified upper earnings limit) but its value has gradually been reduced, and in the medium term, S2P will become a flat-rate top-up to the basic state pension.

Compared to many other countries, such as Germany, the UK has a relatively high level of private pension provision. Between 1978 and 1988, individuals could opt out of SERPS into a defined benefit (final salary) scheme. But, from 1988 onwards individuals could also opt out into a defined contribution (money purchase) pension scheme. Since this time, there has been a growth in defined contribution occupational pension schemes and individual private pensions. Nearly half of the people now entering retirement receive more money from one of these private (occupational or individual) schemes than they do from the state.

The UK system is complicated, but can be summarized as a basic, flat-rate level of state provision with additional saving encouraged through the use of tax incentives. In practice, it has worked much better for people whose employers offered a defined benefit scheme.

Germany

The German pension system was the first formal state pension system in the world, designed by Otto von Bismarck and introduced in 1889. It is very different from the UK system. First, there is a single state scheme, the public retirement insurance (*Gesetzliche Rentenversicherung*). Second, it was designed as a system of earnings replacement rather than simply to protect against poverty in old age. It pays a pension that is roughly proportional to someone's labour income averaged over their life, and is therefore much more generous to high earners than to low earners. When it was introduced, SERPS was also designed on this principle. However, almost as soon as SERPS was introduced its generosity was reduced through successive reforms because of concerns about future costs, and this is the problem now facing the German pension system. And, in the UK, many people opted out of SERPS into a private employer or individual scheme, whereas in Germany, almost all employees belong to the state system.

The German system is funded on a PAYG basis – in other words, pensions are financed out of contributions made by current workers. The contribution rate required to finance pensions today is around 19 per cent of wages. Without reform, this was projected to rise to nearly 40 per cent by 2050. This led to huge pressure for reform, and in recent years, in order to stabilise the contribution rate, the pension has been made less generous by reducing its level and raising the age at which people are eligible to receive it. To fill the gap, the government is using tax subsidies to try to encourage private (occupational and individual) pensions, which currently account for around 10 per cent of retirement income.

Australia

Unlike the UK and Germany, Australia has never had any earnings-related social insurance element. Instead, its pension system consists of a flat-rate means-tested benefit, known as the age pension, and mandatory occupational savings pensions, known as the superannuation guarantee.

The age pension pays a flat amount to anyone who qualifies over the ages of 65 for men and 60 (rising in the future to 65) for women. Income and assets (excluding the home) are taken into consideration in determining eligibility, and many people spend down their assets (and buy bigger houses) to enable them to qualify. Around three-quarters of retirees receive the age pension – and of these, two-thirds get the maximum amount.

On top of this basic, means-tested element is the superannuation guarantee which requires employers to contribute an amount equal to 9 per cent of workers' earnings to superannuation individual accounts. Employees are not required to contribute but can make additional voluntary contributions. This scheme covers more than 90 per cent of employees. To help low-income workers, the government will match every A$1 of superannuation contribution with a co-contribution of A$1.50 (up to a maximum). Benefits may be taken in the form of an annuity or lump sum, with most people choosing to take a lump sum. There is clearly a potential conflict between the superannuation system, which mandates saving, and the age pension, which creates an incentive for people to run down their assets to qualify for the full amount.

Provision

Means testing

In principle, the government could meet its equity objective through the general system of means-tested benefits, which would be paid to anyone in old age who satisfied the income and wealth eligibility criteria. This is the case in Australia. In the UK in 1999, the government introduced more generous means-tested benefits for people over 60, known as the Pension Credit. This has become an increasingly important part of the overall system of income provision for people in retirement – it is more generous than the Basic State Pension and is projected to apply to 70 per cent of pensioners by 2050. Means-tested benefits provide a cost-effective way of targeting limited resources on poor pensioners (compared to, say, an increase in the Basic State Pension). However, they have been criticized heavily for reducing incentives for working-age people to save for retirement. In Australia, where additional saving is compulsory, it has been argued that they provide incentives for people to spend down their assets.

This is known as a moral hazard problem. It is a classic problem with any form of insurance – as noted in an earlier chapter, once people are insured, they will reduce their efforts to avoid the event for which the insurance is provided, whether it is turning off the gas to prevent the risk of fire, or saving to guard against poverty in retirement. It arises because the insurer (in this case the government) cannot monitor perfectly individual actions; the government cannot distinguish between those who genuinely cannot afford to save for retirement, and those who fail to do so. In many cases, moral hazard problems prevent private markets from working efficiently, such as in health care, as we saw in Chapter 2. In this case, however, it is the government that creates the problem by insuring individuals against penury in old age.

It may sound as though people are trying to cheat the system. This is not the case; it is rather that the presence of a government safety net changes the optimal allocation of resources between periods. Going back to our previous example, suppose that the government provides a safety net of £4 for anyone who has an income of less than this in retirement, but that it pays nothing to anyone who has a private income above this level. Individuals can choose to consume their £10 equally in each of periods one and two (and get nothing from the government), yielding total benefit of 80. Or they can consume £10 in period one and, with no savings, receive £4 from the government in period two. This yields a total benefit of 89. It therefore makes sense for people not to save.

The moral hazard problem is unlikely to affect the entire population. There will be some people who would save enough to take their retirement income well above the safety-net level; they would suffer a greater loss of benefit from reducing their retirement consumption to £4 than they would benefit from higher consumption when they are working. The problem applies particularly to people whose retirement incomes would fall just above the level of the safety net. Without further intervention, the result is a higher cost to providing a safety net. However, the government may decide that an appropriate solution is to provide an insurance-based pension, or to compel people to save a portion of their earnings when they are working for retirement, enough to take them above the safety net if they have sufficiently high lifetime earnings.

Social insurance – Pay-As-You-Go (PAYG) versus funded pensions

Apart from cases such as Australia that rely on a pure means-tested system, most governments provide an insurance-based pension (see further discussion in Chapter 9). Everyone receives a pension in retirement (even millionaires) so long as they meet the eligibility criteria – a specified number of years' contributions into the pension fund (as is the case in the UK and Germany), or a residence requirement.

There are, very broadly, two alternative ways a government could run a pension fund. One is to raise revenue from the working population (through taxes) to pay current pensioners. This is known as a *Pay-As-You-Go (PAYG)* system and is how pensions in the UK and Germany are financed. The alternative is to collect contributions from people when they are working and invest them in a fund for the future when they are retired. This is known as a *funded system*. Private pensions are run on a funded basis, but there is no reason why state pensions could not also operate in this way.

The issue of how to fund pensions has become a matter of heated academic and political debate. As we have seen, the existing PAYG systems in many countries have been put under increasing pressure by ageing populations. The basic problem is very simple – there are fewer working-age people to pay contributions relative to pensioners who need to be paid pensions. With generous state pensions, as in Germany, the financing problem is particularly pronounced. Many people have seen funded pensions as the answer to this problem. On the face of it, funded pensions do not suffer from the same financing problem; since individuals make their own contributions, there will always be a pot they can draw on in their retirement. However, if individuals are expected to live longer, then the level of annual spending they will be able to finance out of the pot will be reduced. Funding does not avoid having to make the kind of hard choices outlined by the UK Pension Commission (work longer, save more or face a lower standard of living in retirement). Moreover, the transition from a PAYG system to a funded one would be painful, since it would require one generation to pay not only for their own future pension but also for their parents' pension.

Another argument that has been made in favour of funding is that it allows individuals to enjoy a higher rate of return. In a PAYG system, the return (how much more the pension is worth compared to the contributions) is roughly equal to the rate of wage growth. In a funded system, individuals can invest in the stock market, where returns have historically been higher than wage growth. Also, in a funded system, individuals can be given more choice to invest their savings in a wide range of assets. In general, more choice is usually a good thing, since it allows individuals to align their choice with their preferences. However, given the earlier discussion about information problems in financial markets, there may be some doubt as to whether all individuals are well-placed to make such choices. Moreover, along with the higher expected return of investing in equities comes increased investment risk. Falls in the stock market are not uncommon. A big fall at or close to retirement could have big effects on individuals' incomes in retirement. Finally, an advantage of a PAYG system is that it involves transfers across generations. This means that aggregate risks (cohort longevity risk and inflation risk) can be spread across generations. In a funded system this is not possible.

Regulation

As we have seen, for many reasons, consumers in retail financial markets may not be the rational, well-informed agents of economic models. The decisions they have to make are complex, regarding trade-offs between consumption today and consumption in an uncertain future, and the products themselves are often unnecessarily complicated (with, for example, opaque charging structures). In principle, financial advisers are there to help consumers make the right choices, but they may face incentives that lead them to recommend the wrong products.

These problems provide a rationale for the government to intervene in regulating financial markets. This regulation can be characterized as *process regulation*, since the government sets standards for the process of buying and selling of financial services. Examples of these regulations in practice include regulations surrounding financial promotions – that is, what providers can and cannot advertise about the products they are selling; disclosure requirements, which require companies to provide standardized product information; and suitability requirements, which set standards for advisers making product recommendations. In addition, providers and advisers have to be authorized by the regulatory authority, which makes regular checks to ensure that the regulations are being met.

More recently, the UK government has also introduced limited forms of *product regulation*. This was in response to a concern that the lack of information was preventing consumers from shopping around for financial products – the usual mechanism for driving competition in a market. In 1999, the government therefore introduced stakeholder pensions – individual retirement accounts that had to meet specified standards in terms of charge structure and the maximum level of charges.

The introduction of stakeholder pensions formed part of a policy of 'informed choice'. The UK government was committed to providing a basic level of pension provision, but took the view that, above this level, individuals should determine how much they wanted to save for retirement. The underlying belief was that, if given the right opportunities, including the right products and clear information (including, for example, pension statements that set out explicitly what future pension entitlements would be), people will plan sensibly.

However, the growing body of evidence pointing to problems of procrastination and inertia in individual saving decisions has caused a recent policy shift. In response to the recommendations of the Pensions Commission, the government announced in 2006 that it will introduce a National Pensions Saving Scheme. This offers individuals a simplified, low-cost vehicle to save for retirement. But it is also going to feature *automatic enrolment*; that is, people who are working will be enrolled automatically into the scheme, and will have to choose to opt out. This goes beyond simply providing individuals with information to help them to make the right decisions, and recognizes that individuals may have problems processing and acting on that information. It therefore involves the government taking a more active role in pushing people into saving for their retirement. However, both the Pensions Commission and the government stopped short of compelling people to save above the fairly minimal level of the Basic State Pension.

Although funded out of general taxation, the Basic State Pension is akin to a compulsory minimum level of pension provision (at least for all those in paid work). However, for most people, it will not be sufficient to provide a comfortable level of income in retirement, since it will be worth around 30 per cent of median earnings. Rather, it will provide a platform on top of which the government hopes that people will build additional private savings. As we saw above, in many other countries, such as Germany, the state provides a more generous pension, intended to provide earnings replacement rather than just a basic income. The reasons why this route was not chosen in the UK are largely historical (see Hill 2007) and reflect the fact that many employers already provided fairly generous occupational pensions, although, in the face of financing pressures in recent years, many employers have closed these schemes to new, and even existing, employees.

The argument used against compelling people to save more for their own pension in the UK is that it may force some people to save too much, and to save in a particular form that they might not want to save in. It is a 'one size fits all' policy and, in practice, it may not suit people who have high current spending needs, or those who wish to save for their retirement through accumulating housing wealth. However, it remains to be seen whether the chosen route of informed choice, together with the additional push from automatic enrolment, will be sufficient to overcome the problems of information failure, procrastination and inertia.

Subsidies

Compared to other forms of saving in the UK (such as a savings account in a bank or building society, or money invested directly in stocks and shares), pensions are treated favourably by the tax system. Individuals receive income tax relief on contributions made into a personal private pension. This is partially offset by the fact that they have to pay income tax on the income as it comes out of the fund in retirement, but they can take up to a quarter of the total amount saved completely tax free. Also, since individuals typically have higher incomes when they are working than when they are retired, they will pay less tax on the income withdrawn from the fund than they would have done on income paid into the fund.

This tax relief amounts to a large subsidy for pension saving. The most recent estimates suggest that this costs the government £14 billion, although these estimates are inevitably imprecise, since they involve making assumptions about what people would otherwise have done with their money. Even so, this amount is around one-third of the cost of the Basic State Pension.

Overall, tax incentives have a potentially ambiguous effect on saving. Tax relief increases the return on saving, and this may encourage people to save more, but it also allows them to consume more today as well as tomorrow. This second effect means that they will actually increase consumption and reduce saving today. However, aside from the overall effect on saving, the fact that pensions are more attractive than other forms of saving is likely to encourage people to save in a pension rather than elsewhere. The government therefore uses tax relief to encourage people to save in pension funds. It is desirable for the government if people lock up some of their savings until retirement and save in a form that they later have to annuitise. The tax relief may be necessary in order to persuade people to do this, since they might not otherwise choose a form of saving with these relatively unattractive features.

The current system of tax relief is extremely regressive. It is worth much more to rich individuals than to poorer ones. One reason is that richer individuals save more in pensions. However, it is also because contributions attract tax relief at the individual's marginal rate of tax –which is greater for higher-rate taxpayers.

It has been estimated that half of the benefit went to the top 10 per cent of tax-payers: and a quarter to the top 2.5 per cent. Obviously, the government cannot stop richer people from saving more, although it could place tighter caps on the amount of contributions that attract tax relief. However, it could also make the subsidies relatively more generous to middle- and lower-earners by limiting tax relief to the basic tax rate for everyone. It could also, as it has done with the proposed new National Pension Saving Scheme, have a form of matched pension saving. Under this scheme, for every 4 per cent of earnings saved by the individual, the government will add a further 1 per cent.

SUMMARY

- Pensions provide a means for people to maintain their level of spending when their income falls in retirement. In general, individuals will have an incentive to save some of their income when they are working in order to finance spending in retirement. This overall process is referred to as *consumption smoothing*.

- Government intervention may be required for a number of reasons. First, some individuals may be too poor to afford to save when they are working. Second, the private market may not be able to insure people against certain types of aggregate risks (including inflation risk and cohort longevity risk). Third, saving for retirement may involve making difficult decisions about complicated financial products. Many people put off making such decisions.

- In principle, the government could provide a basic level of support through means-tested benefits. However, this may reduce people's incentive to save for themselves. The main alternative is for the government to provide a system of social insurance.

- One important issue is how generous the pension provided by the state should be. The government could provide a very generous pension, but with an ageing population, this is costly. The alternative is for the government to provide a minimum and rely on additional private saving. Private saving may be encouraged through subsidies or via automatic enrolment mechanisms.

FURTHER READING

The Spring 2006 volume of the *Oxford Review of Economic Policy* provides a number of useful articles on various aspects of pension provision and retirement. See, in particular, the articles by Barr and Diamond (2006) for an overview of the economics of pension provision, Hills (2006) and Banks and Smith (2006) for further discussion of the UK, and Whitehouse and Whiteford (2007) for an analysis of pension systems and reform across the OECD.

Barr (2000) and Barr (2004b) contain an expanded version of the arguments in Barr and Diamond (2006). See also Diamond (1977, 2004) and Feldstein (2004).

The two reports by the Pensions Commission provide an extremely comprehensive overview of the state of pension provision in the UK, as well as an analysis of the problems and suggestions for reform. They are well worth a look and can be found at http://www.webarchive.org.uk/pan/16806/20070802/www.pensionscommission.org.uk/index.html. Hill (2007) also contains a general overview of the UK system.

Brewer *et al.* (2007) contains an analysis of pensioner poverty based on standard income measures, and Dominey and Kempson (2006) has a wider discussion of pensioner poverty, covering indicators of material deprivation.

On the new behavioural economics, see Thaler and Benartzi (2004, 2007) and Choi *et al.* (2004a, 2004b).

QUESTIONS FOR DISCUSSION

1. Suppose that the government is going to introduce a target for reducing pensioner poverty. How should pensioner poverty be defined?

2. Is it fair if women receive a lower annuity income than men in return for the same lump sum?

3. Many governments make helping poor pensioners their main priority in pension provision. What potential problems might this create?

4. If I heavily discount the future and spend all my money when I am young, should the government help me when I am old?

5. Is moral hazard likely to be a problem in the annuity market?

6. 'If people live longer, they need to save more when they are working, work for longer, or face lower incomes in retirement.' Should individuals be left to make the trade-off for themselves?

7. Should pension saving be compulsory?

8. 'Tax relief on pensions is heavily regressive and does little to boost saving.' Should it therefore be abolished?

CHAPTER 5

Housing

For more than thirty years – since the 1970s – the UK government's objective in relation to housing has been for everyone to have 'a decent home at a price they can afford'. This reflects the importance of housing as one of the most basic human needs, and the fact that, if left to itself, the market would be unlikely to meet this need. This chapter explores the market failures that give rise to a need for government intervention in the housing market, and the alternative policy tools that can be used.

Government intervention in the housing market in the UK takes a number of different forms. First, the housing market is heavily regulated, with regulations covering everything from land use to building standards to the quality of accommodation. Second, the government subsidises demand for housing by paying (in part or in full) rent for people on low incomes (through housing benefit) and by giving favourable tax treatment to owner-occupied housing compared to other assets. There are also a number of government schemes offering financial support to particular groups of people buying their own homes, the biggest and most famous of which is the 'Right to Buy' policy, which offered discounts on the market valuation to sitting council house tenants who wanted to purchase their homes. Finally, the UK government provides social housing; that is, housing financed by the government and provided either by the government itself or by not-for-profit organisations at sub-market rents. Historically, spending on provision through social housing was greater than that on demand subsidies. In the aftermath of the Second World War, the government was better placed than the private sector to take on the required level of slum clearance and construction. Over time, however, the balance has shifted to demand subsidies, which at the time of writing account for two-thirds of the total of £16 billion of direct government spending on housing (up from 18 per cent in 1975).

When we talk about housing, we are usually referring to any form of accommodation, whether owned or rented. The government's objective is set in these broad terms, and does not imply a target for people to actually own their homes. However, the affordability of house-buying has become an increasingly salient issue in the UK, following a period of rapidly rising house prices. Since 1996, average real house prices have at least doubled in all English regions and increased relative to average wages, giving rise to concern that owner-occupation is becoming unaffordable for an increasing number of people. This chapter considers possible arguments for why the government might intervene to promote home-ownership in particular, rather than just addressing the wider need for some form of housing.

Objectives

Equity

As defined above, the government's objective in relation to housing is defined principally in terms of equity. Shelter is a basic human need, and it is therefore seen as appropriate that the government should ensure that everyone has some form of accommodation. Of course, this does not justify everyone having a footballer-style mansion or a luxury penthouse in London's Docklands. Nor does it necessarily imply that everyone should own their own home, although there are important equity considerations that are relevant to the issue of home ownership. Housing is increasingly the dominant form of wealth in the UK, and rising house prices will exacerbate further the inequality between owners and non-owners as existing owners see the value of their homes increase. Moreover, with, at the time of writing, house prices worth several times average earnings, there is evidence that inherited wealth (often from house sales) is playing an increasingly important role in financing house purchases, implying that, without government intervention, inequalities in wealth are likely to be transmitted across generations.

However, when people talk about housing as a necessity, they usually mean that there is a *minimum standard* of accommodation that is a necessity of life. This is undoubtedly the official view implicit in the concept of 'a decent home' – namely, that there is a minimum standard of housing below which no family should be allowed to fall. Interestingly, the objective that was adopted in the immediate post-war period was that there should be 'a separate home for every family that wishes to have one', with no reference being made to the standard of the accommodation. The inclusion of 'decent' reflects the fact that, in a more affluent society, the view of what is an acceptable minimum standard has changed and, according to government-defined standards, now includes a kitchen that is less than twenty years old and a bathroom that is less than thirty years old.

Of course, shelter is not the only basic necessity; food and warmth are others. Apart from the case of food stamps in the USA, the way in which governments usually meet these other needs is to ensure that people have enough income to allow them to buy (a basic level of) food and fuel. So, why is housing different? Why does the government deem it necessary to provide housing directly, or to link income support payments directly to housing costs through housing benefit? There are paternalistic reasons why the government may prefer someone to spend benefits on housing rather than on, say, alcohol, although the same would apply to food and fuel. The scale of housing costs is likely to be an important factor, since the amount of cash that someone needs to be able to afford to pay for accommodation is quite large. The level of income support for a couple with children is currently around £200 a week; adding accommodation costs for a family would double this amount. Giving cash handouts of this size with no strings attached may simply be seen as being too generous. Another factor is the huge regional disparities in housing costs (described by Beveridge in his 1942 report as the 'problem of rent'); at the time of writing average rents across England are £120 a week, but are £180 a week in London. Making dedicated payments for housing costs provides a flexible way to take these regional variations into account, although this is not always the case. In Australia and Germany, for example, payments do not vary, while rents do.

Efficiency

There may also be additional efficiency reasons for the government to provide housing that are not present in the case of food and fuel. If someone chooses not to spend their money on food, they are going to suffer the consequences themselves and their decision will have little effect on others (although any subsequent medical costs will have to be borne by taxpayers). However, if they decide not to spend their money on accommodation, the fact that they are living on the street may impact directly on others who live in the area. Put formally, it creates a negative externality by imposing a cost on other people. Clearing the streets of (intentionally) homeless people to avoid the discomfort of those who live nearby may not sound like a particularly edifying rationale for government intervention in the housing market. However, it highlights the fact that individuals' decisions about housing have important consequences for other people, in a way that their decisions about fuel and food do not. Decisions about housing can have negative – and positive – externalities that are likely to make the free-market outcome an inefficient one, since individuals are unlikely to take these external effects into account when calculating the costs and benefits of their actions. As we discuss further in the section below, even if the government did not have a strong equity rationale for intervening in the housing market, there would be a justification on the grounds of economic efficiency.

The market system and housing

The market system is the main means of allocating housing in the UK. At the time of writing, 4 million (out of a total of 22 million) households in England live in social housing (that is, housing provided by the public or not-for-profit sectors). In many European countries, the social rented sector grew rapidly immediately after the Second World War as the government responded to urgent post-war housing needs. In the UK, the social sector peaked at 31 per cent of households in 1979, but a combination of the Right to Buy policy and reduced new building rates had seen it decline to fewer than one in five households in the mid-2000s. By European standards, this is neither unusually large or small. Some countries, such as Germany, have a very small social sector (fewer than 6 per cent of households), while in others, such as the Netherlands, the social sector is far larger (at 35 per cent of households).

Owner-occupation has grown continuously in the UK (and in most other European countries) during the post-war period. In 1951, 30 per cent of homes were owner-occupied. At the time of writing, this proportion is now 70 per cent. Again, this is not particularly high by European standards. The rate of home-ownership is above 80 per cent in Ireland, Spain and Norway. However, there are some countries, such as Germany, Denmark and the Netherlands, where the home-ownership rate is only around half of the country's households.

As was shown in Chapter 1, the market system has several distinct advantages, but in the case of housing, there are a number of reasons why the unregulated market is likely to fail to produce an efficient and equitable outcome. In this section we shall examine some of the reasons for these failures. In addition to the problem of *externalities* already mentioned, there are likely to be problems arising from *imperfect information* and from a lack of adjustment to price changes because of *supply inelasticity*.

Externalities

When individuals decide how much to spend on housing, they are likely to consider only the costs and benefits to themselves. However, their decisions are likely to affect other people in a range of ways, discussed further below, imposing external costs and benefits on others. The failure to incorporate these externalities in the decision-making calculus means that the outcome of individual decisions is likely to be socially inefficient. Where individual decisions create external benefits, there will be under-spending, and in cases where individual decisions create external costs, there will be over-spending.

So, what are these external costs and benefits? One important example is the link between housing and health. It has been fairly well-established that there is a link between the quality of housing and the health of individuals. Disease tends to thrive in damp, cramped, overcrowded conditions. Individuals may have the incentive to spend on housing up to the point where they reap benefits for themselves in terms of improved health, but there are additional benefits for other people living nearby, if the spread of disease is reduced, that will not be taken into account. Health reasons have historically played an important role in motivating governments to take direct action to clear slums, although the government may also achieve its goals through the regulation of, for example, the density and design of accommodation. More recently, in keeping with growing concerns about climate change, housing regulations now also cover fuel efficiency.

More generally, if someone makes changes to the fabric of a house, this will tend to alter the level of satisfaction its neighbours obtain from their own housing. This might be because there are direct effects: neighbours might derive pleasure from seeing the freshly-painted façade of a house because it is better than the grimy old paintwork; or they might take offence at a new conservatory because it obscures their view.

Also, the neighbours' level of satisfaction will be affected if an individual's housing decisions have an effect on the quality of the *neighbourhood* within which the houses are located. Galster (2002) defines neighbourhood as 'a bundle of spatially based attributes associated with clusters of residences'. These attributes are multi-dimensional and may include some or all of the following – the structural characteristics of the buildings in the area, the infrastructure (roads, etc.); the area's demographic and socio-economic profile; the local services (schools, hospitals); and the environment and amenities. The key is that they are spatially based. All the people living in a particular area (as well as local businesses) are consumers of neighbourhood, but, as Galster points out, an important feature of neighbourhood is that the act of consumption may alter the neighbourhood's characteristics. In other words, certain types of household may be attracted to a particular area because of its proximity to certain local services or businesses. In turn, the arrival of these households may change the current demographic or socio-economic profile of the neighbourhood and initiate further longer-term changes in these and other attributes. In this way, one household's consumption of a neighbourhood can generate costs and benefits for others living in the same neighbourhood, and since the quality of neighbourhoods are often defined in a relative fashion, to households in other neighbourhoods as well. Through this process, neighbourhoods can also quickly enter virtuous or vicious circles, whereby improvement begets further improvement, or decline spirals downwards.

An important question for policy-makers is the extent to which neighbourhood characteristics have a direct effect on important outcomes such as education, employment and levels of crime. Assume that the socio-economic profile of a neighbourhood declines. This will have a negative impact on the remaining residents who are now consuming a poorer quality of neighbourhood. In other words, their level of satisfaction with the neighbourhood will go down. But does the deterioration in quality of the neighbourhood also have a direct effect on, say, the employment prospects of neighbourhood residents? Take the people who stay in the neighbourhood. Do they now face worse prospects of finding a job, and their children a poorer quality of education because the characteristics of the neighbourhood have changed? There are a number of reasons for believing that neighbourhood effects might matter. They may operate through a number of mechanisms, including neighbourhood resources (reputation of place, local public services), peer group effects or social norm, as well as exclusion from the informal networks through which people often find work.

However, identifying neighbourhood effects is hard to do in practice. The neighbourhood effect must exist independently of the characteristics of the neighbourhood's residents. Obviously, the concentration of people with low levels of skills in a particular neighbourhood is likely to result in a high level of unemployment, but the presence of a neighbourhood effect would imply that characteristics of the neighbourhood itself were at least partly responsible for the high level of unemployment, in addition to individual skill levels. Dietz (2002) and Durlauf (2004) provide an overview of empirical work in this area.

In the USA, the Moving to Opportunity (MTO) demonstration programme provides an important source of evidence on the potential effect of neighbourhoods. This programme, rolled out in five cities – Baltimore, Boston, Chicago, Los Angeles and New York – provided housing vouchers to a randomly selected group of families living in inner-city areas. These vouchers enabled the families to move out of the inner-city area to a more affluent neighbourhood. The issue at stake is what this change in neighbourhood means in terms of adult and child outcomes. Evaluations of the programme, including Katz *et al.* (2001) have found positive effects for children on behavioural outcomes, health and juvenile crime, but less evidence of positive effects on adult economic outcomes. Moreover, whether the positive effects can be attributed to neighbourhoods or more generally to improved housing quality is unresolved. Nevertheless, the MTO programme highlights that, for policy-makers, understanding the effects of housing and neighbourhoods is important, not only for affecting people's quality of life but also, potentially, for influencing other important outcomes.

If neighbourhood matters, an obvious question is why individual landlords or home-owners do not spend money to try to improve neighbourhood quality. The answer is that any investment they might make is almost certain to yield a poor return because the poor neighbourhood conditions will dominate any improvement they might make to a single dwelling. The existence of strong neighbourhood external costs will deter any future tenants or house-purchasers who would be willing and able to pay the rent levels or house prices that would make improvement worthwhile. Consequently, private individuals are likely to decide against spending money on their property and will thereby contribute to the decline of the neighbourhood.

Only if individuals could be confident that others in the neighbourhood were also going to improve their property would they be likely to consider investments of their own. In this case, it is possible that concerted action on the part of a number of people might result in a sufficient reduction in the level of external cost being imposed by one on another to make individual investments worthwhile. However, uncertainty will usually mean that no one is willing to take the initiative. The essence of this problem – which is sometimes known as 'the prisoner's dilemma' – can be demonstrated in terms of the following simple example.

Suppose there are two landlords, Bert and Ernie, who own two adjoining properties on a certain street. Both buildings have become rather run-down and they are each trying to decide how much to spend on repairs and renovation. For purposes of illustration, let us assume that they have both decided to spend at least £10, 000, and that they are each considering whether it would be worth upgrading the buildings through an additional £10,000 on top of this sum. Let us start by looking at the decision from Bert's point of view. He cannot be sure what Ernie is going to do, and yet he knows that because of externalities the return he receives will depend to a certain extent on Ernie's actions. The factors he will need to consider are summarised in the 'pay-off matrix' shown in Table 5.1.

Table 5.1 Bert's rates of return

	Ernie does not invest	*Ernie invests*
Bert does not invest	4%	6%
Bert invests	2%	5%

The matrix shows that if Bert decides not to invest the extra £10,000 and Ernie decides to do the same, Bert will receive a 4 per cent return on his original investment. If, however, Ernie invests while Bert does not, Ernie's improved building will bestow an external benefit on his property and raise his return to 6 per cent. So if Bert *does not invest* he will receive either a 4 per cent or a 6 per cent return. On the other hand, if Bert decides to invest while Ernie decides not to do so, Ernie's less-well-kept building will impose an external cost on Bert's property and reduce his return to 2 per cent. Finally, if Ernie did invest at the same time, Bert would receive some external benefit and his return would rise to 5 per cent. Thus, if Bert decides to *invest*, he will receive either a 2 per cent or a 5 per cent return. So which option will he choose?

It is likely that Bert will approach the problem in the following manner. First, he will ask himself what is the best strategy to adopt if he thinks that Ernie is not going to invest; the first column of the matrix in Table 5.1 shows that he too would do better not to invest in these circumstances because then he would make a 4 per cent return instead of a 2 per cent return. Second, he will ask himself what is his best strategy if he thinks that Ernie is going to invest; the second column of the matrix shows that, once again, he would do better not to invest in this situation. In this way he would make a 6 per cent instead of a 5 per cent return. Thus, in both cases he will make a larger return by not investing. Because Ernie is faced with exactly the same uncertainties concerning Bert's behaviour, he can be expected to go through a similar decision-making process. If he does, he will reach the same conclusion; namely, that his best strategy is not to invest. Therefore neither Bert or Ernie will invest and they will both make a 4 per cent return. Notice, however, that if they had both invested the extra £10,000, they would both have been better off, because they would each have earned a 5 per cent return! This is the essence of the prisoner's dilemma.

The term prisoner's dilemma derives from the supposed problems facing two prisoners arrested on a joint charge. When they are kept in separate cells, and therefore unsure about each other's willingness to collaborate with the police in return for favourable treatment, they are likely to end up with – from their point of view – a worse outcome than if they had been able to plan a joint defence. By acting independently in situations where they are unsure about each other's behaviour, decision-makers reach an outcome that is less desirable to both of them than one they could have reached had they collaborated. But collaboration between landlords of poor-quality housing is unlikely to take place, especially as it is in any given landlord's interests to appear to collaborate – in order to get his/her neighbour to invest – and then to renege on the deal.

Arguably, these problems may be less severe in the case of owner-occupied housing. If Bert and Ernie were actually living next door to each other, they might (particularly after living next door to each other for a period of time) overcome the co-ordination failure by building up trust. After they had returned a number of favours – borrowing and returning a lawnmower, for example, and inviting each other over for dinner – each could be more confident that the other would keep his word. Home-owners are also more direct stakeholders in their local neighbourhood (compared to private landlords) since they have to live and possibly work in the neighbourhood as well as having a financial stake through housing. This means that the incentive to try to overcome the co-ordination failure is that much greater, giving rise to, for example, residents' committees to try to effect neighbourhood change.

It is also likely that individual home-owners will have a greater incentive to invest in improving a property than have private landlords. Ignoring the effects on neighbourhood, the return on investing in home-improvements can be expressed as an increase in the value of the flow of housing services. For a private landlord, this equates to a higher rent s/he can charge; for a home-owner, it equates to a higher level of satisfaction while s/he is still living in the property. For both, there will also be a higher price when they come to sell the property. Since the home-owner makes the choice of the paint colours and the kitchen units, s/he is almost certain to derive a higher level of satisfaction from improvements than the average prospective tenant is prepared to pay for the same (financial) level of improvements made by the landlord. So long as s/he is planning to stay for a number of years, therefore, the home-owner is likely to derive a higher return from investing in home improvements than is a private landlord, and has a greater incentive to invest.

Imperfect information

Information is a necessary lubricant to keep markets working smoothly. Consumers need information about the quality of products and the prices in the marketplace in order to shop around effectively and drive prices down. In the housing market, however, consumers are not always perfectly informed. The decision to move house may be prompted by a job change, requiring individuals to relocate quickly and to an unfamiliar area. They may lack the necessary information (and the time to acquire and process such information) in order to make a well-informed decision, and may pay over the odds for accommodation. Recent migrants are often at a particular disadvantage. This may be because they have just arrived in an area and have not had sufficient time to acquire the necessary information; or it may be that their lack of education or familiarity with the housing system prevents them from understanding how to acquire it. These information problems may be exacerbated by additional language barriers.

However, private landlords may also face information problems in that they are unable to determine the quality of potential tenants. Consider landlords' objectives, which are to obtain the maximum return on their property. As well as charging a high level of rent, they will want to reduce the time the property is empty, and to keep maintenance and repair costs as low as possible. They would therefore like to find careful tenants who will look after their property (keep it clean and not break the furniture) and who are likely to stay in the property for some time. These are 'good tenants'. However, there is another type – 'bad tenants' – who cause a lot of damage and typically move out after a couple of months. A priori, the two types of tenant are indistinguishable. When prospective tenants come to look round a property, landlords cannot tell whether they are good or bad prospects. This is known as a problem of *asymmetric information* – the individuals know whether they are good or bad tenants, but the information is hidden from the landlords. The bad tenants have no incentive to reveal themselves (since they would be charged a higher rent or excluded from the property altogether), while the good tenants may have problems in identifying themselves. In practice, however, landlords can do various things to encourage good tenants and/or discourage bad ones, such as setting a minimum letting period and requiring a deposit and letters of reference. And, while they cannot identify bad tenants, they can also exclude groups of people on the basis of identifiable characteristics that they (rightly or wrongly) perceive to be possessed by bad tenants. Historically, landlords have excluded people on the grounds of occupation (sailors, for example), ethnicity (the Irish, for example), race, and welfare-dependency, though it is probably stretching things too far to try to justify such discrimination on economic grounds.

Deposits and reference letters are more acceptable ways for landlords to try to overcome the problem of asymmetric information. But they may none the less have unfortunate consequences in denying access to private rented accommodation to people who cannot afford a deposit and are unable to provide a letter of reference. Those on low incomes get support with their rent payments through the housing benefit system, but this does not include the payment of a deposit (which is often one or two months' rent in advance). Those who have been in care or in custody may also lack the means to finance a deposit, and be unable to get letters of reference from employers or former landlords; these groups are given priority in terms of social housing.

While landlords may (reasonably or unreasonably) be trying to protect themselves from bad tenants, the result is that some groups may find themselves excluded from private rented accommodation or restricted to a narrow subset of the private rented sector. This may leave them with a very limited choice of accommodation, and facing unscrupulous landlords who, with a near-monopoly of supply, can charge high prices for poor-quality accommodation. In the 1950s and 1960s, Peter Rachman bought up slums in Notting Hill in London, evicted the sitting tenants and filled the properties with immigrant families who were forced to pay extortionate rents. In large part he was able to do this because these families were excluded by discrimination from renting elsewhere. Although they were clearly being exploited, many of Rachman's tenants defended him because he was the only one to offer them accommodation.

Adjustment problems: supply inelasticity

Chapter 1 described how the market system copes with changes in demand. If demand for a commodity increases there will be an initial rise in its price, which can be expected to encourage some firms to produce more. This increase in supply will satisfy some of the additional demand. As supply increases there will be a tendency for the price to fall gradually from its immediate post-change level until a new equilibrium price is established. In some circumstances, however, there is very little opportunity to increase output in response to rising demand. In these circumstances, demand will remain unsatisfied while prices rise to – and

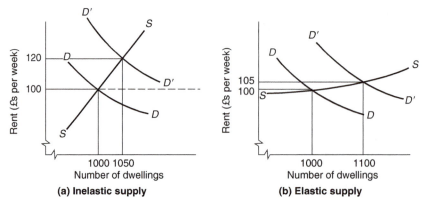

Figure 5.1   Supply elasticity, prices and dwellings.

remain at – the immediate post-change level. If these conditions apply we say that supply is *inelastic*.

The difference between a situation of relatively inelastic supply and one in which the supply response is more flexible (elastic) is demonstrated in Figure 5.1. In both parts of the diagram the vertical axis records the price of housing (in terms of £s rent per week) while the horizontal axis records the number of dwellings demanded and supplied in this particular local market. In the first panel, the point of intersection between the demand schedule (*DD*) and the supply schedule (*SS*), indicates an equilibrium price of £100 per week, at which 1,000 dwellings are demanded and supplied. Now suppose that there is a sudden increase in demand following the migration of additional families into the area. This is depicted by the second demand schedule (*D′D′*). The increase in demand leads to a new equilibrium at which the price has risen to £120 per week and the supply has increased by 50 dwellings. Note that a substantial increase in price (20 per cent) has led to only a small increase in the supply of housing (5 per cent). When supply is inelastic, the bulk of the adjustment to a change in demand conditions will take place through a change in price instead of a change in the quantity.

In contrast, the second panel of the diagram shows how an identical initial equilibrium position, followed by the same change in demand conditions, results in a far smaller price increase and a much larger increase in the supply of housing. Here the price rises to only £105 (5 per cent), whereas 100 more dwellings are supplied (10 per cent). When supply is elastic, more of the change in demand conditions will take place through a change in quantity.

While this illustrates the concept of elasticity in relation to the rental housing market, it is also, of course, extremely relevant to the owner-occupier sector. Inelastic supply is one key factor in explaining why house prices can increase very rapidly. In practice, house price increases are also fuelled by speculation and expectations. If house prices start to increase (because of an increase in demand), expectations of future appreciation increase individuals' willingness to pay more now – increasing demand (and prices) still further. In practice, while earnings are clearly important in determining how much individuals can borrow, there is a lot of flexibility in the size and terms of loans that individuals are prepared to take out (and financial institutions are prepared to lend), which has meant that people are able to finance ever-higher house prices. Obviously, these arguments will also work in the other direction – a small fall in demand is likely to feed through to fairly big reductions in price. The combination of inelastic supply and speculative behaviour by consumers therefore results in the price of housing being quite volatile (big swings up and down) compared to the prices of foodstuffs and services, for example.

The elasticity of supply has important implications for the equity of outcomes in the housing market. This is because, when prices or rents rise, it is the existing owners of properties who benefit, at the expense of their tenants or potential owner-occupiers. If it is impossible to increase the supply of a commodity for which demand has risen, then the owners of the existing stock will be in a monopoly position and will receive monopoly profits. Clearly, this will affect the distribution of wealth, often in ways that penalise lower-income groups, who are less likely to be property owners.

The UK-government-commissioned Barker Review of Housing Supply reported on supply conditions in the owner-occupied sector (see HM Treasury 2004). It concluded that housing output in the UK responds only very weakly to changes in house prices compared to that in other countries. Formal estimates suggest that it is half as responsive as that in France, a third as responsive as in the USA, and a quarter as responsive as in Germany. And, the report suggests, in the UK, responsiveness has been declining over time. In the 1990s, supply responsiveness fell almost to zero (in other words, there was no change in housing output in response to increases in price). Increasing demand has therefore fed entirely through into higher house prices. So, why is housing supply so inelastic? There are underlying problems with the relatively fixed supply of land and with the house-building industry, which we discuss in this section. Government planning regulations, discussed in the next section may exacerbate these problems.

Land shortages

The supply of housing is inelastic because land is in fairly fixed supply, particularly in a relatively densely populated country such as the UK. The problem of land supply is exacerbated by the fact that location is crucial to housing. There is not really a single housing market in the UK – rather a series of local markets. A house in Islington is not a substitute for one in the Scottish Highlands, and it cannot be moved from one place to another. This contrasts with the supply conditions of most other goods. If there is a shortage of a particular model of car in Leeds, for example, but they are plentiful in Manchester, dealers can transport them from Manchester to Leeds. Because such mobility is not possible in the case of housing, supply shortages may persist in some areas while there are surpluses elsewhere. Of course, there will be linkages between different local markets. For example, if there is a shortage of housing in Leeds compared with

Manchester, we may expect prices in Leeds to be higher than those in Manchester. Lower Manchester prices may induce some people to move from Leeds to Manchester, and thus mobility of people may reduce some of the problems posed by the immobility of housing. However, this type of mobility is likely to be limited because the decision to move from one town to another could involve a range of costs including a change of jobs or a longer journey to work, separation from friends, changes of schools for children and so on. The gains resulting from lower house prices would have to be quite substantial to bring about such movements. Fixed costs associated with moving house also tend to lower mobility.

House-building

A further factor that means that supply is likely to be inelastic, at least in the short run, is that it takes some time to build a house – typically, between one and two years. But, there are additional potential problems within the house-building industry that may exacerbate the problem of supply. As already discussed, house prices are more volatile than the prices of most other consumer goods and services. This increases the degree of risk for developers compared to, say, the manufacturers of washing machines, since they will be more uncertain as to whether they can sell their houses at a high or low price, and therefore whether they will make a reasonable return on their development costs. Timing the production of houses and their release for sale is important, because it affects how much the houses sell for; the Barker Review suggested that a 1 per cent increase in house prices can increase profits by up to 8 per cent. Many developers will adopt a wait-and-see approach to building and releasing houses, which may in fact reduce the responsiveness of supply still further.

Faced with uncertainty over house prices, developers are likely to behave fairly cautiously in order to minimize the impact of uncertainty; they will, for example, be reluctant to make long-term fixed commitments. The Barker Review highlighted low levels of investment in capital-intensive technologies, innovation and in the skills of the workforce, who are frequently employed on a subcontracted basis. This lack of investment will further slow down the process of house-building.

In addition to the underlying market risk associated with volatile prices, developers face additional risks linked to the development of particular sites, including problems in obtaining planning permission, problems with construction and so on. These are more likely to occur with the development of brown-field sites (the redevelopment of land that has already been built on), and this may make builders more reluctant to build there.

Government policies

Without government intervention, the housing market is likely to experience a number of problems. Government regulation is important to deal with the externalities of decisions about housing. Also, some form of government intervention is required to address the problem that many people cannot afford to rent or own their own home.

Regulation

A process in which developers were allowed to build anywhere they wanted would be undesirable. Given the externalities in house-building, an unregulated process of development could result in problems of congestion and environmental degradation. Development on brownfield sites may require government intervention because of the risks that the private sector may be unable to take on, while development of greenfield sites (that is, ones previously undeveloped) may require government intervention in order to ensure that there is the appropriate infrastructure (roads, schools, etc.) in place.

For these reasons, government intervention is desirable in housing development in order to bring about an efficient outcome. In particular, government planning regulations designate land for particular uses, deciding that some must be reserved for recreational or agricultural uses, while other land is made available each year for building. However, as highlighted in the Barker Review, the planning process has directly caused a number of problems for the responsiveness of supply. The amount of land that is made available for development is typically determined in line with projected numbers of households in an area – based in turn on population projections, assumptions about living arrangements and estimates of immigration. These projections may turn out to be wrong, and they do not take into account the speculative demand for housing discussed above. This is a fundamental problem in that the amount of land made available is not responsive to changing prices, as would be the case for other goods supplied by the market. The process is politically designed rather than market driven. Land availability is often determined according to annual or five-yearly targets, rather than reflecting changing demand conditions.

Subsidies

In the UK, the government subsidises demand for (private and social) rented housing among low-income tenants through the housing benefit system. The UK system allows the level of subsidy to vary spatially according to local market rents. Independent rent officers determine, on a case-by-case basis, how much of the actual rent on a property will be covered by housing benefit, based on their judgement of what is reasonable in an area for the size of property that the family needs. In this way, the system of housing support in the UK takes into account regional variation in rents. However, this is not the case in all countries. In Australia and Germany, for example, the amount of demand subsidy does not vary by location. This may mean that, in practice, low-income households are priced out of some areas.

The total amount paid in housing benefit in the UK is quite large (£13 billion in 2004–5) – more than is paid in pure cash support through income support and income-related job seekers allowance (£8.1 billion). Given the underlying regional disparities in rents, relatively more goes to high-price areas, such as London and the South East (which together get 43 per cent of the total budget).

One of the main advantages of demand subsidies, compared to the system of government-provided social housing described below, is that it allows individuals a degree of choice. Housing is not a uniform commodity, but a complex bundle of individual attributes, including the number of rooms in the property, access to outside space, interior fixtures, and location. Whereas with social housing, individuals are typically presented with a single take-it-or-leave-it option, with demand subsidies, they are given some leeway in finding accommodation that better matches their underlying preferences over the different attributes. In addition, the housing benefit system is flexible. If someone's housing needs change because of altered family circumstances, or because they need to relocate for employment, then their benefit will adjust relatively quickly (compared to social housing) to their new housing needs.

In principle, housing benefit should enable the UK government to meet its target of providing people with accommodation since it directly subsidises housing for those on low incomes. However, there are a number of reasons why it might not be effective. First, take-up is only around 85 per cent of those who are eligible (although the amount claimed is greater, at around 90 per cent, because those who do not claim typically qualify for smaller amounts). Second, as we have already seen, information problems in the private rented sector may lead to landlords setting conditions (deposits, reference letters) which some people are unable to meet. Other groups may have problems securing private-sector rented accommodation or be excluded because they are thought to represent bad tenants. Third, the system is relatively less generous to some groups, particularly young, single adults, covering only the cost of a room in shared accommodation. If people are unable or unwilling to take such accommodation, preferring a bedsit or one-bedroomed flat, then their full housing costs will not be covered.

A common criticism of housing benefit is that it provides little incentive for those eligible to shop around to find the best rent. If someone else is going to pay the full cost of the accommodation (within reason) then a person gains nothing if s/he finds somewhere just as suitable that costs £10 a week less. The absence of any incentive to find cheaper accommodation reduces the competitive pressure in the marketplace and results in rents being higher than they would otherwise be. An alternative is a voucher system, such as the one operating in the USA, which pays a fixed (although locally-varying) amount towards housing costs. This provides an incentive to shop around to find accommodation within the voucher limit. There is an even stronger incentive to shop around in a new system of local housing allowances trialled in the UK in 2003. Here, fixed housing allowances were set for different-sized properties in each area, based on private rents. Each claimant received the full value of the allowance (adjusting for income) and was allowed to keep the difference if they found somewhere at a lower price. Not only does this create a strong incentive to shop around, but it also allows people to trade-off housing against other goods (such as food or children's clothing), according to their preferences.

In practice, levels of housing benefit, vouchers and local housing allowances will tend to limit low-income tenants to below-average price (and quality) accommodation. Exclusions by landlords may further limit the choice for housing benefit recipients. The result may be a concentration of low-income households in poor and poorly-serviced neighbourhoods, with implications for their quality of life and, possibly, education and employment outcomes because of the negative externality effects of living in a deprived neighbourhood.

Another potential disadvantage with demand subsidies are the disincentives they create for work and saving. The government wants to target the benefit on those who need it – namely, those on low incomes. But, there will be some point in the income distribution where the government wants to stop paying the benefit. In the UK, housing benefit is gradually withdrawn (above a threshold level of income) at a rate of 65 per cent. This means that, for each additional pound above the threshold, a person will lose 65 pence of housing benefit, implying that their net gain from the additional pound is only 35 pence. This is equivalent to a 65 per cent marginal rate of tax, higher than the 40 per cent paid by higher rate taxpayers in the UK. Overall, the system ensures that people are better off if they work, rather than not working, but the size of the gain to working may be quite small. The same argument applies to saving, since the benefit is withdrawn in line with people's savings, as well as pension income. In his recent report on social housing, Hills (2007) pointed out that in areas where rents are higher (London and the South East, for example), the earnings range over which these disincentives apply is correspondingly greater, since it takes longer for the full amount of housing benefit entitlement to be withdrawn. In the case of London, even those on average earnings may still find themselves facing the 65 per cent effective tax rate.

In principle, demand subsidies could be used to support owner-occupied housing as well as rented accommodation. In the UK, support for low-income owner-occupiers has been cut back. People taking our mortgages after October 1995, with just a few exceptions, receive no government support to help with covering interest payments for the first nine months they are on means-tested benefits. The presumption was that the private insurance market would increasingly fill the gap, though there is little evidence that this is the case. In other countries, including the USA, housing vouchers can be used for house purchase as well as to cover rents. Since the year 2000, another form of demand subsidy for owner-occupation – mortgage interest tax relief – has also no longer been available in the UK. Before the year 2000, home-owners received tax relief on their mortgage interest payments (up to a maximum), thus reducing the effective price of owner-occupation. Similar systems of tax relief are still in operation in a number of countries, including the USA and Ireland. Other countries provide explicit support for owner-occupation, with measures ranging from the provision of additional support for first-time buyers to support for the purchase of municipally owned units. In Australia, for example, first-time buyers are eligible for a one-off (non-means-tested) grant of $A7,000.

Provision

Social housing refers to housing provided by the public sector (or increasingly, the not-for-profit sector) at submarket rents. Prior to the Second World War, fewer than 10 per cent of households in the UK lived in social housing. There was a huge expansion in the post-war period, as the public sector was better-positioned than private landlords to take on the enormous task of re-construction. By 1975, social housing accounted for nearly a third of all homes, but has since declined to fewer than one in five as a result of the Right to Buy scheme and sharply reduced new building rates. Within the social housing sector, there has been a shift in provision in the UK from local authorities to not-for-profit housing associations. In many other European countries, non-governmental organisations play an important role in providing social housing. In the Netherlands, for example, which is among the European countries with the largest social housing sectors, all provision is by not-for-profit housing associations, although the government sets rent controls. In Germany, private organisations are responsible for providing most of the social housing, and receive direct subsidies from the government in return for setting submarket rents for a prescribed period of time.

An important question is whether there is a continuing role for the provision of social housing alongside demand subsidies. Demand subsidies have the attraction of enabling individual choice and providing flexibility, although decentralisation of provision from government to housing associations and private providers may have a similar effect. We have already seen that there are some groups who may effectively be excluded from the private rented sector. Other vulnerable groups may not be able to deal with the process of finding somewhere to live and applying for demand subsidies. Reflecting this, people deemed to be in priority need for housing in the UK include those formerly in care or custody, those who are escaping from violent partners, and those who are pregnant. However, these groups are fairly small in number – and in many cases their short-term needs could be met through temporary housing.

On the question of efficiency, we would expect social housing to be able to increase supply elasticity. In the context of Figure 5.1, demand subsidies will obviously result in a shift in the demand curve, which, in the absence of any supply response, will feed through entirely into higher prices. Supply-side subsidies, on the other hand, should result in a genuine increase in supply, which will shift the supply-curve to the right – and lower prices. Moreover, the public sector should be able to undertake building programmes that more risk-averse private developers might reject (although evidence on building times does suggest that private housing is built rather more quickly than council housing). However, in the public sector, building decisions will be made by politicians and bureaucrats. They will be driven by political and fiscal concerns, rather than responding to consumer demand, which was the central criticism of the Barker Review. Making non-governmental organisations directly responsible for provision may help to resolve some of these issues, though not if politicians retain ultimate control.

On average, for low-income groups, social housing is likely to be of higher quality than privately-rented housing. In the market, quality will be driven by competition, but, for the reasons already discussed, low-income groups may face a relatively limited choice. Hills (2007) finds that, among low income renters, standards of accommodation are higher in the social rented sector than in the private sector. Because social housing is provided at submarket rents, then it avoids (or at least reduces) the work disincentive problem discussed above. People on low incomes in social housing receive help in paying their rent in the form of housing benefit. However, because the level of rent is lower than that in the private sector, the amount of rent is tapered away over a narrower range of earnings. Thus, the high effective marginal tax rate applies to a lower level of earnings, improving the incentives to work (and save). In spite of this, Hills (2007) found no evidence that those in social housing were more likely to work than those in the privately-rented sector. One potential problem is that people in social housing are unlikely to be allocated a house in a new area automatically if they move – they may have to join a lengthy waiting list. This may make them reluctant to move, and their relative lack of mobility may reduce their chances of finding a job, since they will be searching in a narrower geographical area.

In principle, the government might use social housing as a way of influencing neighbourhood composition, providing and allocating housing in a way that encourages a wider social mix. That was certainly part of the original thinking behind social housing, as this 1949 quote from Aneurin Bevan (then Minister of Health with additional responsibility for housing) makes clear: 'We should aim to introduce what has always been the lovely feature of the English and Welsh village, where the doctor, the grocer, the butcher and the farm labourer all live in the same street . . . the living tapestry of a mixed community.' While social housing has always catered more for people with low incomes, at its peak it did provide homes for people across the whole scale of income distribution, including 20 per cent of people in the top 10 per cent of the income distribution, according to Hills (2007). However, this is far from the case at the time of writing. In the UK, as in a number of other European countries, the shrinking of the social sector has meant that social housing is increasingly concentrated at the bottom of the income distribution scale, and in poor neighbourhoods (and often among immigrant families). In the UK, the Right to Buy policy was taken up more by relatively better-off council house tenants, in better areas, and in houses rather than flats. The remaining, smaller supply of social housing is increasingly allocated on a needs basis rather than the length of time on a waiting list. The result is that the majority of social housing is now located in areas of high deprivation.

SUMMARY

- The government's objective of providing decent homes that people can afford largely reflects an equity objective and the fact that shelter is a basic human need.

- However, government intervention is also motivated by efficiency considerations. Individuals' decisions about housing – where to build houses, where to live, how much to spend on upkeep and so on – affect other people. It is unlikely that a pure market system would produce an optimal outcome.

- Government planning regulation, although necessary for these reasons, is seen as exacerbating the underlying problem of inelasticity of supply, resulting in volatile house prices.

- Governments can achieve their equity objective either by subsidising demand directly (housing benefit) or by providing social housing. Housing benefit offers people choice about where to live and what type of rental housing to choose.

However, it may push up the price of housing and may create disincentives for work, particularly in areas of high housing cost. Some individuals may also effectively be excluded from the private rental sector because of landlords' requirements for deposits and/or letters of reference. Social housing is largely free of these problems. However, people in social housing are relatively immobile and may be stuck in relatively deprived neighbourhoods.

FURTHER READING

Both Oxley (2004), and O'Sullivan and Gibb (2002) are useful textbooks that provide further coverage of many of the topics covered here.

There have been two government-sponsored reviews of the housing market in the UK which contain much interesting and useful material. The 2004 Barker Review of Housing Supply focused on problems in the supply of owner-occupied housing (see HM Treasury 2004) http://www.hm-treasury.gov.uk/consultations_and_legislation/barker/consult_barker_index. cfm. John Hills' 2007 report focuses on social housing, but also looks more widely at arguments for government intervention in the housing market (see Hills, 2007).

Whitehead (2002) discusses the economics of social housing, while Whitehead and Scanlon (2007) provide information on social housing in Europe. Giles et al. (1996) contains detailed evidence on the characteristics of people living in the social rented sector, and their work incentives.

Galster (2002) and, more technically, Durlauf (2004), provide a good introduction to the economics of neighbourhoods, while Dietz (2002) and Durlauf (2004) summarise the available empirical evidence on the existence of neighbourhood effects. See also Katz et al. (2001) for an evaluation of the Moving to Opportunity demonstration programme.

QUESTIONS FOR DISCUSSION

1. The Barker Review recommended that the government should set a target for the affordability of home-ownership. Do you agree, and how should this be defined?

2. Is it discriminatory for private landlords to refuse to house people who have recently left prison?

3. 'The price of housing is high because the price of land is high.' Discuss.

4. If there is a positive externality to home improvements, should the government provide a subsidy scheme for such improvements?

5. The key worker scheme offers subsidised loans to people working in the UK public sector to help them buy their own homes. What is the rationale for such a scheme, and what effects is it likely to have?

6. How can governments shape neighbourhoods? Should they try?

7. Should the government subsidise owner-occupation, and if so, how?

8. Is there still a role for social housing?

CHAPTER 6

Crime

In 2005–6 the UK government spent over £30 billion on public order and safety, including £15.5 billion on policing, £5.8 billion on the courts and administration of justice, and £3.6 billion on prisons and managing offenders. Until fairly recently, however, crime has not been a major area of study for economists – and some may still feel that it is not an area where economic analysis can be of much use. There is a separate academic discipline, criminology, that is concerned with the incidence and forms of crime as well as its causes and consequences, and sociologists and psychologists have long been interested in crime. A particular focus of interest within these other disciplines is the extent to which criminals are born or made – whether criminal activity is the result of 'bad homes' (and other bad experiences, particularly in childhood), or 'bad genes'. Following the seminal work of Becker (1968), however, economists have added another dimension to the debate by considering whether crime may be a result of 'bad incentives'.

This chapter looks at what economics has to offer as a tool for analysing crime prevention. Following other chapters, it looks at what society's objectives might be in relation to crime control, focusing on efficiency and equity, but adding another social objective, that of civil liberties. It asks whether these objectives will be met under a pure market system, before considering alternative forms of government intervention.

Objectives

This section looks at what quantity of resources the government should devote to crime prevention, and how it should allocate them. Three objectives are usually cited in relation to crime control – the two objectives of efficiency and equity, as in other areas, but also another social objective, the preservation of civil liberties. That is, an ideal system of crime control would be one that reduces crime as far as possible, that spreads the benefits of crime reduction as fairly as possible, but, in doing so, preserves the liberties (of movement, of privacy and so on) that society deems to be essential.

Efficiency

Is it desirable – even if it were possible – to try to achieve a zero level of crime? According to police statistics, 5.4 million crimes were committed in England and Wales in 2006/7. This almost certainly understates the total number of crimes, since the police figures only capture crimes that are actually recorded by the police. There are many reasons why individuals may not report crimes to the police – in the case of theft, the value of the item stolen may be quite small; they may think there is little point reporting a crime if they don't think the police will be able to solve it; or, in some cases, they may fear retribution. And, even if individuals report a crime, the police may not actually record it. Like other administrative data, police statistics will be affected by the rules governing the recording of data. Some incidents reported to the police may not be recorded officially because they may not fall into a notifiable offence category, or because there is insufficient evidence.

As an alternative, governments make use of individual survey information to obtain estimates of the number of crimes committed (in the UK, this is done through the British Crime Survey – BCS). Individuals from a representative sample of the population are asked whether they have been the victim of a crime in the previous twelve months, and to give details of the crime. For the crime types it covers (personal and household crime), this approach can provide better estimates of the extent of crime, because it includes crimes that are not reported to the police and crimes that are not recorded by them. The figures are also a better indicator of crime trends, because they are unaffected by changes in levels of reporting to the police, and in police recording practices. However, for obvious reasons, this approach cannot be used to collate reliable homicide statistics. It also excludes crimes termed as victimless (for example, possession of drugs); surveys do ask people about drug-taking, but the responses may be unreliable. According to the BCS, there were approximately 11.3 million crimes against adults in 2006/7.

So, is it a sensible objective for the government to reduce this level of crime to zero? Reducing crime has obvious benefits, but there are costs to engaging in preventive activities, such as increased police patrols. This consumes resources that could be used for other goods and services. The efficient level of crime prevention needs to take into account the costs as well as the benefits. Society should engage in crime prevention up to the point where the costs of engaging in further control begin to outweigh the benefits.

This can be illustrated by a simple example. Suppose that there is only one policy tool for reducing crime: through police patrols. The government's problem is to determine the efficient number of police patrols. It knows the benefits of such patrols in terms of the number of crimes prevented during a year and it can express these benefits in terms of a monetary value. Neither of these assumptions is straightforward, as we discuss in more detail below. However, the government is assumed to know both the monetary value of the additional reduction in crime resulting from each additional patrol – the marginal social benefit (*msb*) – and the cost of an extra patrol in terms of recruitment, wages, taxes, uniform and so on – the marginal social cost (*msc*). In this case, we can

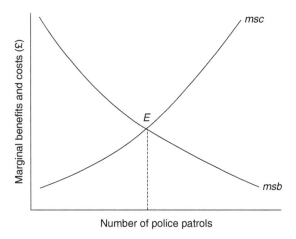

Figure 6.1 Costs and benefits of police patrols.

draw the diagram shown in Figure 6.1, familiar from previous chapters. This shows, on the vertical axis, the *msb* and the *msc* expressed in pounds (£) and, on the horizontal axis, the number of police patrols. The *msb* curve slopes downwards, reflecting the reasonable assumption that benefits from increasing the number of police decline the more police are currently on patrol; the *msc* curve slopes upwards on the assumption that the additional costs of recruiting more police increase with the size of the force (because of, for example, the need to pay higher wages to attract more people to apply).

Figure 6.1 allows us to determine the efficient number of police to employ. To the left of the point of intersection of the two curves (*E*), the *msb* is greater than the *msc* – in other words, employing another police recruit generates benefits in excess of the costs, so it clearly makes sense to continue to expand the police force. To the right of the point of intersection, however, the *msc* is greater than the *msb* – in other words, the costs of employing another police recruit would be greater than the benefits it would generate. The point of intersection, *E*, represents the efficient level.

In theory at least, determining the optimal level of policing – and hence the associated efficient level of crime – is relatively straightforward. In practice, the government may have a fairly good idea about the *msc* curve, but may face greater uncertainty over the *msb* curve. The marginal benefit in pounds of employing an additional policeman (or more generally devoting more resources to crime prevention) depends on two things – the relationship between more resources and crime reduction, and the monetary benefit of that reduction. We discuss each of these in turn.

The supply of crime

A contribution of the Nobel-prize-winning economist, Gary Becker, was to model the individual's decision to commit a crime as a cost–benefit calculation. In other words, committing a crime is in a sense a rational choice. What this means is that, in deciding whether or not to commit a crime, the individual considers the expected return from doing the crime. This in turn depends on the rewards if successful (that is, the person is not caught), the penalty if unsuccessful, and the probability of being caught (as well as the probability of being prosecuted). The individual then compares this expected return from the crime with the return from the alternative, which is primarily legitimate employment. In some models, crime and legitimate employment are seen as being mutually exclusive alternatives, but in practice, many people combine employment with crime. Nevertheless, committing a crime is likely to affect what someone can earn through legitimate employment. Not only will crime reduce the effort someone can devote to a job in the short term, but, over the longer term, when people are considering their lifetime earnings, the probability of being caught will have a big impact on their career prospects.

Becker's economic model of crime yields a number of important insights. First, it implies that individuals will respond to 'negative incentives' to commit crime. Employing more police will increase the probability of being caught and will reduce the level of crime, as will imposing tougher sentences. Imprisoning more people reduces crime, because those who would otherwise commit crimes are now locked up. This is known as the *incarceration effect*. However, the model implies that imprisoning more people caught committing crimes is likely to have a second – deterrent – effect because it reduces the expected return to crime.

The model also implies that opportunities in the labour market are crucially important for crime rates. Freeman (1996) argues that one cause of the rise in crime in the USA has been the collapse in demand for unskilled men. This group has seen their relative wages fall by around 30 per cent since the 1970s, making crime relatively more attractive. A number of studies have shown that wage rates, rather than unemployment rates per se, are correlated with crime rates (see Grogger 1998; and Machin and Meghir 2004). This means that improving the employment prospects of unskilled workers in order to raise the pay-off from legitimate employment is an alternative way of attempting to tackle crime rates.

There is a growing body of evidence to support this economic approach to crime. The studies already cited show that crime rates are sensitive to labour market opportunities (and wage rates in particular). Freeman (1996) also presents evidence that young men who commit crimes have a lower perception of the risk of being caught, have a higher assessment of the potential rewards from crime, and have fewer opportunities in the legitimate labour market. Of course, the model does not imply that only economic incentives matter. Some of the rewards from crime may be non-financial, and for many people they will be negative (such as guilt and remorse). Since the benefits from crime are likely to be immediate, while the penalties (fines, imprisonment and potential loss of future earnings) come later, the extent to which individuals discount the future will also matter (see Chapter 4 for a further discussion of individual discount rates). Individuals will also vary in their degree of risk aversion – for some people, a very small probability of being caught and punished will have a big effect on whether they commit a crime, while others will only be deterred if there is a very high probability of being caught. Some of these factors are likely to be inherent to the individual; and environmental factors, including the process of socialisation within peer groups, may also be important. Glaeser *et al.* (1996) argue that the huge disparities in crime rates between 'high crime' and 'low crime' areas cannot be explained simply by differences in economic, demographic and other factors, and is instead the result of social interactions or peer effects. They find that these effects are larger for some crimes (petty larceny and theft) than for others (murder). Thus, bad genes, bad homes, bad neighbourhoods and bad incentives can all play a role in determining criminal behaviour. While Becker's economic model of crime predicts that incentives matter, it is highly likely that people facing similar incentives will behave in very different ways because of these other factors.

In order to determine the *msb* of spending additional resources on crime prevention, the government needs to know not just that increasing police patrols will reduce crime, but also by how much. How is it possible to estimate the effect of spending additional resources on reducing crime rates? In practice, there is considerable variation in resources devoted to crime over time and across countries (or, in the case of the USA, across states within a country). One possibility might therefore be to compare crime rates between periods (or areas) with high levels of policing and those with low levels of policing, to determine the effect. The big problem here is one of reverse causation; the direction of causation may run from crime levels to policing, rather than the other way round. A comparison of US states, for example, would show that areas with high levels of policing (and tough sentencing) typically have above-average crime rates. But, of course, this does not show that spending more money on the police increases crime rates, but that high levels of crime tends to lead to higher spending on the police. In economics, this is referred to as an *endogeneity problem*. We are interested in the causal effect of a potential determinant of crime rates (spending on the police) on the outcome, but this determinant is itself affected by the outcome. In the absence of random policy experiments (spending more money on police in randomly chosen areas and observing the effect on crime) other approaches are required to try to disentangle the causal effect. In order to determine the effect of police spending on crime, one US study exploited the fact that spending on the police varied over the gubernatorial and mayoral electoral cycles to identify the effect on crime rates. Another has focused on the effect of increased police presence following a terrorist attack on other crimes in the same area.

The costs of crime

As well as knowing the effect that additional spending will have on reducing crime levels, the government needs to translate this into a monetary value to determine the *msb*. Of course, the benefits of reducing crime are related directly to the costs of crime, so this is equivalent to obtaining a monetary value for the social costs of crime. These social costs include not only the direct financial costs incurred by individuals, but also the cost of pain and emotional suffering to individuals directly affected, and the wider effects on other members of society through factors such as the fear of crime. The social costs therefore include direct expenditure costs, as well as the best estimates of the value of the less tangible impacts of crime.

This kind of cost–benefit calculation is frequently criticised on the grounds that it involves trying to place a monetary value on things that cannot – or should not – be valued in a financial way (such as human life). However, as we have seen, it is virtually impossible to make sensible decisions about how much to spend on crime prevention without some judgement about the value of that spending. At the very least, spending money on crime prevention involves a trade-off, since the money will not be spent on something else that also has a value. Putting a monetary value on the costs of crime can therefore be seen as an attempt to make explicit the implicit assumptions that would otherwise underlie spending decisions. Of course, as we shall see, it involves a number of assumptions, and the figures are far from being estimated precisely. Nevertheless, it is an essential step in achieving the objective of efficient resource allocation – both in determining the overall level of resources to devote to crime prevention, and the allocation between different types of crime.

In assessing the costs of crime, there is a fundamental distinction between genuine resource costs and transfers between individuals in society. Take the theft of a mobile phone, for example. At first sight, putting a financial value on this loss might seem relatively straightforward, since it could be captured by the replacement cost or purchase cost of the phone. However, this ignores the fact that while there is a cost to the victim of losing the phone, there is a direct gain to the thief. Since both victim and thief are members of society, the effects of the theft for both need to be taken into account. It may seem an illogical conclusion, but in a strict cost–benefit analysis, there is no overall social cost, since the loss to the victim is directly offset by the gain to the thief. In practice, the UK government does include the value of the property in assessing losses resulting from theft. Their argument is that this transfer is unwanted or forced. However, the same argument might apply to transfer payments made through the government benefit system, which some people certainly do not regard as voluntary. It might be argued that, because the thief is breaking the law, s/he should have no place in the cost–benefit analysis (technically referred to as having 'no standing' in the cost–benefit analysis). However, the idea that someone who breaks the law ceases to be part of society is not one that everyone would be comfortable with.

However, a theft does have wider consequences beyond the simple transfer of a phone from one person to another, which are likely to give rise to genuine costs – including the inconvenience of having to buy a replacement, the cost of any insurance that the person had to cover the possibility of theft, the psychological costs to the victim, any wider effect on the level of fear of crime in the area, and so on. In thinking about the social costs of crime, it is helpful to distinguish three types of costs:

- *Anticipation costs* that are incurred in anticipation of crimes occurring and fall mainly on potential victims.

- *Consequential costs* that are incurred as a direct consequence of criminal events and fall mainly on the victims, but also on public services that are brought in to deal with the consequences, such as the health service.

- *Response costs* that are incurred in response to the crime and fall mainly on the criminal justice system.

Anticipation costs include defensive expenditure on security measures such as burglar alarms, fencing, lighting, security guards and so on. They also include the direct expenditure cost of engaging in precautionary behaviour designed to minimise the probability of being the victim of a crime (such as taking a taxi when it would be cheaper to walk). These clearly involve genuine resources that would not be spent in the absence of crime, although, in some cases, precautionary behaviour may be tied up with other benefits (it may be preferable to take a taxi when it is raining, for example; and, perhaps more significantly, paying more to live in a neighbourhood with a lower crime rate may also be motivated by access to better schools). Spending on insurance is another anticipation cost. Insurance is largely a transfer of resources from potential victim policyholders to actual victim policy-holders. However, there is a genuine resource cost involved in the administration of insurance policies. Finally, fear of crime involves potentially large, but more intangible, costs. Fear of crime may have a direct effect in reducing people's quality of life. An attempt could be made to estimate the size of this effect by, for example, comparing the prices of otherwise identical houses in high crime and low crime areas. In principle, this differential would measure directly individuals' willingness to pay to avoid crime, although, as already noted, low crime areas may have other benefits, such as good schools. Fear of crime may also have an important indirect effect on people's behaviour, preventing them from doing what they would otherwise do – not going out at night for fear of being mugged, for example, and therefore missing out on an enjoyable evening.

The individual victims of crime bear many of the consequential costs. As has already been discussed, in the case of property theft, the cost to the individual arising from the loss of an item is directly offset by a gain to the thief, assuming that both value it equally. If the stolen items are not insured, the incidence of the cost falls directly in the victim; and if they are insured, there is a further transfer of resources from other people within the insurance pool. Note that while these are all transfer payments and do not count as a cost to society as a whole, we may still care about who gains and who loses for equity reasons – as well as believing that it is morally wrong to obtain transfers by force. Of course, if the property is damaged or destroyed (a case of joy-riding rather than vehicle theft as such), then it does count as a genuine social cost. And, as already mentioned, the victim may incur costs of time through dealing with the consequences of a crime (reporting it to the police, making an insurance claim, buying a replacement item).

Some crimes may have very substantial emotional and physical impacts, and result in a reduced quality of life for the victims. These impacts include any direct physical injuries, but also include feelings of vulnerability, loss of sleep and so on. These impacts generally far outweigh the financial costs, but are harder to place a monetary value on. The amounts given to victims of violent crime in compensation are not a wholly reliable guide, since they are determined by administrative criteria that may not take into account fully the individual's loss. Estimates of benefits from health improvements are frequently used in health expenditure analysis, and these can be used as a guide, although the loss of health sustained as a result of crime may be qualitatively different. As well as the costs to the victims, there may be additional costs imposed on the health service and on victim support services. These are far easier to quantify in terms of the resources used to staff and run these bodies.

The response costs represent the resource costs in catching criminals and bringing them to justice. These include the costs to the police, the costs of running a court system and the costs of staging a trial (including legal costs and the costs of jurors' time). They also include the costs of the prison and probation services, and the costs of incarceration to the offender – and his or her family.

The UK government has recently tried to estimate the total cost of crime in England and Wales (Brand and Price 2000). The total figure is around £60 billion. This takes into account most of the individual costs discussed above, but does not include the cost of the fear of crime or the impacts on quality of life. It does, however, count the theft of property (technically a transfer) as a cost. While inevitably imprecise, this figure is useful, since it highlights the scale of the problem. Also useful are differences in costs between different types of crime, since these reveal how the government should think about prioritising spending within the overall crime budget. Violent crimes (violence against the person and common assault) account for slightly less than a quarter of all crimes when measured by number of offences, but when the social cost is taken into account, they comprise nearly 60 per cent of the total cost of crime. Theft, on the other hand, accounts for 42 per cent of crimes, but only 14 per cent of the cost of crime.

Equity

Efficiency is not the only objective society might have in deciding on the allocation of resources for crime control. Notions of fairness enter very strongly into the area of crime prevention and criminal justice. However, here we are less concerned with defining what are 'just' outcomes, than with considering an equitable allocation – that is, a distribution of resources between individuals (or areas) that results in a fair distribution of benefits.

In most countries, crime is not allocated evenly across different areas, but is far higher in some areas than others. In England and Wales, levels of burglary, vehicle theft and violence in rural areas have been consistently lower than in urban areas since the 1980s. Also, the risk of being a victim of crime varies geographically by the level of deprivation; generally, people living in more deprived areas are more likely to be a victim of crime than those living in less deprived areas. People living in deprived areas are also more likely to suffer the experience of a genuine loss as a result of burglary and theft, since they are much less likely than wealthier people to have home and contents insurance. The incidence of crime also varies by ethnic group. Adults from a mixed race or Asian background are more likely than those from other ethnic groups to be victims of crime in England and Wales. For Asians, this largely reflects their (younger) age group, while mixed race people still have a higher risk of being a victim of crime after allowing for both their age and the type of area in which they live. Rather than allocating resources evenly across different areas and groups, it may be considered equitable to allocate resources to try to achieve a more equal distribution of crime rates, or to achieve an equal (proportionate) reduction in crime. In both cases, this is likely to mean allocating more resources to areas of high crime, which are also likely to be deprived areas.

In this case, it is hard to say, a priori, whether the efficiency and equity objective are likely to conflict. As we have seen, it is socially efficient to allocate resources where the marginal social benefit is highest and/or the marginal social cost is lowest. One of the key determinants of the marginal social benefit is the type of crime committed – so much depends on the patterns of regional variation in individual types of crime. If violent crime is highest in deprived areas, then both efficiency and equity considerations would result in a high level of resource allocation. However, it may be relatively costly to tackle crime in areas of high deprivation if the underlying causes involve a complex combination of economic factors, and peer group and neighbourhood effects.

Liberty

Unlike the other areas of government intervention we have looked at in this book, there is a third important objective that deserves discussion – that of civil liberties. In thinking about how to tackle crime control, governments need to be mindful of preserving individual liberties. Few people would want to live in a police state, even if it was able to yield low crime rates at low cost. In some cases, arguments about civil liberty strengthen the case against ineffective criminal measures – the introduction of identity cards has been widely criticised as being a huge waste of public resources as well as a potential threat to individual liberties because of the increase in the amount of data available to the government.

More generally, however, preserving individual liberties may potentially conflict with the attainment of efficiency. This conflict reveals itself in designing a criminal justice system. In general, any system is unlikely to operate perfectly, but will suffer from two different types of error (known as Type I and Type II errors). A Type I error involves wrongly convicting an innocent person, while a Type II error involves wrongly freeing someone who is guilty. An efficient system would try to minimise Type II errors; it would have a very high probability that the guilty would be convicted, since a high conviction rate is an effective method of controlling crime. A system that is concerned with individual liberties, on the other hand, would work on the basis of a far lower probability that the guilty are convicted, since it would aim to minimise Type I errors.

Defendants will have extensive protection in order to minimise the possibility of people being punished for crimes they did not commit, while accepting that, as a result, many of those who are guilty will escape.

The market system and crime prevention

The current system of crime control involves a mix of private and public spending. As we have already seen, individuals bear much of the direct expenditure costs of crime, and much of this spending is directed at reducing the likelihood of crimes occurring – or at least to reduce the likelihood that the crime will be committed against a particular person or property. Private spending on defensive measures (burglar alarms, guard dogs, private security) is substantial. In the case of crimes against property, it is roughly equivalent to the amount that the government spends through the police and criminal justice system.

There are many areas of law (contract, tort and property law, for example) where enforcement is carried out almost entirely privately, and the role of the state is simply to provide a court system. Historically, the private enforcement of the law used to be more widespread in England (and in many other countries), extending even to criminal law. Central and local governments paid bounties for the apprehension of criminal offenders, who were caught by private agents. A publicly-provided police force was a relatively recent introduction.

Economic analysis can provide some useful insights into whether crime control should be publicly- or privately-provided. In general, it shows that there is an economic efficiency case for some form of government intervention, since the market is unlikely to provide the optimal level of crime control. The reason is related to the externalities associated with measures taken by individuals to reduce crime.

Suppose there is a private agency offering 'police' patrols to anyone who is prepared to pay for them. Individuals will choose to buy these patrols up to the point where the financial cost of an extra patrol (the marginal private cost) is equal to the benefit in terms of the reduced probability of crimes being committed against them (the marginal private benefit). However, if an individual pays for a police patrol to pass by his/her house on an hourly basis, this will not only reduce the probability that his/her house will be burgled, but it is also likely to reduce the probability that his/her neighbours' houses will be burgled – and probably all the houses in the street. Employing a police patrol therefore has external benefits to other people who live in the same area. The presence of these external benefits will imply that the market outcome will not be socially efficient. Since individuals only take into account the private benefits, and not the wider social benefits, they will tend to demand too few police patrols.

Against this, it could be argued that this analysis grossly understates the number of patrols that would be purchased under a system of private provision, since, if each individual on the street faces the same cost–benefit trade-off, then each will choose to purchase the same number of police patrols, implying a far greater total number of police patrols for the street. In practice, however, this is unlikely, because of the *free-rider problem*. If your neighbours can benefit from your provision of police protection, they are not likely to buy their own. Instead, they will trust that you will provide enough to protect them – in other words, they will choose to free-ride on your purchase of police patrols. And if you make the same calculation about your neighbours, then the same argument applies – you choose not to buy police patrols yourself, hoping to free-ride on others. The outcome is that no one will buy any police patrols – clearly a sub-optimal outcome, given the benefits in terms of crime reduction. (This is the same as the problem of the prisoner's dilemma, discussed in relation to housing in Chapter 5).

Police patrols have two features that give rise to this problem. One is that they are non-rival. This means that one person's consumption of a commodity does not reduce the amount that is available for other people to consume. Although one person pays for the police patrol and benefits directly from it, his/her neighbours will derive a very similar level of benefit. This is very different to the case of apples discussed in Chapter 1, where one person's consumption of an apple directly precludes anyone else from consuming it. The other feature is that police patrols are non-excludable. This means that it is impossible for an individual who is consuming a commodity to prevent anyone else from consuming it. If person A buys police patrols, s/he cannot stop his/her neighbours from benefiting from them. Again, apples are different – if a person purchases an apple, s/he can stop other people from consuming it. Goods that possess these two characteristics – non-rivalry and non-excludability – are defined by economists as *pure public goods*. The classic example of a pure public good is street lighting – if provided, everyone benefits equally from it and no one can be prevented from benefiting from it. And, as we have seen, police patrols are very similar. With pure public goods there is a prima facie case for government intervention since, if left to the market, free-riding will result in under-provision. Note, however, that many goods and services that are provided publicly (including health, education, public parks and libraries) are technically not pure public goods.

Government policies

These arguments imply that some form of government intervention is required on efficiency grounds, although they do not necessarily dictate that governments should *provide* crime prevention services directly. As we have seen in previous chapters, governments can finance (or regulate) private provision without having to provide the services directly themselves. Indeed, in a famous paper, Gary Becker, together with another economist, George Stigler, argued that the process of law enforcement should be privatised (Becker and Stigler 1974).

Their main concern with a publicly-provided system was that it was, by design, prone to corruption. Since the financial gain to the police of enforcing the law is typically less than the financial value of the penalty to the offender, there exists the potential for the offender to bribe the police. If the victims had to pay for enforcement, this would give rise to the free-rider problems discussed above, so a purely private system (i.e. privately financed and enforced) would be inefficient. Becker and Stigler's solution was for the state to offer rewards to private enforcers for capturing offenders. These rewards would be paid for out of fines charged to offenders. If the offender is too poor, the government might pay the enforcers a bounty and then imprison the offenders. To prevent over-zealous enforcement, the enforcer would have to compensate any innocent person they apprehended. In addition to removing incentives for corruption, Becker and Stigler argued that it would also result in cost-effective crime control, since the rewards would provide both the incentive to work out the least-cost enforcement methods and the incentive to use them.

However, there seems to be something inherently wrong with the idea of a system of private bounty hunters to apprehend offenders instead of a police force. Ultimately, the objection may be moral and lie with a reluctance to allow private-sector agents to use the force that is sometimes necessary to capture offenders. The tactics required to gather information, capture violators and prevent reprisal may also include covert operations as well as force. There may be a strong case for restricting the use of such tactics to a single, government-run agency. The Mafia offers a strong example of some of the risks in a privatised system of law enforcement.

Judge Richard Posner, writing together with William Landes, raised the following economic efficiency objection to Becker and Stigler's proposal (Landes and Posner, 1974). They argued that the potential deterrent effect of punishment depends both on the severity of the punishment and on the probability of being caught. Since there are two variables, it is necessary to choose some 'mix' of the two. One could imagine punishing theft by catching half the thieves and fining them £100 each, by catching a quarter and fining them £200 each, or by catching one thief in a hundred and hanging him or her. Assuming that each of these alternatives achieves the same deterrent effect, how to decide which alternative is best? Aside from equity and liberty considerations, the most efficient mix is the one that gives rise to the greatest deterrent effect at the minimum cost. Landes and Posner argued that it is relatively cheap to increase the severity of punishment and relatively expensive to increase the probability of punishment. The cost-effective method therefore involves increasing the severity of the punishment rather than the probability of being punished. The greater the punishment, the fewer criminals have to be caught in order to maintain a given level of deterrence – and catching criminals is costly. This means hanging a thief – or at the very least locking him/her up for a very long time. There is a clear trade-off here between efficiency and civil liberties.

Landes and Posner argued that the problem with Becker and Stigler's privatised system of enforcement is that it prevents the government from choosing separately both the severity of punishment and the probability of punishment, and therefore from achieving the optimal mix. The government can determine the fine that the offender has to pay, which acts as the reward for the private bounty hunters, but they then respond by deciding how much effort they are going to devote to catching the offender. If the government sets a high fine, it cannot simultaneously have a low probability of the offender being caught. Instead, the private agents will respond to the high fine by devoting a lot of effort to catching the now very valuable offender and the probability of capture will be correspondingly high. Within the privatised system proposed by Becker and Stigler, there is no way to increase the severity and lower the probability at one and the same time.

Landes and Posner's argument relies on there being a trade-off between severity and probability, but, in practice, this may not work in quite the way they suggest. They would argue that the most cost-effective system would impose very severe punishments, but with a very low probability of being caught. But, for criminals, if the probability of conviction drops, they may be sufficiently short-sighted to ignore the severity. For the criminal justice system, the greater the severity of punishment, the greater the procedural safeguards normally become. If the severity of punishment increases, there may be a greater desire to reduce Type I errors. So, as the severity of punishment increases, the judicial system may respond by making the probability of punishment ever smaller. Moreover, we may feel that there is something inherently wrong with a system that imposes very severe punishments with a low probability of being caught. It may be seen as unfair that some offenders are punished when so many others get away with their crimes.

However, as well as the important moral objection outlined above, there are other difficulties attached to relying on private enforcement. If a reward is generally available, then competing bounty hunters may devote wasteful effort to trying to capture offenders. They may also under-invest in enforcement technologies, such as computerised databases of fingerprint records, which may constitute natural monopolies. In general, therefore, there are strong economic and other arguments for a police and criminal justice system both paid for and run by the government.

SUMMARY

- It is unlikely to be optimal to have a crime-free society. Instead, the government should consider the costs as well as the benefits of crime control in determining the overall level of spending to devote to crime reduction, and the allocation of that spending to different types of crime.

- In the area of crime, the preservation of civil liberties is likely to be an important government objective, alongside efficiency and equity.

- Economic models of crime treat criminals as rational agents who respond to incentives. These include both the probability and size of punishment, but also the rewards from 'going straight'. However, these models recognise that people will respond in very different ways to the same set of incentives.

- It has been suggested that combining a low probability of being caught with a very severe punishment offers a cost-effective means of reducing crime, but there may be good reasons for not adopting this approach in practice.

- It has been argued that a system of private bounty hunters could be a cost-effective way of apprehending criminals, as well as reducing opportunities for police corruption. However, there is a strong case for the government to have a monopoly over the use of force.

FURTHER READING

There are no useful introductory textbooks covering the economics of crime. A good, if brief, introduction is contained in Friedman (2001). Other overview articles contain some technical material, though often this can be ignored without missing the main points, including Freeman (1999) and Dilulio (1996), which provide overviews of the subject, and Ehrlich (1996) which focuses on the supply of crime and the effect of punishment.

A number of papers provide evidence on the effect of economic incentives on crime. Levitt (2004) is probably the most accessible and provides a useful summary. See also Freeman (1996), Grogger (1998) and Machin and Meghir (2004).

Brand and Price (2000) provides comprehensive coverage of the social costs of crime. See also Gibbons (2004) for a particular application to evaluating the cost of property crime in London.

QUESTIONS FOR DISCUSSION

1. The government has estimated that the total cost of crime is at least £60 billion, yet it currently spends only £30 billion on public order and safety. Should spending therefore be substantially increased?

2. How might you obtain an estimate of the cost of the fear of crime?

3. Are victimless crimes (for example, drug-taking) costless?

4. Do you agree with the Landes and Posner argument that even petty thieves should be locked up for a very long time if they are caught?

5. 'Since vehicle theft simply involves the transfer of a car from one person to another, it is a less serious offence than joy-riding.' Do you agree?

6. Which is worse – wrongly convicting someone who is innocent, or failing to convict someone who is guilty?

7. If someone steals my idea, I go to a private lawyer; if someone steals my car, I go to the police. Why are these two types of theft dealt with in very different ways?

8. How would you measure the efficiency of the police force?

CHAPTER 7

Road Congestion

In 2005 more than 500 billion kilometres were driven by all road vehicles, compared to 77 billion in 1955, and journeys by car have accounted for almost all of the increase. There has been a tenfold increase in the number of kilometres driven by cars since the 1950s, largely because of rising levels of car ownership. In 2004, 75 per cent of households in the UK owned their own car, compared to just 31 per cent in 1961. By 2004, more households had two or more cars than had no car at all.

Of course, individuals derive enormous benefit from having access to a car. Having a means of transport is crucial for participation in many mainstream activities of society, including employment, consumption and leisure activities. And private cars offer a number of advantages over other forms of transport, including the benefit of door-to-door travel, privacy, a guaranteed seat, a flexible route and, often, a faster journey time. However, using a car is not without its costs. These include an increase in road traffic accidents, and the potential damage to the environment. But by far the biggest cost arises from the problem of increasingly congested roads, which have caused average vehicle speeds to fall, particularly in urban areas. In London, Britain's worst congested city by some considerable margin, the average speed of trips across the city had fallen by the 1990s to below that at the beginning of the nineteenth century, when journeys were made by horse and carriage or by tram. In inner London, drivers spent more than 30 per cent of their time stationary, and more than half of their time driving at speeds of less than 10 miles per hour. This level of congestion led, in February 2003, to the introduction of the London Congestion Charge, a compulsory payment to drive in a defined inner London charging zone between the hours of 7.00 am and 6.30 pm, Monday to Friday. The scheme has been successful in reducing the volume of traffic within the charging zone, and a number of other cities within the UK are now considering adopting similar road pricing schemes.

This chapter considers what the government's objectives are in tackling road congestion. It looks at why the free market is unlikely to meet these objectives, and then considers a number of alternative policies, including road-building and regulation, as well as road pricing. We also look at how the London Congestion Charge has worked in practice.

Objectives

As we show below, it is unlikely to be the case that eliminating congestion altogether is the desired outcome. Instead, the government needs to determine the optimal level of road use, based on efficiency and equity objectives.

Efficiency

The basic objective is to allocate the scarce road network in an efficient manner, taking into consideration the benefits and costs of different kinds of road journey.

Benefits of road travel

Different forms of travel are rarely valued in their own right, but are necessary to satisfy other demands. Of course, there are exceptions – taking a Sunday drive on a deserted road around a Scottish loch may be valued purely for itself – but, for the most part, individuals do not get direct utility or pleasure from time spent travelling. Instead, the demand for travel is a *derived demand* – so-called because it is derived from the final demand for other activities. For example, in the case of business and commercial traffic, it is necessary to move raw materials and semi-finished goods to the factories where they will be incorporated into finished products ready for consumption, and then to move these finished goods to the shops from which they will be sold to customers. The demand for this transport is therefore derived from consumers' demand for final goods and services. Similarly, in the case of private travel, getting to work is necessary in order to earn money, getting to the cinema is necessary in order to watch a film, and so on. Transport is not unique in this – health care, discussed earlier in this book, has similar properties. People do not value painful medical intervention for itself; what they value is the gain in health status that will follow the treatment. Similarly, people do not usually value driving; what they value is the activity, or the monetary reward of the activity, they are travelling to or away from.

What this means in practice is that the benefit that individuals derive from a trip, and hence their demand for the trip, will be related to the benefit they derive from the final activity. Thus trips along the same stretch of road involving commercial deliveries to shops, private shopping trips, commuting journeys to work and so on will all yield different levels of benefit. This will need to be borne in mind when deciding on the way in which the scarce road network should be allocated. It is common sense that a more efficient allocation of the road network will allow people who derive the greatest benefits to make their journeys. And, if a charge is going to be made for using a particular stretch of road (and/or at a particular time of day), people who derive the greater benefit will be more willing to pay the charge.

So far, this discussion of the benefits of travelling has said nothing about the mode of transport individuals choose to take when they make a journey. Typically, there will be more than one option alongside driving, including walking, cycling and using public transport. Individuals will decide which to take on the basis of the costs and benefits of each of the alternatives available to them. As already noted above, driving has the advantages of door-to-door travel, privacy, guarantee of a seat, a flexible route and, usually, a faster journey time; while an alternative form of public transport, such as a bus, has the advantages of (often) being cheaper overall, resulting in no parking problems, and offering an opportunity to be involved in other activities (for example, reading) while travelling. The level of benefit someone derives from a journey by a particular mode of transport will depend on their preferences for each of these characteristics. If (in general, or for a particular trip) someone places a high value on flexibility and hates depending on timetables, they will tend to value a car trip more highly; but if, on the other hand, they enjoy reading a newspaper or magazine while travelling, and find driving stressful, they will prefer the bus.

Costs of road travel

The costs of driving can be divided into the private costs to the driver and the costs that driving imposes on other people, including other drivers and wider members of society.

The private costs include the direct, monetary costs of the fuel, and the increased wear and tear on the vehicle, but also the cost of the driver's time spent making the journey. Valuing the cost of time is a hugely important issue in transport, because it represents a major portion of the costs. While time itself does not have a direct monetary cost – it is not bought and sold in a 'time marketplace' – it is a scarce resource (there are only 24 hours in a day) and so has a direct opportunity cost. For example, time spent on work-related travel has an obvious cost, since it is usually less productive than time spent at work. But time spent on commuting also represents a cost – most people would prefer (and would therefore be willing to pay something for) an extra half-hour in bed in the morning instead of fighting traffic on the way to work, or for an extra half-hour gained in the evening as a result of a shorter journey home.

It is essential to be able to place a monetary value on the cost of time in order to determine the efficient level of road journeys, so how is this done in practice? For journeys made as part of an individual's work (excluding commuting), the time spent is assumed to come at the expense of productive time spent at work. The monetary cost is then the value that an employer puts on an hour of the individual's time at work, which is captured by the gross (that is, inclusive of taxes) hourly wage rate paid to the worker (plus a mark-up for other employment-related costs). This should be a reasonably good measure of an individual's productivity. If the individual were less productive than this, then the employer would start to lose money and would start to reduce employment; if the individual were any more productive, then it would make sense for the employer to hire more workers, and this would tend to bid up wages. The

Department of Transport has used survey information on average wages to derive an estimate of the value of time spent on work-related journeys, equal to £18 an hour.

But not all journeys are work-related. What about other types of trips – for example, commuting or those that are leisure-related? In these cases, not all of the time spent making the journey comes at the expense of time spent productively in the workplace. Instead, it substitutes for time that individuals would otherwise spend on leisure activities (including lying in bed!). There are a number of approaches to placing a monetary value on this time. One is to ask people directly how much they would be willing to pay, for example, for an extra half an hour in bed each day. This approach, known as *contingent valuation* or *stated preference*, has a number of obvious drawbacks, because the questions are purely hypothetical, but it can be of some use when there is no other information available. Another possibility (known as *revealed preference*) is to look for situations where individuals reveal through their behaviour how much they value their leisure time – for example, by choosing to pay a toll to cross a road bridge that will save them an hour in trip time, rather than driving the long way round. Using both these approaches, the Department of Transport has estimated the value of time spent on non-work-related trips at £5 an hour.

As well as the private costs to the driver, there are a number of costs that driving imposes on other people. These are *external* costs, or *externalities*. One such externality is the cost of repairing roads damaged by the passage of vehicles. In the case of public roads, this is borne directly by the highways authority, though since this is funded out of government money, the real burden of the cost falls on taxpayers. In practice, the damage that a vehicle does to the road depends on the axle load (that is, the weight per pair of wheels), which means that almost all damage is caused by heavy vehicles such as trucks, rather than by cars. One possible solution is to regulate axle loads. Also, by imposing a vehicle tax that relates to the cause of the road damage and hypothecating the revenues to the highways authority, the government can make drivers bear much of the burden of this cost.

Another source of externalities is that driving imposes a number of environmental costs, including increased noise and air pollution. At the time of writing, 15 per cent of the world's emissions of carbon dioxide are from motor vehicles, and in developed countries, this figure is 40 per cent. Vehicle emissions are argued to be responsible for 50 per cent of nitrogen oxide in the atmosphere, a precursor to acid rain. The scale of the environmental externalities will depend on the type of car and also the type of fuel, as well as the length of the journey, and when and where it takes place.

Driving also imposes *accident externalities*, arising from the increased risk of accidents. Each journey implies an additional risk of an accident for the driver, but, apart from health costs borne by the state, this is purely a private cost and something that the driver will have factored into his/her individual cost–benefit analysis in deciding on the mode of travel (and whether to travel at all). However, there is also an increased risk of accident for others (including other road users and pedestrians), that the driver will not have taken into account. This risk of accident is likely to depend on a number of factors, including distance travelled, where and when the journey took place, and other traffic on the road. Since most estimates of the value of a life are high (the Department of Transport estimate at the time of writing is £1.3 million), the external accident costs are likely to be substantial, although there is considerable uncertainty over the relationship between each additional car journey and the increased risk of an accident.

Finally, there are external *congestion* costs. These are the costs that an individual's decision to drive imposes on other drivers through the increase in the volume of traffic on the road. The more vehicles there are on the road, the less freely traffic flows, and average journey times rise. Congestion is measured formally as the difference between the actual speed at which traffic flows and the free flow reference speed (measured, for example, at night). If an individual drives on a road that is at or near to capacity in terms of free-flowing traffic, then his/her journey will add to the problem of congestion and impose a cost on other drivers. This cost is mainly in terms of longer journey times, but also increased uncertainty over journey times (if the person has to be at work by 9.00 am, and the journey takes on average half an hour, but can take up to an hour when the roads are busy, s/he will need to leave at 8.00 am to ensure getting to work on time) and increased wear and tear to other cars. Recent estimates have suggested that congestion costs account for more than 70 per cent of the total external costs of driving. Importantly, not all roads are congested all of the time and these external congestion costs will vary enormously across different roads and by time of day.

Equity

There are a number of equity considerations that are likely to be relevant to a discussion of road use. As noted above, access to some form of transport is likely to be necessary if individuals are to participate in the mainstream activities of modern society, and this can be used to justify the existence of a minimum level of provision of transport, access to which is open to all, irrespective of income, age, race or sex. While most would agree that access to a minimum standard of transport is important, far fewer would argue that this minimum should include access to cars for all. However, there are some groups for whom access to cars is particularly important, such as those living in remote rural areas with no public transport, and the disabled, who are unable to use public transport easily. Any scheme, such as road pricing, that attempts to limit car use should take the needs of these groups into consideration.

Judgements about the equity of particular outcomes commonly refer to the distribution across rich and poor. This particular concept of fairness is known as *vertical equity*. It demands the unequal treatment of unequals (rich and poor) to achieve a fairer (more redistributive) outcome. Alternatively, *horizontal equity* demands the equal treatment of equals. In the case of road pricing, a 'fair' outcome (in terms of horizontal equity) would be one where all drivers in the same situation paid the same. However, this outcome could be deemed 'unfair', or regressive, since it would mean that poorer households using a car are likely to pay a relatively higher proportion of their incomes than richer households who use one. Since car ownership rises with income, the overall burden of a road pricing scheme across the income distribution is likely to be fairly flat, but among the poorest households, those who do drive will be relatively harder hit.

We return to these equity considerations in the discussion of road pricing below, but in the next section, we focus purely on whether the market system will deliver an efficient outcome.

The market system and road use

Given the benefits and costs of road use discussed above, we can consider whether the market system will deliver an efficient level of road use. This occurs when the total net benefit (total benefits minus total costs) is maximised. Thus we need to take into account the level of benefit associated with each journey, and the costs, both private and external, that it generates. For simplicity, and because they constitute the greater part of the external social costs of road use, we focus our discussion on the costs associated with congestion. Similar arguments apply to environmental and accident externalities.

When there are few vehicles on a particular road at a particular time, each vehicle will be able to travel freely at its chosen speed – subject to speed restrictions – without impeding other vehicles. However, as the flow (which we can express as vehicles per minute) increases, beyond a certain point, the vehicles will begin to delay each other; and these delays will tend to become greater as the flow continues to increase. The road becomes congested. As additional cars join the flow, they slow it down and impose costs on others. The simple numerical example shown in Table 7.1 indicates the nature of the problem.

The first column shows the flow of vehicles per minute. To keep the arithmetic simple, we have shown these in units of a single vehicle per minute. In

Table 7.1   Vehicle flows and time costs

Vehicle flow (cars per minute)	Journey time per vehicle (minutes) = marginal private cost	Total journey time, all vehicles [(1) × (2)]	Increase in total journey time as flow increases by one vehicle	Extra journey time imposed but not borne by the last vehicle [(4) − (2)]
(1)	(2)	(3)	(4)	(5)
1	10	10		
2	10	20	10	0
3	10	30	10	0
4	10	40	10	0
5	11	55	15	4
6	13	78	23	10
7	16	112	34	18
8	20	160	48	28
9	26	234	74	48
10	34	340	106	72

practice, such increases would probably have a negligible effect on costs; however, the principle is not affected by the unit of measurement adopted. The second column shows the time it takes for each vehicle to travel along the road at different levels of flow. This is the marginal private time cost per vehicle for the journey. When there is no congestion, the journey time taken by each vehicle is 10 minutes. This situation prevails up to a flow of four vehicles per minute. Beyond this point, congestion begins and journey times become longer. At five vehicles per minute the journey takes 11 minutes, at seven vehicles per minute it takes 16 minutes, and at ten vehicles per minute it takes over 30 minutes.

However, the important point to note is that, when additional vehicles join the stream, they slow down *all* the traffic. It is not just the additional vehicle that travels at the new, lower speed, but also the traffic that was on the road before the increase in flow. For example, when the flow increases from four to five vehicles per minute, the journey time for all motorists becomes 11 minutes. Hence we may say that the additional motorist has imposed a *congestion cost* on the original motorists.

If we look at columns (3), (4) and (5) in Table 7.1 we can see the extent of congestion costs. Column (3) shows the total journey time taken by all vehicles. For example, at a flow of four vehicles per minute, total journey time is 40 minutes (4 × 10); at five vehicles per minute it is 55 minutes (5 × 11), and so on. Column (4) shows the increase in total journey time as the flow increases by one vehicle; for example, if we look at the row showing five vehicles per minute, we see that the increase from four to five vehicles adds 15 minutes to the total journey time (55 – 40). This sum of 15 minutes is attributable to the fifth vehicle that joins the flow. However, the fifth vehicle itself takes only 11 minutes to make the journey – see column (2), so the difference between 11 minutes and 15 minutes – 4 minutes – represents the extra journey time the fifth vehicle imposes on other motorists. This extra journey time is shown in column (5).

Up to this point we have been concentrating on the way that journey times change as *additional* vehicles join the flow; that is, we have been looking at the change in journey time attributable to the *marginal vehicle*. If we put a monetary value on the time spent travelling, then we can express these journey times as costs and derive the additional cost attributable to each vehicle that joins the flow. This is termed the *marginal cost*. At each level of flow this can be broken down into two components: the private marginal cost and the congestion (or external marginal) cost. Together they comprise the social cost arising from the marginal motorist's journey; that is:

marginal private cost + marginal congestion cost = marginal social cost

An alternative way of presenting this information, which shows the distinction between private and social costs very clearly, is to depict it in the form of a chart. This has been done in Figure 7.1. The horizontal axis shows the flow of vehicles per minute on the road. The vertical axis measures the marginal cost of using the road. In Table 7.1, we showed the travel times for each vehicle in minutes. To convert journey time into monetary costs, we assume that each minute spent travelling costs each motorist 5p. (For the purpose of the example, we

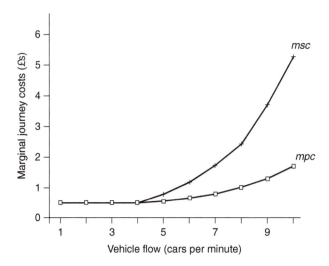

Figure 7.1 Vehicle flow and marginal journey cost.

ignore any differences in value of time between different travellers). The two curves in the chart show the way marginal private costs (*mpc*) and marginal social costs (*msc*) change as the vehicle flow on the road increases. Up to a flow of four vehicles per minute there is no congestion. Therefore, the cost per vehicle journey is 50p (= 10 minutes at 5p per minute) for each of the first four vehicles. Because there is no congestion, marginal private cost equals marginal social cost. At a flow above four vehicles, congestion sets in, and the marginal social cost associated with each vehicle becomes greater than the marginal private cost by an amount equal to the marginal congestion cost. For example, at a flow of eight vehicles, marginal private cost equals £1.00 (= 20 minutes at 5p per minute) whereas the marginal social cost equals £2.40. The marginal congestion cost thus equals £1.40 (= 28 minutes at 5p per minute). This means that the eighth vehicle to join the flow imposes a cost of £1.40 on all the other vehicles as well as incurring a cost of £1.00 itself. As can be seen from the figure, when the flow increases and congestion becomes more serious, the divergence between private and social costs becomes larger. Hence, at a flow of ten vehicles per minute, the marginal congestion cost equals £3.60.

If we turn now to benefits, we need to consider all potential drivers who might make the road trip (not just those who in fact *do* make the journey) and the possible benefits that each would derive from doing so. As already discussed, these possible benefits will depend on the journey's purpose and the driver's preferences for travelling by car compared to using the main alternatives. We can rank all potential road users according to the possible benefit they would derive from their car journey to get the typical pattern of demand shown in Figure 7.2.

On the horizontal axis of the chart we show the number of vehicles per minute travelling along a road, and on the vertical axis we show the level of benefit that each additional motorist would derive from using the road. We assume

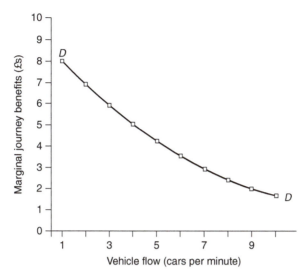

Figure 7.2   Vehicle flow and marginal journey benefits.

that each motorist is able to express his/her level of benefit in terms of money (this is referred to as the *willingness to pay* for a journey) and that this is known to the economist. The curve *DD* expresses this information. It shows that the first motorist – for example, someone travelling on a work-related trip who needs to be at a meeting in half an hour's time – values the journey at £8.00. The fourth motorist – for example, someone who is travelling to work but does not mind being late – values the journey at £5.00, while the eighth road user – for example, someone who is going to do some shopping – attaches a value of only £2.40 to it. Each point on *DD* indicates the level of benefit that would be received by the last motorist to join the flow. Therefore we can say that it indicates the level of benefit obtained by the *marginal* vehicle user or, put another way, it is a *marginal benefit* curve. We have so far discussed only the private benefits, though there are unlikely to be any additional social benefits to driving and so, in this case, marginal private benefits (*mpb*) equal marginal social benefits (*msb*).

Bringing the costs and benefits information together in a single chart, as in Figure 7.3, we can see what an efficient level of road use would look like, and how it compares to what would arise under the market system. Once again, the diagram measures the flow of vehicles per minute and records costs and benefits in terms of £s.

Given the cost and benefit schedules presented above (and ignoring the external costs) we expect a market equilibrium flow of ten vehicles per minute. The intersection of the *DD* and *mpc* curves at this traffic volume indicates that the tenth driver to join the flow attaches a value of £1.70 to his/her journey. This is equal to the private costs s/he incurs in making the journey. (This cost is found by multiplying the time spent travelling for this tenth motorist – 34 minutes, by the cost per minute – 5p). Hence this traveller will find it just worthwhile to

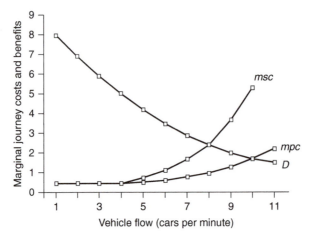

Figure 7.3 Marginal costs, benefits and road use.

make the trip. No further potential motorists will join the flow, because they do not value the journey as highly as the cost they would have to incur.

However, we can see from the chart, that £1.70 is not the total addition to costs arising from the tenth vehicle's journey, since there are congestion costs that it imposes on others. These are depicted by the difference between the *msc* and *mpc* curves; that is, £3.60. Thus the benefit that the tenth motorist obtains is less than the total costs (private plus external costs) of his/her journey. If the flow were to be reduced below ten vehicles, the discrepancy between *mpb* (= *msb*) and *msc* would be reduced, until at a flow of eight vehicles per minute, *msb* would equal *msc*. At this traffic volume, the benefit derived by the last motorist to enter the flow (£2.40) is equal to the sum of the costs s/he imposes both on him/herself and others. This is the efficient level of road use.

This analysis makes clear that a system of road use that does not require the car user to take into account the total costs of his/her actions – including the costs imposed on others – will lead to an excessive number of vehicles using the roads. The fact that the market system results in an inefficient outcome arises as a result of the discrepancy between the private costs faced by the potential motorist and the external costs (including environment and accident external- ities as well as congestion costs) that are imposed on others. Figure 7.3 also shows that the efficient level of road use is not one where all congestion is elim- inated, and traffic is free-flowing. At the efficient level of traffic flow – eight cars per minute – there are still congestion costs, indicated by the gap between the *mpc* and *msc* curves. However, at this level of efficiency, the marginal social cost is equal to the marginal social benefit.

Government policies

Faced with a level of congestion arising from the market system that is too high from an efficiency perspective, what should a government do? We discuss three possible options, including increasing the capacity of roads (and other forms of transport), regulating the number of vehicles, and rationing through road pricing. Our discussion in this section is largely theoretical; details of particular road pricing schemes (the London Congestion Charge and the Singapore Electronic Road Pricing system) are described in the next section.

Provision

Congestion arises as a result of there being too many vehicles on a limited road network. It has been argued that one solution is to build more roads, or to widen existing roads. This is not always possible in congested urban areas, but may be feasible for congested inter-urban routes. Of course, road-building is a costly activity, but the financial costs of expanding the road network may well be lower than the projected costs of increased congestion (estimated to be an annual £22 billion by 2025).

It is helpful to analyse the effects of road building, using the framework set out in the previous section. If capacity increased, the level of vehicle flow at which the marginal private cost of an additional journey began to rise (also the point at which the marginal private and social costs began to diverge) would be pushed out to the right, to a higher level of vehicle flow. In principle (and ignoring environmental and accident externalities), it would be perfectly possible to increase capacity sufficiently such that the flat part of the marginal private cost curve intersected with the demand curve. At this point, the market system would deliver an efficient outcome. Of course, the level of demand would be higher following the increase in capacity, since the marginal private cost is lower at higher levels of vehicle flow. But, there would be no external congestion costs associated with this higher level of demand.

However, the effects of increasing capacity do not stop there. The demand curve shown in Figure 7.2 is based on the benefits to individuals of driving, compared to using alternative forms of transport, under the old, restricted capacity road network. If capacity increased, then driving would become more attractive compared to alternative forms of transport. The demand curve would then shift to the right, to lie parallel to the old demand curve shown in Figure 7.2, reflecting the fact that the marginal benefit from an additional journey is higher at each level of vehicle flow. At this new, higher level of demand, the old problem of congestion is likely to return, and the chances are that the government will find itself back to square one. The government cannot build its way out of the congestion problem.

Another possibility might be to reduce the level of congestion caused by cars by improving alternative forms of transport. This is known as a *second-best policy*, since it tries to deal with an inefficiency in one sector (car travel) by introducing taxes or subsidies in another, closely-linked sector (public transport). Expanding the overground or underground rail network is likely to be expensive, and not always possible, but increasing the level of subsidy for buses is a feasible option. However, it faces a number of potential problems. Much of the evidence suggests that the demand for bus travel has an extremely low *price elasticity of demand;* that is, demand increases by only a small amount in response to fare reductions. Hence even quite large subsidies may have very little effect in practice. Moreover, even if they are made substantially cheaper, buses are unlikely to be very attractive on congested roads, since they will be slow and unreliable. The experience with the London Congestion Charge suggests that the introduction of the congestion charge was crucial to increasing bus use, as well as increased spending on bus services, because it improved their speed and reliability as well as increasing passenger numbers. It is possible to generate a 'virtuous circle' – more passengers mean improved services mean more passengers – but it took the introduction of the congestion charge to initiate the process. Without an additional mechanism for reducing congestion, there is also a danger that, if additional bus subsidies did increase the number of passengers and so initially reduce road congestion, new motorists would then take to the roads and in the end traffic would rise to the point where congestion was equal to that prior to subsidisation. These arguments suggest that increased subsidies for buses are unlikely, on their own, to result in substantial reductions in congestion.

Regulation

The problem of congestion is that there are too many cars on the road. Under the market system, there will be ten cars, compared to the efficient level of eight. One way of achieving the efficient volume of cars is to impose direct limits on the number allowed to drive at any one time. The government could, for example, simply ban the ninth and tenth car from driving at all or, perhaps more realistically, ban them from driving into the congested urban area. Of course, this rather arbitrary system is likely to face a number of problems. Say the government allowed 25,000 cars to drive into a city each day. This would create increased congestion early in the morning as drivers competed for the 25,000 places and, for the 25,001st driver, there would be the cost of a wasted journey.

A scheme is currently in operation in Athens that bans cars from entering the centre of the city on specific dates of the month according to the date and the last digit on their number plate. If the date is even and so is an individual's number plate, he/she can drive in the centre. Similarly, if the date is odd and so is the number plate, the driver is permitted to drive in the centre. Otherwise, cars have to be left at home. Ostensibly, this system might seem to be fair, since there is no charge that might fall relatively more heavily on low-income households, and the criteria for determining who is allowed to drive on any given day are arbitrary (and therefore affect all drivers in the same way). In practice, there have been a number of problems with the scheme, including a high demand for number plates, and for second cars. Also, even if the scheme had worked perfectly, it would not have achieved an efficient outcome because it does not allocate the scarce road network according to the benefit that people derive from using it.

Looking at Figure 7.3 helps to make this clear. The outcome under the market system is inefficient, not just because the number of car journeys is too high, but because some trips – specifically the ninth and tenth – are undertaken even though the marginal benefit of those trips does not exceed the marginal social costs. However, the government has no way of knowing a priori who the ninth and tenth drivers are. A system of quantity rationing simply bans two trips, but not necessarily the ninth and tenth trips. Instead, it might be the first and second trips that are banned, in which case there is a lot of benefit lost to those potential road users. As we shall see in the next section, the main strength of road pricing is that it rations the scarce road network according to consumers' willingness to pay, and hence the benefit they derive from using it.

Road pricing

Road pricing in various forms has a long history in the UK. Tolls and turnpikes date back to the time of Charles II, when the first turnpike road (part of the Great North Road) was authorised in 1663. However, the aim of this form of road pricing (and more recent examples, including the Dartford Crossing, the Severn Bridge, and the M6 Toll, which opened in 2003) was not to address the problem of congestion, but to finance construction and maintenance. One consequence of imposing tolls may have been to reduce demand compared to the toll-free level of road use, but the aim was to generate revenues rather than to achieve an efficient level of road use. The discussion in this section will focus on road pricing as a measure to address the inefficiency arising from congestion.

Drivers in the UK already pay two types of tax – the vehicle excise duty, which raised nearly £5 billion in 2005–6, and hydrocarbon oil duty (or fuel duty), which raised £24 billion in 2005–6. So why is an additional tax needed to deal with congestion?

The answer lies in the design of the two existing taxes, and the fact that neither is well-targeted at the problem of congestion. The vehicle excise duty is a flat-rate charge for using (or keeping) a vehicle on the road that, since 1998, has varied by type of engine or carbon dioxide emissions. It is therefore a tax on vehicle ownership rather than use; it is payable in full even if the car is simply parked on a road for the entire year. However, what matters to the motorist when considering a particular journey, and to the government concerned with the social costs of that journey, is the extra cost the journey is going to incur – that is, its *marginal cost*. Vehicle excise duty has no effect on marginal costs. So while the tax may make some contribution to rationing road use – by reducing the demand for car ownership – it is not well-suited to reducing congestion.

Hydrocarbon oil duty (or fuel duty) is a specific excise duty applied per litre of fuel, varying by type of fuel. The amount of tax paid will therefore relate to the amount of use made of the roads. But, the amount of tax paid will be the same per litre of fuel whether the journey is made on deserted country roads, or in the busy centre of a city. Journeys in congested conditions tend to increase petrol consumption, but this is an indirect mechanism for reducing congestion.

The current taxes, while they raise a substantial amount of revenue, are a very blunt instrument for tackling the problem of congestion. They are good at some things, such as representing the relative infrastructure costs of different types of vehicle, influencing the choice of fuel and encouraging individuals to switch to more efficient vehicles. But they are not targeted at the external cost of congestion, which varies by when and where a journey is made. It has been estimated that the total amount of tax that road users pay covers the costs of the road infrastructure three or four times over. But, the incremental costs of each journey, which matter for individuals deciding whether to drive, are far greater than the incremental taxes that drivers pay. It is this latter discrepancy that road pricing seeks to address.

The basic principle behind road pricing is very simple, and it is easy to see how it works by considering Figure 7.3. The basic problem is that, under the market system, the ninth and tenth trips are undertaken even though the marginal cost (including the cost of congestion) is greater than the marginal benefit. The obvious solution is to make individuals face the true total marginal cost – raising the marginal private cost of a journey to the level of the marginal social cost. This would ensure that only those drivers who valued their journey at or above its marginal social cost would drive, and the level of road use would be efficient. In terms of Figure 7.3, this would be achieved by levying a tax of £1.40 per vehicle if the flow was eight vehicles. This would mean that the private cost incurred by the eighth driver (that is, the one who, after ranking, is shown to value the journey least highly of the eight on the road) would be raised to its marginal social cost level of £2.40. Faced with a new tax-inclusive private cost that was above the level of benefit they would derive, the ninth and tenth drivers would no longer choose to drive on that road at that time, and might choose to make their journey at another time, or by another means of transport, or not at all.

The theory underlying road pricing is straightforward. But implementing such a scheme in reality is much more complicated. The cost and benefit curves that were drawn in Figure 7.3 are stylised examples, and are rarely know with any certainty in practice. In order to design an efficient system of road pricing, applied just to a single road at a single point in time, the government needs an understanding of the relationship between traffic flows and congestion (and of the value of changes in congestion), and an understanding of the value that different (potential) drivers attach to their journeys.

In practice, implementing road pricing will also be complicated by the fact that the cost and benefit curves will vary across roads and by time of day because of variation in traffic flows. If the *DD* curve in Figure 7.3 intersected the cost schedule at a traffic volume of four vehicles or less, reflecting the demand for road use at off-peak times, for example, no tax would be necessary, since the marginal social cost would be equal to the marginal private cost. Because of fluctuations in traffic flow at different times of the day, taxes will need to be applied on the same stretch of road at some times but not at others. And, they will need to be applied on some roads and not on others, and at different levels according to the degree of congestion. In practice, huge differences exist in congestion costs. Newbery (1990) estimated that urban centre areas at peak hours have an average congestion cost of ten times the average over all roads, and more than a hundred times that of the average motorway or rural road. In an efficient tax system, these differences would need to be reflected in variation in the tax rates.

Finally, assuming it has the necessary information to set charges at an efficient level, the government needs a secure and reliable method for collecting and enforcing charges. We discuss in the next section how this has been achieved in practice.

But before doing so, we return to the issue of equity. The introduction of road pricing creates winners and losers. The people who continue to use the roads will gain through faster and more pleasant journeys. This will apply both to those people who previously travelled by car and those who travelled by other modes of transport, such as bus or bicycle. However, the reduction in congestion will have been achieved by deterring some car users from making their original journeys. Some will make the journey by an alternative means; and others will reschedule their trips at different times or by different routes. Some may cease to make the trip altogether. On balance, these people who have changed their behaviour are likely to suffer a loss in benefit from the introduction of a congestion charge. Will different groups bear the costs in different amounts?

Congestion charges reduce the volume of traffic by rationing through price. This is efficient (compared to quantity rationing) since it allows those who derive a high level of benefit from the activity to carry on doing it, while those who derive a lower level of benefit will stop. To put it another way, those who derive a high level of benefit are willing to pay the charge. However, in practice, people's willingness to pay also embodies their ability to pay. We would therefore expect those on higher incomes to be more likely to pay the charge and carry on driving, while those on lower incomes would be more likely to experience a loss in benefit as they switch to a less-preferred alternative. Also, as already discussed, there may be a concern that, for those on low incomes who do continue to drive, the tax represents a relatively greater proportion of their income. Finally, there are some groups, such as those with a disability, for whom access to a car is considered to be particularly important, indeed necessary, for participation in the activities of mainstream society.

The revenues raised by road pricing, if they form part of general revenues, represent a transfer of resources from one group in society (charge-payers) to another (all taxpayers). The revenues are not one of the benefits of the scheme. But, in principle, and has been the case with the London Congestion Charge in practice, the government could address some of the distributional concerns by choosing to allocate the revenues to a particular cause, such as public transport, that would benefit the less well-off disproportionately.

Road pricing in practice

The London Congestion Charge was introduced on 17 February 2003. A £5 flat-rate day charge was imposed for driving into or within the inner London 'charging zone' (including the best-known shopping, business and tourist areas) between 7.00 am and 6.30 pm, Monday to Friday (excluding bank holidays). This was increased to £8 a day from July 2005. A number of vehicles are exempt, including those used by disabled individuals, bicycles and motorbikes, and buses and taxis registered in London. Residents have a 90 per cent exemption and do not pay at all if their vehicle is parked for the day.

The charge can be paid in advance on a daily, weekly or annual basis, or on the day of travel. Around 110,000 charge payments are made each day. Payment can be made in a number of ways, including via the internet, telephone and text as well as through retail outlets. When paying, individuals are required to submit their vehicle registration number, which is then entered into a central database. Automatic Number Plate Recognition (ANPR) technology at the boundaries and strategic locations within the zone is used for checking and enforcement. Where a vehicle owner has not paid, the registration number is then checked against the Driver and Vehicle Licensing Agency's (DVLA's) central register, and a Penalty Charge Notice is issued (the fine is £50 if paid within two weeks, £100 if paid within one month and £150 thereafter).

The implementation of the scheme has not been without its problems. The costs of running the scheme have been twice as high as expected, reflecting problems with compliance and enforcement. The costs of setting-up and running a scheme typically do not feature heavily in the standard diagrammatic analysis of road pricing, yet, in practice, they have proved to be substantial and, according to some estimates, are equal to nearly two-thirds of the total benefits from reduced congestion.

An alternative charge collection system is in operation in Singapore – the Electronic Road Pricing System – introduced in 1998. Like the London congestion charge, this also operates a single zone scheme. However, payment is made via an on-board unit (OBU) installed in each car. When the vehicle passes under the gantries, the system automatically identifies the vehicle (using ANPR) and deducts an appropriate amount from the user via the smartcard inserted in the OBU, which can be topped up via the internet or at designated outlets. In principle, this technology could be used to vary the charge by time of day, although, in the Singapore scheme, charges are assessed only quarterly, based on average city speeds.

Yet more sophisticated charging methods involve distance charging based on positioning technology. In principle, such a system could be used to charge individuals for using all points of the road network, since it records time of day and distance travelled; however, the technology is not yet developed enough to be rolled out.

The fact that the London Congestion Charge is a flat rate makes the scheme simpler to operate. In theory, it may not be that inefficient, given the particular nature of congestion in London which, prior to the introduction of the charge, was broadly constant at all times of day with little of the usual variation in average traffic speeds between standard peak and off-peak times.

The initial assessments of the effect of the Congestion Charge show that it was effective at reducing traffic flowing into the charging zone – by up to 33 per cent in the case of car traffic. Of the reduction in numbers of people driving, more than half were estimated to have switched to public transport (mainly buses); a quarter diverted around the congestion charge zone; 10 per cent used other forms of private transport, taxis and bicycles; while 10 per cent stopped travelling or moved their journeys to other times of the day. In total, the level of congestion is estimated to have decreased since the introduction of the congestion charge, and there has been a greater than expected increase in the number of bus passengers. As already discussed, the introduction of the congestion charge was accompanied by a number of measures to improve the buses (financed out of the revenues), and it appears to have been the combination of the congestion charge and the expanded service that has led to the rise in use.

In spite of problems with the costs of the scheme, the London Congestion Charge is broadly seen as being a success. Not least, it represents a huge achievement in setting up and running the largest road pricing scheme in the world, with little vocal opposition. Many other cities in the UK and worldwide have been taking notes, and similar schemes are likely to be implemented elsewhere. With improvements in positioning technology over the coming years, further extensions of road pricing seem inevitable.

SUMMARY

- Road congestion is a growing problem. It is estimated to account for 70 per cent of the total social costs associated with driving.

- In principle, there is an optimal level of road traffic determined by the costs (including congestion and other social costs) and benefits of driving. Estimating the costs of congestion requires putting a monetary value on the time spent sitting in traffic.

- There are a number of ways the government could cut congestion. These include building more roads, or increasing public transport, regulating the number of vehicles allowed to drive on congested roads or through a system of road pricing.

- Compared to the alternatives, road pricing is more likely to reduce traffic and to allocate the scarce road network efficiently. The London Congestion Charge, introduced in 2003, has been successful at reducing traffic volumes in London by up to 33 per cent.

FURTHER READING

Newbery (1990) offers a good introduction to the economics of road pricing, including a detailed discussion of the different social costs associated with road use. More up-to-date material can be found in the Department of Transport (2004) 'Feasibility study of road pricing in the UK': http://www.dft.gov.uk/pgr/roads/roadpricing/feasibilitystudy/studyreport/. Annex A contains the economic case for road pricing, while Annex C provides details on charging technologies and existing schemes.

Blow et al. (2003) and Leape (2006) provide useful overviews of the London Congestion Charge. Further information, including annual evaluation reports, can be found on the Transport for London website: http://www.cclondon.com/. Proud'homme and Bocajero (2005) and Mackie (2005) provide opposing views on the social costs and benefits of the Congestion Charge.

There are a number of interesting papers that discuss how to value costs and benefits; see, for example, MVA et al. (2003) on the valuation of time, or Portney (1994) and Diamond and Hausman (1994) on contingent valuation.

QUESTIONS FOR DISCUSSION

1. Is a system of quantity rationing, such as the one operating in Athens, a more equitable means of dealing with congestion than a system of price rationing, such as the London Congestion Charge?

2. What are the social costs and benefits of the London Congestion Charge?

3. What factors are likely to be important in determining the success of similar road pricing schemes in other cities in the UK, and worldwide?

4. The value of lives saved is an important part of the benefits of road safety measures. How might economists go about trying to place a monetary value on a life saved?

5. Discuss in what ways setting a toll to raise revenue to finance the building of a road would differ from setting a toll to address the problem of congestion on a road.

6. In Singapore, private car ownership is limited through a licence bidding system which has restricted car ownership to 10 per cent of the population. How does this compare to congestion charging as a means of rationing road use?

CHAPTER 8

Climate Change

Climate change has become an increasingly prominent social problem world-wide. The stark conclusion of the *2006 Stern Review on the Economics of Climate Change* was that, if the world does not act,

> the overall costs and risks of climate change will be equivalent to losing at least five per cent of global GDP each year, now and forever. If a wider range of risks and impacts are taken into account, the estimates of damage could rise to 20 per cent of GDP or more ... Our actions now and over the coming decades could create risks of major disruption to economic and social activity, later in this century and in the next, on a scale similar to those associated with the great wars and the economic depression of the first half of the 20th century.

The Review called for governments around the world to spend 1 per cent of global gross domestic product (GDP) per annum (equivalent to US$450 billion) on cutting carbon emissions in order to avoid the worst effects of climate change.

Economics was central to the *Stern Review*'s analysis of the costs and benefits of climate change mitigation. While environmentalists – and increasingly politicians – may call for something to be done to save the planet, taking action to slow down or reverse the process of global warming has costs. Some of the concern about the costs of climate change is because developing countries are likely to be particularly hard hit – any money spent on reducing carbon emissions could be spent on funding programmes to combat malaria or AIDS, or to increase technological or human capital to ensure that these countries are better able to adapt to global warming in the future. The UN has estimated that US$75 billion would be enough to give every person in developing countries clean drinking water, sanitation, basic health care and education right now. Some argue strongly that this would be a better way to spend money than on actions to reduce global warming. Resolving these debates is some way beyond the scope of this chapter, but we show how economics can help to provide a framework for thinking about these issues.

It is important to recognise that climate change is quite different from many of the other social problems considered in this book. Compared with health care, education, road congestion or pensions, for example, which are largely domestic issues, climate change is an international problem. Greenhouse gases emitted in one country affect the global environment, with consequences for people living in other countries. Moreover, if one country unilaterally takes action to control its greenhouse gas emissions, the benefit could be more than outweighed by increased emissions elsewhere. Neither the problem nor the solution is restricted to a single country. Also, climate change is intergenerational, since actions that are taken today will have important consequences for future generations. Deciding on the appropriate level of climate change mitigation to undertake now involves valuing costs and benefits that fall across different generations – possibly several hundred years into the future. How those future costs and benefits should be weighted compared to costs and benefits borne today has been a central issue in the climate change debate. The simple cost–benefit framework can be extended to accommodate both the international and intergenerational aspects of the problem, but ultimately moral as well as economic judgements are likely to be involved.

The focus of this chapter is on climate change and how to reduce carbon emissions – the main driver of global warming. However, much of the analysis is more widely applicable to other environmental problems.

Objectives

As before, efficiency is a central objective for government policy. The *Stern Review* sought to quantify and monetise the costs of climate change in order to determine the efficient level of emission controls. Judgements about equity – between people within a country, across countries, and across different generations – are also important in the climate change debate.

Efficiency

The basic efficiency problem with climate change is that many activities undertaken by individuals as consumers (for example, driving or flying) or producers (for example, manufacturing or energy production) result in an external cost to the environment, which is not reflected in their private price. These costs are known as *negative externalities*. As discussed in previous chapters, since private individuals do not have to pay these costs themselves, the resulting level of consumption or production is inefficient – the total cost to society, including the effect on the environment as well as the private costs, is greater than the (private) value.

As well as being seen as a problem of over-consumption or over-production, the efficiency problem can also be viewed as a suboptimal level of spending on measures to tackle environmental damage. It may be possible for consumers and producers to reduce the amount of pollution associated with their activities by various means – investing in cleaner technology or switching to liquid petroleum gas, for example – but this will involve some financial cost. From society's point of view, it is worth reducing emissions so long as the cost is less than the damage prevented. However, if individuals do not bear the cost of environmental damage directly, they have no incentive to prevent it. The externality problem can therefore be viewed either as an inefficiently high level of consumption and production, or an inefficiently low level of pollution control.

Since much of the climate change debate is about spending money to reduce emissions (rather than directly cutting back on consumption or production), this is the focus of our analysis. The problem can be illustrated by means of a simple example. Suppose that a computer factory produces ten units of carbon emissions at its current level of computer output. Because the costs of this pollution are borne widely by society and not directly by the computer manufacturer, they will have no bearing on the decision of how many computers to make, which will instead be determined by the expected price of computers and the private costs of making computers.

If the computer manufacturer could reduce the level of carbon emissions (but produce the same number of computers), then society would gain from the reduction in pollution. This is illustrated in Figure 8.1, which plots the marginal damage costs (MDC) schedule associated with different levels of carbon emissions. These are the costs to society arising from each additional unit of carbon emission – the tenth unit of carbon, for example, yields damage costs equal to £30. These damage costs also represent the benefit to society of reducing carbon emissions by each additional unit. So, if the firm can reduce carbon emissions from ten to nine units, the benefit to society will be equal to £30. The curve is upward-sloping, since the effect of each additional unit of carbon emission depends negatively on existing levels of carbon concentration in the atmosphere.

However, in order for the firm to reduce its level of carbon it needs to spend some money – investing in cleaner technology, for example, or switching to a more expensive, but cleaner, energy source. These costs are shown in the marginal abatement cost (MAC) schedule which plots the additional cost incurred

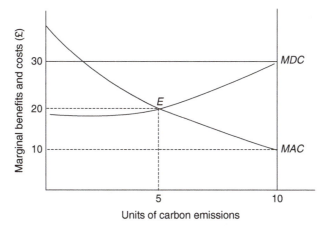

Figure 8.1   The costs and benefits of pollution abatement.

in reducing carbon emissions from their current level. The *MAC* curve shows that, at the current level of ten units of carbon emissions, it would cost £10 to reduce emissions by one unit. The *MAC* curve is downward-sloping, since it is assumed that firms are likely to have to spend increasing amounts of money in order to drive down their carbon emissions further towards zero.

At the current level of ten units of carbon emissions, the cost of reducing emissions by one unit (£10) is far less than the benefit to society (£30). Overall, there would be a gain to society from spending money to reduce carbon emissions below this level. The figure makes it clear that it would not be optimal to reduce the level of emissions to zero since, at this point, the marginal abatement cost is greater than the marginal damage cost. The efficient level of carbon emissions is five units, at which the marginal cost to society of cutting emissions by another unit is exactly equal to the marginal benefit. At levels of emissions above this, the cost of cutting emissions (*MAC*) is less than the benefit (*MDC*), so it makes sense to cut emissions. At lower levels of emissions, however, the benefit from cutting emissions is greater than the cost of doing so.

However, while it is easy to define in principle the efficient level of investment in carbon reduction, as in other policy areas it is far harder to do this in practice, particularly because of the international and intergenerational nature of the problem. Take marginal abatement costs. The costs most usually used in cost–benefit analysis are the expenditure costs of investment in cleaner technology, but this is not the end of the story. If firms spend money on pollution abatement, this will have additional consequences, either for their profitability (and whether they remain in business), or for the prices they charge consumers. To the extent that higher prices result in consumers changing their behaviour (switching expenditure from 'dirty' to 'clean' goods), the expenditure costs will in fact overstate the abatement costs. If some firms are forced out of business, this may impose additional short-term adjustment costs on local economies because of the resulting unemployment.

If firms have to spend money on pollution abatement, then the higher cost is likely to be passed on to consumers, resulting in reduced consumption. However, in principle, investment in energy-saving technology could result in an overall reduction in price, causing an increase in demand for the final product, which will offset some of the energy savings. This is known as the *rebound effect*, or the *take-out effect* and it comes about when improvements in efficiency reduce fuel use and cost for a given activity, such as heating a house or making a car journey. The reduced cost of fuel encourages the greater use of fuel – for example, for a warmer house, more or longer journeys – and the greater use will offset some of the direct energy savings from the improvement in efficiency. This is less likely with carbon taxes (discussed further below), because the lower total cost of energy from the increase in efficiency is offset by the higher cost from the tax.

In practice, the cost of reducing emissions may be uncertain. There may be uncertainty today over the effect of new, cleaner technology applied to particular industries, but more fundamentally, given that many of the costs of climate change will occur a long way into the future, there is additional uncertainty over what the cost of abatement might be in the future. Arguably, with greater investment in researching and developing clean technologies, the cost of reducing carbon emissions will be driven down over time. If the cost of reducing carbon emissions is much cheaper in five or ten years' time, then, given the long-term nature of the problem, a firm might want to carry out relatively more emissions reduction in the future, when it is cheaper. A perfectly legitimate strategy is not to spend money on reducing carbon emissions today, but to invest in productive technology and human capital and to postpone abatement until tomorrow, when the cost will be lower (and when the damage from climate change is greater). This is known as the *climate-policy ramp*, since it involves deliberately ramping up over time the level of policies to slow down global warming.

There is also a huge amount of uncertainty over the magnitude of the *marginal damage costs* (also known as the *social cost of carbon*). This arises for a number of reasons:

- uncertainty over the linkage between carbon emissions and global temperatures;

- uncertainty over the valuation of damages arising from rising global temperatures;

- how to value costs and benefits accruing to people in different countries; and

- how to value costs and benefits accruing to people across different generations.

We discuss each of these in turn.

Modelling linkages

Placing a value on the effect of carbon emissions on the environment involves modelling a number of linkages: How do emissions affect atmospheric concentrations? How do atmospheric concentrations affect the global temperature? How does the global temperature affect regional climate and weather? And how do climate and weather have direct impacts on people? Each of these linkages has to be modelled separately. There is genuine scientific uncertainty over the precise effects, and each stage is therefore likely to involve a number of parameter assumptions. The result is a range of different estimates for the environmental impacts, which may include the possibility of environmental catastrophe. One important issue is how to deal with these low-probability, but very severe, outcomes. Their impact is potentially devastating. Should the analysis be based on the worst case scenario (which could involve spending a large amount of resources on reducing global warming), or only the most likely outcome?

Valuing impacts

The next stage is to place a monetary value on the impacts of global warming. These impacts are potentially wide-ranging and include effects on crops and livestock, on property, on individual health (including the possibility of death), and on quality of life. In some cases, global warming will have positive benefits (people typically like warmer, sunnier weather) which will need to be taken into account. Some impacts are relatively straightforward to place a monetary value on, since there is already a market valuation that can be used – the value of crops lost because of drought, for example, or the cost of replacing possessions destroyed by a flood. For many other potential outcomes (including the effects of disease and death), there is no obvious market price. Instead, a value has to be derived using either revealed preference methods or contingent valuation methods (see Chapter 7 on road congestion for a further discussion of these methods).

Several studies have tried to estimate the value of health improvement and the value of a life. These studies are legitimate, since governments and individuals often make explicit or implicit judgements about how much to spend in order to improve health or save lives. But, the range of estimates obtained is fairly wide and varies depending on the approach used and the data. Other potential outcomes – including the effects of social unrest and migration (so-called *socially contingent impacts*) are even more uncertain, but are potentially very large. In practice, because of the differing levels of precision attached to these different types of costs and benefits (market, non-market and socially contingent), they can, as in the *Stern Review*, be presented separately. The 5 per cent figure quoted at the start of this chapter referred only to the market costs, which can be estimated with some degree of precision. Including environmental and human health impacts raises this figure to 11 per cent. No attempt was made by Stern to infer the cost of socially contingent outcomes. Presenting a minimum cost in this way places a lower bound on the amount of spending on climate mitigation policies that is justified.

There is also a degree of uncertainty because many of the costs occur in the future – and sometimes a long way in the future. The estimated costs take the world as it is now, but, if the effects of climate change become more severe, it is likely that people will respond by changing their behaviour in order to minimise the adverse consequences (by not building houses on flood plains, for example, or by switching to weather-resistant crops). The financial costs of these activities are a legitimate cost of climate change, but these are likely to be far smaller than the outcomes that the behavioural changes are intended to avoid. Factoring these behavioural responses into the analysis will yield smaller, and arguably more realistic, estimates, but also introduce a further degree of uncertainty.

Cross-country comparisons

Climate change is global in its impact. Carbon emissions in one country will affect global temperatures, and this will affect people living in other countries. Most people are agreed that the worst effects of climate change will be felt by people living in developing countries. This is because of their geography, their greater dependence on agriculture, and because, with fewer resources, they are less able to adapt to the consequences of climate change. Moreover, because their incomes are already low, the adverse consequences are likely to hit particularly hard. Because of the diminishing marginal benefit from additional income (see

Chapter 4 on pensions), a £1 loss for someone with an annual income of £100 is greater than a £1 loss for someone with an annual income of £10,000.

The simple cost–benefit framework can be extended to deal with these distributional issues. If there is a concern that the value of a £1 loss to someone in Senegal is greater than the value of a £1 loss to someone in the USA, it is possible to apply weights that raise the value of each £1's costs and benefits in Senegal relative to those in the USA. However, deciding what those weights might be is more controversial. One possibility is to base the weights on individuals' own behaviour in avoiding adverse outcomes – how much are they prepared to pay (through an insurance premium, for example) to avoid a loss of £100, for example. But these studies are typically conducted in developed countries, and may not be more generally applicable to cross-country comparisons. Another possibility is to conduct the following thought experiment (known as 'Okun's leaky bucket') to determine the appropriate weight. Suppose that a policy-maker implements a policy to help the poor that costs a rich person £100. Because some of the money will leak out of the system, the poor person will be made £X better off, where £X is less than £100. The crucial question is this – how big would £X have to be for the policy to go ahead? Are we happy for the poor person to be just £1 better off, or £10, or £50? Achieving consensus on this is likely to be quite hard in practice.

Intergenerational issues

Another crucial issue is how to value costs and benefits that occur a long way into the future. The damage caused by one unit of carbon emitted today lasts for over 400 years. Indeed, the damage done in the immediate future is relatively small; but it rises quickly, peaking in around 100 years' time, and then gradually declines. So, cutting carbon emissions today will have very little positive benefit at the present time, but will yield benefits for hundreds of years to come. In everyday decisions, individuals (and governments) discount the future, as was discussed in Chapter 4. They place less weight on costs and benefits occurring in the future compared to costs and benefits today. In part, this discounting of the future reflects the possibility that people may not survive that long; it may also reflect people's impatience to have things now rather than later. On average, the market interest rate (paid on money deposited in savings accounts, for example) reflects the extent to which people discount the future since it is the necessary increase in money tomorrow that people require in order not to spend their money today. It has also been argued that the market interest rate is the appropriate discount rate to use, since it reflects the general market return on productive capital. Anything that involves investing today in return for future benefits has an opportunity cost, in terms of the next best alternative that the money could have been invested in to yield a productive return. The benefits therefore need to be at least as great as those that could be obtained through the alternative investment. This is why some people argue very strongly that investing in productive human or technological capital represents a better use of scarce resources today than investing in climate change mitigation policies.

In practice, there is a range of market rates of return reflecting either the return to saving or the risk-free rate of return on capital. These are different because of tax reasons. Using the market rate of return gives a discount rate of at least 5 per cent. If the discount rate is at this level, however, benefits or costs occurring 100 years into the future are discounted away almost to nothing. This means that most of the benefits of reducing carbon emissions today are given a zero weight in the cost–benefit analysis. Many people are uncomfortable with this outcome. Moreover, there are a number of reasons why current market rates of return may be inappropriate to use in making long-term government decisions, not least because there may be considerable uncertainty about what the market rate of return will be over the horizon where the costs and benefits accrue. Among the arguments against using market rates are that they reflect the decisions of imperfectly informed individuals acting in their own interests and considering only their own lifetimes. Market outcomes may also be affected by a limited number of very wealthy individuals. By contrast, the government has to consider the interests of several generations, and must take into consideration the interests of every member of society, and it may have superior information about the social (rather than the private) return to alternative forms of investment.

At the other extreme, it has been argued that the government should not discount costs and benefits to future generations at all, and indeed that it is morally wrong to place less weight on the interests of future generations compared to people living today. This would mean that the government should put an equal weight on £100-worth of benefits occurring in 500 years' time as it does on £100-worth of benefits occurring today. In this case, all the benefits of cutting carbon emissions today are included in the cost–benefit analysis, and this massively increases the payoff to engaging in activity to reduce global warming. The policy implication would be to invest much more heavily in climate change mitigation. Very broadly, this is the approach taken in the *Stern Review* – although it does allow for a very small probability of global extinction caused by, say, an asteroid hitting the planet.

There may be strong moral reasons for believing that future generations should be treated equally with current generations in a cost–benefit analysis. However, doing so gives rise to some rather tough conclusions. Nordhaus (2008) illustrates this by means of a 'wrinkle experiment'. He puts this as follows: Suppose that scientists discover a wrinkle in the climate system that will cause damage equal to 0.1 per cent of global consumption starting in 2200 and continuing indefinitely. If the interests of future generations were given equal weight in a cost–benefit analysis, then removal of this wrinkle would justify a reduction in current consumption of up to 56 per cent. This is not something that many people today would be happy with.

At the very least, we may believe that future generations will be better off than we are, implying that a 0.1 per cent reduction in consumption will have a smaller welfare loss in the future than it would today. This thinking lies behind an alternative approach to discounting that is based on the expected future growth rate. Essentially, it argues that we should discount future benefits (and costs) to the extent that we expect future generations to be richer than we are.

This means that future costs and benefits are down-weighted compared to today's, but involves discounting at the underlying economic growth rate, which is typically less than the market rate of return.

A final point about valuing and discounting future costs and benefits. The underlying approach to analysing the costs and benefits of climate change taken by the *Stern Review* is a welfarist one. It involves a consideration of the effects of policies on the welfare of individuals, with actions today based on whether or not they improve the sum of individual welfare (today and in the future). When considering costs and benefits in hundreds of years' time, there is no real certainty that individual welfare will be determined in the same way as it is now. The value that individual costs and benefits are given in the analysis reflects today's valuations (and in turn, the preferences of society today). But, as Nordhaus argues, in several hundred years' time, individuals are likely to consume goods and services that are unknown today, while there will have been enormous technological advances affecting healthcare. Who knows how these future generations will value the benefits from reducing carbon emissions in 2008.

Equity

The previous discussion of the efficient level of climate change mitigation has already raised important equity considerations. The assessment of the scale of the benefits to be gained from reducing carbon emissions depends critically on how to weight benefits for developing countries and benefits occurring to future generations. In turn, this involves largely subjective judgements about how to treat fairly rich countries compared to poor ones, and future generations compared to the current one.

Another important equity issue is which countries should bear the costs of reducing carbon emissions. The *Stern Review* concluded that total spending should equal 1 per cent of global GDP, but this total needs to be allocated in some way across different countries. At first sight, the issue of who should pay might seem simple: since it is the polluter who creates the problem, it should be the polluter who pays. For a developed country such as the USA, the 'polluter pays' principle is fairly uncontroversial. The USA is the world's largest polluter – it is also one of the world's richest countries. But, what about China and India? These fast-developing countries are contributing increasingly large quantities of pollution – China is expected to pull ahead of the USA as the world's number one polluter by 2010. But is it fair that they be required to spend a lot of money on reducing carbon emissions when their per capita incomes are still below those of the USA and Western European countries? Should they spend money on reducing carbon emissions when millions of people live in poverty in these countries? For these reasons, both China and India were exempted from the terms of the 2006 Kyoto Protocol, which set mandatory standards for the reduction of greenhouse gases. This might seem fair. But, if some countries are exempted, while their competitor nations are required to comply, does this create an unfair playing field in terms of international trade? Some might think it fair that China and India get the same terms of trade as the USA and Western European countries enjoyed at a similar stage in their development. But if China and India can produce goods more cheaply than these other countries as a result of not having to implement carbon emissions standards, then both will be able to secure more of the world's demand, resulting in a concentration of heavily-polluting industries within these countries. In the literature, this is known as the 'pollution-haven hypothesis'.

Another potential equity concern relates to the distribution of the costs of climate change mitigation within an economy. The 'polluter pays' principle would suggest that firms should bear the cost, but, as we have seen, this is not the end of the story, since the actual incidence of the cost will fall elsewhere. The costs of pollution abatement may result in lower profits for the firm, in which case the cost is borne by shareholders (who in turn may be pension funds investing the money of millions of relatively small investors). Some firms may be forced to go out of business, in which case some of the costs will fall on people who lose their jobs in high-pollution industries. Also, firms may try to pass on some of the costs to consumers in the form of higher prices. In the case of many high-polluting goods, such as domestic fuel, the impact will be regressive, since low-income households tend to spend a higher share of their total income on fuel than do those with higher incomes. This should not necessarily prevent governments from introducing such policies (although in the UK, increasing taxes on domestic fuel have been resisted on exactly these grounds), but there may be a need to compensate such households via the rest of the tax and benefit system.

The market system and the environment

The *Stern Review* suggested that climate change threatens to be the greatest-ever market failure. As discussed above, market failure arises because private actions generate negative external costs. Because individual agents do not face those costs, they have no incentive to limit their activities or to reduce the level of pollution. Given the problem, it may seem impossible for the market to reach an efficient outcome without government intervention. However, in a now famous paper, the Nobel-prize-winning economist, Ronald Coase, argued that an efficient outcome was indeed achievable by the market.

Consider the costs and benefits of pollution abatement shown in Figure 8.1, and assume that there is a single polluter – the computer manufacturer – and a single pollutee who suffers the full costs of the pollution. Because the polluter does not face the costs of environmental damage directly, there is no incentive to reduce the level of carbon emissions below 10. However, the pollutee does face the full costs, and does have an incentive to try to do something. It is plausible that the pollutee will react by trying to persuade the computer manufacturer to reduce its level of carbon emissions. Since the most forceful form of persuasion is likely to be a financial inducement, the pollutee could offer a deal to the computer manufacturer whereby it paid for the costs of reducing carbon emissions. From the diagram, it is clear that the pollutee would have an incentive to do this since it suffers £30 worth of costs from the current level of carbon emissions, whereas the firm only requires compensation of £10 to invest in carbon reduction. In fact, the pollutee has an incentive to compensate the polluter for carbon reduction up to the point where the required level of compensation necessary to get the polluter to reduce carbon emissions by an additional unit is equal to the marginal benefit derived by the pollutee. This occurs at point E, where the marginal cost of abatement is equal to marginal damage cost – in other words, at the efficient level of carbon emissions.

This argument is powerful. It suggests that, if this kind of bargaining takes place between the parties involved, an efficient level of pollution-generating activity will be achieved without the need for government intervention. Moreover, there is another way in which an efficient outcome might be reached. We have assumed that the pollutee has no rights over the clean air that has been polluted. In this case, the pollutee will have an incentive to pay the polluter to stop polluting. But what if the pollutee does have such a right, in which case s/he can sue the polluter for the damages caused? Rather than paying the damages, the polluter will find it cheaper to reduce the level of carbon emissions. It will continue to reduce the level of emissions rather than pay compensation up to the point where the cost of abatement is greater than the damage caused – the efficient level of carbon emissions.

The key point of Coase's argument was that the market could reach an efficient outcome. All that was needed was a clear definition of who has a right to do what – whether the pollutee has a prior right to clean air, or the polluter has a right to pollute. After that, as we have seen, it does not matter who has the right, in order to reach an efficient outcome. This result is known as *the Coase theorem*. However, in the absence of a clearly defined right to clean air, it would be the pollutee who bore the costs of reducing carbon emissions, since the pollutee would be required to pay compensation, an outcome that might be objected to on equity grounds.

In practice, however, there are a number of barriers to the efficient solution being reached. First, the example outlined above assumed one polluter and a single pollutee. In practice, most cases of pollution involve large numbers of firms or individuals who pollute, and a large number of individuals who suffer the consequences; in the case of climate change, these are worldwide. Trying to negotiate a deal between polluters and pollutees in this case would be extremely costly, if not impossible. In some cases, the costs of negotiation and enforcement could exceed the potential gains from Coasean bargaining. In other cases it might not be possible to reach a private deal – for example if there were opportunities for some affected parties to *free-ride* on others, bearing none of the costs but gaining from the actions of others. In the case of climate change, many of the affected pollutees will be part of future generations and may not yet be born. In this case, it is not clear who will bargain on their behalf.

Another problem is that the model assumes that property rights are clearly defined – in other words, that both polluter and pollutee know whether the polluter has the right to pollute or the pollutee has the right to clean air. If these property rights are well-defined, it is clear who should be paying whom, but if property rights are not clearly defined, bargaining may be extremely costly or not possible at all. Also, there needs to be full information and non-strategic bargaining. In order for the pollutee to know that it is worth offering a deal, s/he needs to know the marginal abatement cost schedule. But the polluter may try to act strategically to maximise his or her gain.

Moreover, even if the polluter and pollutee could bargain their way to an efficient solution, there might be objections to the market solution on equity grounds. If the pollutees do not have well-defined property rights, they will have to pay compensation to the polluter. This is the complete opposite of the 'polluter pays' principle, and it may strike many as unfair that the pollutees have to bear the financial cost.

These practical problems have caused many to dismiss Coase's theorem as merely a theoretical curiosity, of little or no practical relevance. There are occasional real-life examples – the citizens of a Swiss town paid compensation to an Austrian nuclear power company not to site a power plant close to the border. But, given the international and intergenerational nature of global warming, we would not expect the market to deliver an efficient outcome; some form of government intervention is required.

Government policies

The two main forms of government intervention in the area of environmental policy have involved the direct regulation of the quantity of emissions that firms are allowed to release (often known as a command and control approach), and the use of economic incentives (taxes and tradable permits). We discuss these different approaches in turn, but first we deal briefly with the possibility of direct provision by the government.

Provision

In principle, the government could directly take over pollution-generating industries. Since the government represents the interests of everyone in society, it would then have an incentive to run the industries at a level at which the net social costs of output of each good produced was equal to the net social benefits, where social costs include pollution and damage to current and future generations. Historically, government ownership of modes of transportation (for example, trains and buses) and of utilities (for example, electricity and water) has been justified on the grounds that government provision may bring the level of output closer to the efficient level. However, the success of these enterprises in achieving an efficient level of output is far from clearly established. Part of the problem is likely to be that the government may have competing priorities, including growth.

Regulation

Historically, regulation (known as command and control) has been the most common form of controlling pollution. In principle, this provides a very simple and straightforward way to reduce the level of emissions to the efficient level. Consider Figure 8.1. Assuming that the government knows the marginal abatement cost schedule and the marginal damage cost schedule, it can determine the optimal level of carbon emissions and regulate firms to produce only that level. In practice, this would be achieved by granting the computer manufacturer a permit to produce exactly five units of carbon.

Of course, as we have discussed, there is a degree of uncertainty about both of these cost schedules. In practice, therefore, the government is unlikely to be able to regulate output precisely to the optimal level of emissions. However, this problem is not unique to the command and control approach, but will also affect the setting of the efficient level of taxes.

It may also be costly (or even impossible) to monitor emissions levels accurately. This may give rise to a number of problems – again, these are likely to affect economic incentives as well as regulation. First, if the government cannot measure a firm's emissions, it will not be able to regulate them. Instead, it will have to choose to regulate a proxy, such as the inputs to the manufacturing process. In practice, governments have typically chosen to regulate (and tax) fuel inputs according to their carbon content rather than carbon emissions. The regulation will only be truly effective if there is a clear and direct relationship between inputs and emissions. Regulating or taxing inputs rather than emissions may also reduce the incentive to invest in technologies that improve the emission content. A second problem is that if there is imperfect or infrequent monitoring, this will reduce the firm's incentive to comply with the regulations (and to declare its tax liability accurately).

A more general problem with regulation is the possibility of *regulatory capture*. This term is used to describe a situation where those being regulated may be able to persuade the regulator to act in their interests, rather than in the interest of society as a whole. In the case of environmental pollution, this would involve setting the regulated level of pollution above the socially optimal level. However, in spite of its name, this problem is not absent in the case of economic incentives. The basic problem is that the government can be manipulated by individual firms, or by the industry, into behaving suboptimally. This may be in the form of setting lax regulations, or tax rates that are too low to achieve the efficient level of emissions.

In fact, as we shall see below, the main argument against the command and control approach is that it less likely to achieve a cost-effective reduction in emissions.

Taxes

Rather than imposing directly an allowed quantity of emissions on a firm, an alternative way of achieving an efficient level of pollution avoidance is to set a price on emissions and allow firms to adjust the quantity they produce. This charge is effectively a pollution tax. This is a direct solution to the externality problem, where under-investment in pollution abatement is caused by the fact that individual consumers and producers do not face directly the environmental costs of their activities. By imposing a tax on emissions, the government forces individuals to take these costs into account.

Going back to Figure 8.1, the government could achieve an efficient level of carbon emissions by imposing a tax of £20 on each unit of carbon emitted. The result of this would be that the computer manufacturer would choose to reduce emissions to five units – and pay tax on these emissions. At a level of emissions above this, it is cheaper to reduce emissions than to pay the tax, since the marginal abatement costs are less than £20. However, at a level below this, the manufacturer would rather pay the tax, since it is cheaper than further reductions in carbon emissions.

In practice, in setting the tax, the government will face many of the same problems as in regulating the quantity of emissions. As before, there will be uncertainty over both the marginal abatement cost schedule and the marginal damage cost schedule, which may result in the tax rate being set inefficiently too high or too low. If the government wants to achieve a target quantity of carbon emissions (as is the case with countries complying with the Kyoto Protocol, for example), then quantity regulations are clearly a more reliable way to do this. In setting a tax, the government relies on firms' responses to determine the quantity reduction.

Under conditions of uncertainty, it has been shown that regulation may be preferable to taxation depending on the relative slopes of the marginal damage cost schedule and the marginal abatement cost schedule.

Suppose that the MAC schedule is fairly flat compared to the MDC schedule, as in panel (a) of Figure 8.2. In this case, setting a tax rate that is slightly too high (or too low) can be very costly. The optimal level of pollution abatement is shown by quantity q^* and cost level c^*. If the government sets a tax rate that is slightly above this, at the level c, for example, then firms will respond to the tax rate by moving along the MAC schedule to q, which is a long way below the optimal level. In this case, firms engage in too much carbon emission reduction. The opposite argument would apply if the tax rate were slightly too low. In this case, quantity regulation can work more effectively to achieve the optimal level of emissions.

In the case of panel (b), however, where the MAC schedule is relatively steep compared to the MDC schedule, price regulation is likely to work better. In this case, setting a regulated quantity that is even slightly too low (q compared to q^*) will result in a very high abatement cost for the regulated industry compared to the benefits of reducing emissions (c compared to c^*).

The main strength of a system of environmental taxes compared to quantity regulation is that it achieves a given level of reduction in emissions in a more cost-effective way. In practice, not all firms are likely to face the same marginal abatement cost schedule. For some, it may be relatively cheap to reduce carbon emissions (low-cost firms), while for others it may be relatively more expensive

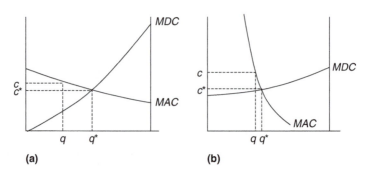

Figure 8.2   Quantity versus price regulation.

(high-cost firms). Ideally, the government would like low-cost firms to cut emissions further than high-cost firms, since this reduces the overall cost of pollution reduction (and allows more resources to be spent on other productive activities).

It is possible to imagine a system of regulation that would achieve this. If the government possessed information concerning the costs of pollution control for all the polluters, it could identify low-cost firms and compel to them to cut emissions further than high-cost firms. However, the information requirements to do this properly are very large, since the government needs to know individual firms' *MAC* schedules. Getting the information from firms is not easy, since they have an incentive to respond strategically and to misrepresent the costs of cutting carbon emissions in order to gain a permit to produce more emissions.

Instead, taxes do away with the need for the government to possess information about individual firm abatement costs in order to achieve cost-effective pollution reduction, since high-cost firms will respond automatically to a uniform tax rate by cutting emissions by a lesser amount than low-cost firms. This is illustrated in Figure 8.3, which shows the marginal abatement cost schedules for two firms – a low-cost firm and a high-cost firm. With no government intervention, both firms produce ten units of carbon emissions. Suppose the government wants to reduce the level of emissions by half – in other words to reduce total industry emissions from 20 units to 10 units. It could do this by giving each of the firms a permit to produce five units, but this would not be the most cost-effective route. The cost to the low-cost firm of cutting emissions from five units to four is less than the cost to the high-cost firm of cutting emission from six units to five. If the low-cost firm produced four units of carbon and the high-cost firm produced six units, this would be cheaper overall than if both produced five. Generally, it makes sense for the low-cost firm to cut its emissions by more than the high-cost firm. If the government sets a common tax rate *T*, firms will respond to the tax by moving along the marginal abatement cost curve to the point where the marginal cost of abatement is equal to the tax rate. In this case, the low-cost firm will reduce emissions to two units, since above this level it would prefer to reduce emissions rather than pay the tax. The high-cost firm, on the other hand, will only reduce its emissions to eight units since, below this level, it would rather pay the tax than cut emissions further. The tax automatically achieves a more cost-effective mix of pollution reduction

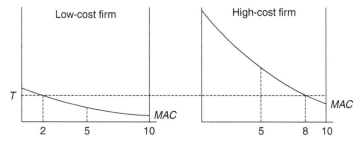

Figure 8.3 The effect of taxes on emissions.

across firms, without the government needing information on the cost structure of individual firms.

In principle, as already discussed, the same cost-effective outcome could be achieved via regulation as through taxation. However, the effect on the relative costs faced by each firm would be quite different. Under a system of regulation, the low-cost firm could end up paying more than the high-cost firm – an outcome that might be seen as quite unfair. To see this, consider that the total costs of abatement paid by each firm are represented by the area under the MAC curve between the actual level of carbon emissions and the maximum level (ten). If the low-cost firm is forced by regulation to cut emissions to two units, while the high-cost firm is allowed to produce eight, the total cost of abatement is higher for the low-cost firm.

Under a system of taxation, however, each firm is required to pay tax on each unit of emission that it produces. The tax liability for each firm is represented by the area under the tax line T between zero and the actual level of emissions. The total cost faced by each firm includes the cost of reducing emissions and the cost of paying tax on the remaining emissions. In this case, the total cost faced by the high-tax firm is greater.

This leads on to another advantage of taxes compared to regulation, which is that they offer a continuing incentive for polluters to cut their pollution. Under regulation, once polluters have cut emissions to the permitted level, they have no incentive to make any further reductions, and indeed may be concerned that if they do cut the costs of abatement, their regulated level of emissions will be lowered further. Under a taxation scheme, however, each unit of emission carries a price tag – an inducement to attempt to cut the costs of treatment.

Another important difference between regulation and taxation is that imposing taxes yields revenue for the government. Historically, the amount of money raised through environmental taxes has been relatively small. However, they are likely to become increasingly important in the future, and may be seen as an attractive way to raise revenue, given current environmental concerns. Some countries, such as Sweden, have used revenue from green taxes to cut taxes on labour. Some see this as the substitution of 'good taxes' (ones that address an externality) for 'bad taxes' (ones that create a distortion). However, it is important to bear in mind that green taxes are not costless, and that in many cases the cost falls disproportionately on low-income houses. Also, if green taxes are genuinely intended to reduce emissions, they may not be a reliable source of revenue in the long term.

Emissions trading

There is another alternative to direct regulation and taxation, and that is emissions trading. As with regulation, this involves the government setting a limit or cap on the total amount of emissions by issuing a fixed number of permits. However, rather than being allocated to firms by the government, these permits are auctioned off through a market in which firms bid for the right to pollute. In principle, firms that face relatively high costs of reducing emissions will be prepared to pay a higher price for permits, and they will pay for the right to pollute more. As with taxes, therefore, this ensures that relatively more emissions reduction is carried out by low-cost firms, achieving a given level of emissions reduction at a lower cost. The end effect is the same, but with one important difference: the price is set by the firms themselves by bidding against one another. Emissions trading is sometimes referred to as 'free market environmentalism', because it involves a market solution to environmental problems.

There are a number of active trading schemes, of which the largest is the European Union Emission Trading Scheme, created in 2005 in conjunction with the Kyoto Protocol. The programme caps the total amount of carbon dioxide that can be emitted from large installations, such as power plants and carbon-intensive factories, and covers almost half of the EU's carbon dioxide emissions.

In practice, the initial allocation of permits to firms under this scheme was determined by a 'grandfathering' provision – in other words firms received an allocation in proportion to their historical emissions (rather than by an auction process). Firms could then decide whether to continue to pollute at this level or to reduce emissions below their allocated level and sell their remaining permits to another firm. Grandfathering is politically attractive, since it reduces the initial cost on industry – which may prevent some firms from going out of business. Compared to an auction, however, governments lose potential revenue by allocating permits by grandfathering. It also has the rather perverse effect of awarding bigger allowances to firms that have historically been the greatest polluters. Grandfathering may help with the initial implementation of the scheme, but it has also been argued that the initial allocations under the EU trading scheme were too generous, evidenced by the fact that the trading price fell to a very low level. In the second phase of the scheme, beginning in 2007, the EU has been much tougher with allocations.

Other criticisms of emissions trading point to the costs associated with the actual trading process, which are likely to be far greater than the costs of administering a tax. There is also a danger that market prices may be unstable and therefore unpredictable, which would damage long-term planning in the industry.

SUMMARY

- In principle, there is an efficient level of climate change mitigation that involves balancing the costs of reducing carbon emissions against the benefits of reducing global warming. This is far from easy to do in practice, and raises a number of hugely complex issues.

- First, there is huge uncertainty about the impact of climate change. Should we plan for the very worst-case scenario, or only for the most likely outcome?

- Second, the problem and solution are both global in nature. This may require making judgements about how to weigh costs and benefits across people living in different countries.

- Third, the benefits of reducing global warming will be felt mainly by people living in several hundred years' time. How should we weight their interests against those of people living today?

■ All these issues involve more than just academic debate. They are fundamental to answering the question of how much we should be spending on reducing carbon emissions today. This matters because any money spent on reducing carbon emission could be spent on other things, such as tacking AIDS or reducing poverty.

■ There are broadly three approaches to tackling carbon emissions – regulation, taxes and tradable permits. The main advantage of taxes and tradable permits is that they should reduce emissions in a more cost-effective manner, compared to regulation. Governments are increasingly moving towards these market-based solutions.

FURTHER READING

Cropper and Oates (1992) provides a comprehensive introduction to environmental economics. Pearce (2003) is a good introduction to the economics of climate change. The final report of the *Stern Review* itself is accessible and contains a wealth of detailed theoretical and empirical material. It is available at http://www.hm-treasury.gov.uk/Independent_Reviews/stern_review_economics_climate_change/sternreview_index.cfm. There are numerous articles that discuss the Stern report, including Nordhaus (2007, 2008) and Dasgupta (2006)

Up-to-date information on environmental taxation can be found in Fullerton *et al.* (2007). Ekins and Barker (2001) and the Royal Society (2002) also contain discussions of economic instruments for tackling carbon emissions, including carbon trading.

The Copenhagen Consensus is interesting because it discusses climate change alongside other global problems that might be tacked, including AIDS and poverty. See Lomberg (2007) or http://www.copenhagenconsensus.com

QUESTIONS FOR DISCUSSION

1. Should the optimum level of pollution be zero?

2. It has been argued that 'no estimate is better than some estimate'. Do you agree, with regard to the social cost of carbon?

3. Do you agree that 'The *Stern Review* should be read as a document that is primarily political in nature'?

4. 'Positive discounting leads to the tyranny of current generations, while zero discounting leads to the tyranny of future generations.' Which is worse?

5. Does the Coase theorem have anything useful to say about climate change?

6. Is it meaningful to say that the polluter should pay?

7. Should China and India be exempt from international agreements to cut greenhouse gases?

8. Tradable permits combine the best of both worlds – the desired level of pollution at the least cost. Do you agree?

CHAPTER 9

Poverty and Welfare

In March 1999, the then British prime minister, Tony Blair, announced a commitment to end child poverty within twenty years (later revised to halving child poverty within ten years). By setting an explicit target for reducing poverty, this commitment opened a debate about how to define poverty, with some commentators wondering if child poverty had something to do with the slums and rags of Dickensian times. This chapter discusses possible ways of measuring poverty, and some of the issues this raises. It also explores the related concepts of inequality and social justice.

The chapter also discusses alternative forms of government intervention to redistribute resources. The traditional welfare state was heavily criticised in the 1980s and 1990s. It was accused of creating a culture of dependency and of being rife with abuse and fraud, and seen by some as being part of the problem, rather than the solution, since it was said to undermine incentives to work and save. A number of policies have since been introduced that are intended to overcome these disincentive problems, including asset-based welfare, the National Minimum Wage, and in-work benefits, such as the UK Working Families Tax Credit.

Measurement issues

Measuring income and wealth

Before considering how to define and measure poverty, it is important to spend some time thinking about the basic units of measurement – income and wealth. While both terms are part of everyday language, in economics they have precise meanings. Barr (2004b) defines income as the 'flow deriving from a stock of wealth'. Therefore the natural starting point is to consider wealth. In everyday language, wealth typically refers to *financial wealth* (money in a savings account, stocks and shares and so on), and sometimes to *physical assets* (land, houses, valuable paintings, and consumer durables such as cars and television sets). More broadly, individuals' wealth also encompasses their *human capital*, which is their set of marketable skills, generally arising as a result of a mixture of innate talent – David Beckham's football skills, for example – and investment in education and training. (There is a discussion of the acquisition of human capital in Chapter 3.)

Each of these three types of wealth yields a flow of income. Stocks of financial wealth yield a flow of money in the form of interest on money in a bank account and dividends paid on shares. Physical assets can give rise to a flow of money (in the case of machinery used to produce chocolate bars which are then sold, for example), but the 'income' can also be in the form of a flow of services from durable goods such as housing, cars and televisions. Human capital also yields income in the form of individuals' earnings. But it can also give rise to non-money 'income', such as when individuals devote their time to leisure or to home production (including child care). This is important to recognise, since individuals may often make choices about how to spend their time that make them poorer in pure monetary terms, but may make them better off in terms of enjoyment of increased leisure time.

In principle, we would like to measure all three forms of wealth and their associated income flows. Barr (2004b) defines individuals' full money income as their money income together with their non-money income (including job satisfaction, enjoyment of leisure and the value of the flows of services from durable goods). Since individuals' money income reflects not only their underlying wealth, but also what they choose to do with their wealth, the idea of full income better captures their opportunity set. In practice, of course, this is extremely difficult. How should we value time spent looking after children, or the flow of services from owning a car? For these reasons, only money income is generally used as a measure of an individual's income. But, it is important to recognise that this is only a partial measure.

Typically, measures of poverty or inequality take into account not just the individual's income, but also the income of the household within which the individual lives. This makes sense. Clearly, someone with an individual income of £10,000 is likely to enjoy a different standard of living if living alone compared to living with a partner who has an income of £100,000. However, assigning household income to both members makes an assumption that they share their resources equally, something that most studies tend to reject. In practice, a couple earning very different amounts may not share their resources 50:50, but may enjoy different living standards within the same household.

Also, if using household income as the basis for determining the standard of living of household members, there needs to be some adjustment for household composition. Take two households, each with a household-level income of £20,000, but one has a single resident and the other a couple with two children. The members of these two households will have different standards of living and we would expect those in the second household to be worse off financially.

One possibility is simply to divide household income by the number of household members – in which case the income of the person in the first household would be £20,000, while each person in the second household would be assigned an income of £5,000. However, while it may not be quite true that 'two can live as cheaply as one', it is probably the case that two do not need twice as much income as one to reach the same standard of living. There will be some economies of scale in households with more than one person; spending on some items such as accommodation and electricity, for example, will not be twice as high for a household with two members as for a single person.

Typically, rather than deriving simple per capita figures, household incomes are adjusted to take into account household size and age composition (adults and children) by means of *equivalence scales*. Each household is assigned an equivalence scale based on its composition. The idea is that dividing household income by its equivalence scale (rather than the number of people in the household) will produce an adjusted (equivalent) income that would yield the same level of benefit as the same unadjusted household income for a single person. Under the commonly-used OECD-modified equivalence scale, for example, the household head is assigned a value of 1, additional household members are assigned a value of 0.5, and each child a value of 0.3. Under this scale, a two-adult household with an income of £30,000 is assumed to be as well off as a one-adult household with an income of £20,000, and as a two-adult, two-child household with an income of £42,000. Underlying equivalence scales are technical assumptions about economies of scale in consumption (which in turn can be assessed empirically using data on spending patterns across households). However, they can also reflect *value judgements* about the priority assigned to the needs of different individuals such as children or the elderly. Clearly, the choice of equivalence scales can make a big difference to the numbers of people in poverty, and the types of households. Increasing the value for each child in an equivalence scale, for example, will reduce the level of equivalised income for households with children, and cause more of these households to fall into measured poverty.

Measuring poverty

Very few countries have formally adopted official measures of poverty. Only the UK and the USA have official poverty statistics. The Canadian government regularly publishes information on the numbers of households falling below varying income thresholds, while the Australian government does the same thing on an irregular basis. In much of Northern Europe and Scandinavia, however, the debate instead focuses on setting the appropriate level for minimum government benefits, and the issue of social exclusion.

In the UK and the USA, the approach to measuring poverty is to define a poverty line, and label anyone falling below this line as being 'poor'. The extent of poverty can then be measured by counting the number of people who fall below the line. On the face of it, this approach appears to be simple and straightforward, but in fact it is quite the reverse. The key issue is defining what 'poor' means, which in turn involves a number of value judgements.

Poverty may be defined in relative or absolute terms. A *relative definition* defines the threshold for poverty in relation to the general standards of living that prevail in society – usually a constant percentage of average income. By contrast, an *absolute definition* tries to define the standard of living necessary for bare subsistence. This is the approach taken in the USA, where the official poverty index is defined as the income required to buy 'a subsistence level of goods and services'. This level has been held constant in real terms since it was introduced the 1960s. As incomes have grown in real terms, the poverty threshold has fallen relative to average incomes – from 48 per cent of median family income in 1960 to 29 per cent in 2000 (see Smeeding 2006).

However, absolute definitions are not completely independent of social norms. As far back as 1776, Adam Smith argued that

> by necessaries I mean not only the commodities which are indispensably necessary for the support of life, but whatever the custom of the country renders it indecent for creditable people, even of the lowest order to be without . . . in the present time, a creditable day labourer would be ashamed to appear in public without a linen shirt.

What is defined as the subsistence level in the USA is certainly well above what would be needed to survive in Sub-Saharan Africa, for example. The World Bank and the United Nations Millennium Development movement define poverty in Africa and Latin America using an income threshold of US$1 or US$2 per person a day. The US standard is several times this level.

Absolute standards are criticised on the grounds that it is unacceptable for people simply to be able to afford to survive while everyone else in society can afford to live very comfortable lives. In the 1960s, Herman Miller, at the US Bureau of the Census, declared that 'we will, in time, eliminate poverty statistically, but few people will believe it, certainly not those who continue to have housing, education, medical care and other goods and services which are far below standards deemed acceptable for this society'. But how far should relative poverty go? In a recent survey, almost half of the children surveyed in Britain thought that a child is poor if they do not have a mobile phone. How would this sound to someone in Sub-Saharan Africa, who is barely able to afford enough food to survive?

In the UK, the official definition of poverty is household income below 60 per cent of the median. This is a relative measure, since poverty is defined relative to standards of living in society at the time. The median household income is a measure of average income that takes the income of the household in the middle of the income distribution. In 2006, the median income was £363 a week, compared to a mean (or mathematical average) income of £445. The mean is higher than the median because it is affected by a relatively small number of very high incomes at the top of the income distribution. According to this measure, there were 12.7 million individuals living in poverty in 2006, or 20 per cent of the population. This is below its peak of 25 per cent in 1997 (see Brewer *et al.*, 2007).

Using a within-country threshold of 50 per cent of median income, Smeeding (2006) compares poverty across a number of countries. With a poverty rate of 12.4 per cent, the UK is ahead of the USA (at 17.0 per cent), Ireland (16.5 per cent) and Italy (12.7 per cent). But, it is behind Canada (11.4 per cent), Germany (8.3 per cent), the Netherlands (7.3 per cent), Sweden (6.5 per cent) and Finland (5.4 per cent). Applying the same US absolute poverty standard across these countries, the UK emerges as having the highest proportion in poverty (12.4 per cent) with the USA second (8.7 per cent). The difference in the proportion in poverty under the two measures is driven by differences in incomes between the countries. In the UK, fewer people than in the USA are poor when compared to average income within the country. But more people are poor in the UK than in the USA when defined by the same absolute poverty measure, because incomes are higher in the USA. The fact that Finland performs well under both measures reflects the fact that incomes are relatively equally distributed, and that it is a rich country.

These kinds of headcount measures are useful for giving an overview of the numbers of people who are in poverty, and making comparisons over time. But they have their limitations. For example, they say nothing about the 'depth' of poverty – in other words how far people are below the poverty line. It only takes £1 for someone to move from being poor to being not poor. Are the people who are poor a long way below the poverty line, or are they just below it? There is a danger that measured poverty can be relatively easily reduced by increasing the incomes of people just below the line, without doing anything to help those who are a long way below.

Both the USA and UK assess poverty in terms of current household income. This is relatively straightforward to understand, and the data are easily available. However, income is by no means a perfect indicator of poverty. As we have already seen, money income partly reflects individuals' choices about how to allocate their total wealth between employment and leisure. Also, individuals' money incomes may vary over their lifetimes. There are some groups with low money incomes, whom we probably do not think of as being poor – students, for example, who are likely to enjoy high earnings later in life. Incomes may also fluctuate from one period to another because of short periods out of employment, or because of variable self-employment income. Ideally, we might like a measure of lifetime income rather than a snapshot at a single point in time. In some cases, spending may be a better indicator of living standards, since people will often smooth their spending through periods of temporary income fluctuations.

More fundamentally, there is a concern that single measures of current income or spending may fail to capture the more complex nature of poverty. It has been argued that poverty is not just about money, and that focusing solely on income (or current household spending) may miss important aspects of what it means to be poor. As an alternative, deprivation indices combine a number of indicators of poverty or, more specifically, relative deprivation. These indices are intended to capture the multi-dimensional nature of poverty by defining a set of things that are considered to the basic norm in current society. Relative deprivation is defined as not having access to these things as a result of a lack of financial resources (known as enforced deprivation). Much of the work on deprivation indices follows the ideas of Townsend (1979). His initial index, developed in the UK in the 1960s, focused on items such as food, refrigerators, indoor baths and holidays. Clearly, whether or not someone is deprived on each of these indicators is likely to be linked to their income (and much of Townsend's initial work focused on the relationship between income and relative deprivation). But, people may face temporary fluctuations in income and not be deprived by these indicators because they can draw on other financial resources. Others with low incomes may have these needs met through more complex systems of support involving family and the local community.

Deprivation indices are absolute in the sense that the same indicators apply from year to year, but relative in that the initial choice of indicators is likely to reflect expectations prevailing within current society (and the set of indicators is likely to be updated from time to time). The UK government is currently integrating deprivation indicators into its measure of child poverty, and has introduced a new set of questions into the main government survey for measuring poverty that cover the following indicators: being able to afford to keep a home warm and in repair; replace or repair electrical goods and worn-out furniture; have two pairs of shoes; a holiday away from home; a hobby or leisure activity and entertain friends or family for a drink or a meal; and have money to spend on self, regular savings and home insurance.

McKay (2004) notes two possible concerns with deprivation indices. One is that it may not be easy to reach common agreement on what indicators should be included in the index. The other is that different demographic groups vary in the extent to which they define themselves as not meeting an indicator by choice rather than because they cannot afford it. To address these concerns, measures of poverty based on deprivation indices are often combined with standard income measures.

There is also considerable interest in measures of neighbourhood poverty or deprivation. This reflects the fact that poverty is typically concentrated into a relatively small number of geographical areas, and that these concentrations can have important neighbourhood effects for the people who live in deprived areas (see Chapter 5 on housing for further discussion on this point). This has given rise to multiple indices of deprivation that apply to a geographical area, encompassing income, employment, health and disability, education, skills and training, barriers to housing services, living environment and crime.

Loosely related to the idea of relative deprivation, an alternative conception of poverty has been proposed by the Nobel-prize-winning economist, Amartya Sen, through his idea of capabilities. He has argued that a person's quality of life is determined by his/her *capability* to achieve certain valuable 'beings' and 'doings'. These encompass very basic functions (being well-nourished, adequately clothed, sheltered and warm). It also includes a level of health and education necessary for an individual to achieve his/her capabilities, as well as political freedom, social interaction and emotional state, such as being able to appear in public without shame. The concept of poverty is then defined in terms of being deprived of these capabilities. This clearly goes much further than the relative deprivation indices. Not only does it encompass more than just meeting material needs; it also embraces a positive approach to freedom in that the individual must be *free to* achieve certain things as well as being *free from* constraints. Sen did not set out an explicit list of capabilities, though such capabilities have been proposed by other authors (see Nussbaum, 1999). The idea of capabilities also underlies the United Nations' Human Development Index, although this includes a relatively limited set of indicators covering income, health and education.

Measuring inequality

Inequality is a concept distinct from poverty. Poverty is concerned with defining a standard of living below which individuals are said to be poor, while inequality is concerned with describing how resources are distributed among individuals within society – and how many resources one group have compared to another. If poverty is defined in absolute terms, it is possible for there to be complete equality, and for everyone to be poor (and equally, for there to be complete inequality and for nobody to be poor). In the case of relative poverty, since the definition of poverty is related to the general standards of living that prevail in the society, then inequality and poverty are much more likely to be linked in practice. In an unequal society, it is more likely that there will be a group of people falling below the acceptable poverty threshold.

One way to measure the degree of inequality in a country is by looking at how concentrated total resources are in the hands of a relatively few people. In practice, this can be done by calculating the proportion of total resources that fall into the hands of the top 1 per cent, the top 5 per cent and so on. This is shown for wealth in the UK in Table 9.1.

The data in Table 9.1 can tell us a lot about the distribution of wealth in the UK. First, that it is distributed unequally. The wealthiest 1 per cent of the population

Table 9.1   Distribution of total wealth, UK

Year	Share of total wealth held by . . .		
	Top 1% (%)	Top 10% (%)	Top 50% (%)
1911	70		
1926	60		
1936	55		
1954	43	80	
1966	33	69	97
1976	21	50	92
1986	18	50	90
1996	20	52	93
2004	21	53	93

Note: Total wealth includes financial assets and housing.
Source: HM Revenue and Customs, Distribution of Personal Wealth, various years, http://www.hmrc.gov.uk/stats/personal_wealth/menu.htm

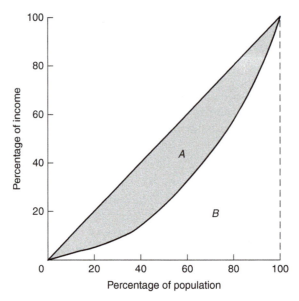

Figure 9.1 Lorenz curve of income distribution (UK).
Source: Atkinson (1989).

hold a disproportionately large share of the total wealth. Even today, the least wealthy half of the population hold no more than 10 per cent of the total wealth between them. And the results are more skewed if housing wealth is excluded from the estimates, since this form of wealth is more evenly distributed. Second, the degree of inequality is relatively low today by historical standards. Contrast 2004, when the wealthiest 1 per cent of the population held 21 per cent of all wealth, with 1911, when the wealthiest 1 per cent held 70 per cent of total wealth. Comparing 1986 and 2004, however, shows that wealth inequality gradually increased over this period.

Another way of showing the degree of inequality is to draw a Lorenz curve for the entire distribution. This is illustrated in Figure 9.1, which plots the percentages of national income received by different percentages of the population when the latter are cumulated from the bottom. That is, it plots the percentage of income received by the lowest 20 per cent, the percentage received by the lowest 40 per cent, the lowest 60 per cent and so on. If there were full equality – such that the lowest 60 per cent of the population received 60 per cent of the national income, or the lowest 80 per cent received 80 per cent – then the Lorenz curve would lie along the diagonal of the diagram. Hence, the further the curve is away from the diagonal, the further is the distribution from full equality, and so the greater the inequality. We can therefore obtain an indicator of the extent of inequality in a distribution by observing the position of the Lorenz curve.

A summary measure of the amount of inequality implicit in a Lorenz curve can be obtained by use of the *Gini coefficient*. This is calculated by dividing the area between the Lorenz curve and the diagonal by the area of the triangle formed by the diagonal and the axes. In Figure 9.1, it is the area A divided by A plus B (the non-shaded area). As the Lorenz curve moves further from the diagonal, area A becomes larger relative to $A + B$, and the Gini coefficient approaches one, indicating greater inequality; as the Lorenz curve moves closer to the diagonal, A becomes smaller relative to $A + B$, and the Gini coefficient approaches zero, indicating greater equality.

The Gini coefficient is useful because it facilitates comparisons. We can compare the Gini coefficient for the distribution of wealth in 2004, which was 0.67, with the income Gini, in which was 0.35. This shows that wealth is less equally distributed than income. We can also make comparisons over time. The income Gini increased from 0.33 in 1997 to 0.35 in 2006; thus income inequality increased in the UK at the same time that the headcount measure of poverty fell.

Statistics such as the Gini coefficient therefore provide useful summary statistics. But it is just that – a summary statistic. It attempts to summarise a vast amount of information concerning differences in peoples' incomes by compressing that information into a single number. In the process of this compression, inevitably, some pieces of information are emphasised while others are ignored. While the Gini coefficient tries to condense information on the whole distribution, we may be particularly concerned with the degree of concentration in the hands of a few, or with access to resources among the least advantaged group, say the lowest 20 per cent. These concerns depend on one's values; and there is no objective method of measuring the extent of inequality.

Measuring income mobility

Poverty and inequality measures both give a 'snapshot' of individuals' living standards at a particular point in time. However, we may feel that this is not quite the end of the story. For example, as we have already seen, some people are likely to move into and out of poverty over the course of their lives, and even from year-to-year. Also, we may feel very differently about an unequal distribution of resources if there is a lot of movement within the overall distribution, and if everyone has an equal chance of making it to the top.

This suggests that we may also be interested in measuring the dynamics of incomes over time and, in particular, measuring income mobility. This can be done at the level of individual income mobility – comparing individuals' positions in the income distribution from one year to the next. Or it can be done at the level of intergenerational income mobility from one generation to the next – comparing the extent to which there is a correlation between the parents' position in the income distribution and that of their children. These measures of income mobility are central to the concept of social justice, discussed further below.

The data requirements to produce measures of income mobility are much greater than those for snapshot measures of poverty and inequality. Measures of individual income mobility require data that follow the same individuals over time, and collect income information each year. Intergenerational mobility measures require information on both parents and their children. Typically, empirical analyses of intergenerational mobility have used cohort studies – that

Table 9.2   Intergenerational income mobility

Father's quartile	Son's quartile			
	Bottom	2nd	3rd	Top
(a) Complete immobility				
Bottom	1	0	0	0
2nd	0	1	0	0
3rd	0	0	1	0
Top	0	0	0	1
(b) Complete mobility				
Bottom	0.25	0.25	0.25	0.25
2nd	0.25	0.25	0.25	0.25
3rd	0.25	0.25	0.25	0.25
Top	0.25	0.25	0.25	0.25
(c) From the NCDS				
Bottom	0.34	0.30	0.24	0.13
2nd	0.29	0.31	0.25	0.14
3rd	0.30	0.24	0.24	0.21
Top	0.06	0.14	0.27	0.52

Source: Data on the NCDS from Dearden *et al.* (1997), summarised in Johnson and Reed (1996).

is, surveys which follow a particular birth cohort of children into adulthood, collecting information on their parents around the time of birth.

One of the most straightforward ways to present information on income mobility is via a transition matrix. This is shown for intergenerational mobility in Table 9.2 (exactly the same steps would be followed for individual income mobility). First, the income distributions for both children and parents are divided into *N* equally-sized groups – in this case, four groups or quartiles. The transition matrix then relates the position in the income distribution of the father to the position of the income distribution of the child. Across the top is the income quartile to which the son belongs, and down the side is the income quartile to which the father belonged. Since the quartiles are equal-sized, both rows and columns add to one. Reading across a row shows the position that the sons of fathers belonging to a particular quartile reached, while reading down a column shows where the sons in a particular quartile came from. Panel (a) illustrates the case of complete immobility. In this case, all the sons of fathers who were in the lowest income quartile finish in the lowest quartile. Panel (b) illustrates the opposite extreme of complete mobility. In this case, sons of fathers who were in the lowest quartile finish equally distributed across the four quartiles. Panel (c) presents evidence on income mobility for children in the UK National Child Development Survey (NCDS) – a cohort study of all children born during one week in March 1958. For the children, the income information was collected in 1991, when they were 33 years old.

From these figures it is clear that there is some degree of mobility. Of sons born to fathers in the lowest income quartile, only a third were themselves in the lowest quartile. But, at the top of the income distribution, more than half of sons born to fathers in the top quartile were also in the top quartile. This implies a degree of asymmetry in mobility – it appears to be easier to get out of the bottom than it is to move down from the top. Clearly, as with inequality measures, income mobility measures are likely to be overlaid with value judgements about whether different types of mobility are more or less desirable. Another judgement concerns the number of groups into which to divide the population. Using broad groups, such as quartiles, may conceal important information about movement within groups. Using narrower groups (such as deciles) is likely to generate much more movement, although some of this may be more apparent than real, as it involves small changes in income, and even in measurement of that income.

It is possible – and sometimes desirable – to have a single summary measure of income mobility. This facilitates comparisons over time and between countries. The information in the transition matrix can be summarised in a single measure of the overall proportion of people who remain the same quartile (in panel (a) this is 1.0; in panel (b) it is 0.25; and in panel (c) it is 0.35). An alternative, with a continuous variable such as income, is to calculate the correlation coefficient between parents' and children's incomes. However, as with income inequality, summary measures condense a large amount of information into a single statistic.

Objectives

In other chapters, we have discussed the government's objectives in relation to efficiency and equity. Efficiency is not irrelevant – historically, poor relief was motivated largely by a desire for a healthy labour force (positive externality), and by fear of social unrest (negative externality). Also, as we shall discuss in the next section, there are likely to be market failures that prevent the private market for unemployment insurance from working efficiently. These would motivate government intervention even in the absence of equity concerns. However, much of the government's involvement in the area of poverty and welfare is likely to be to promote a fair or equitable distribution – although there may well be disagreement about exactly what is a fair outcome.

Minimum standards

For some, the interests of equity might be served simply by ensuring that there is a basic minimum standard of income below which no one is allowed to fall. This view essentially underpinned the initial post-war welfare state in the UK, designed by Beveridge. Its purpose was to provide a minimum level of social insurance for when people were unemployed, disabled, retired or widowed. Reflecting the fact that the minimum level may depend on individuals' needs, it also offered additional support for families with children. However, this minimum standards approach is fairly limited in its ambitions, since it offers mainly temporary income relief. This may have been appropriate in the immediate post-war period, when relatively well-paid employment was available for most people (or at least for men) who wanted it, but it may not be enough to address the underlying causes of the poverty of the twenty-first century, which include limited opportunities for the low-skilled, and the breakdown of families. The concept of social justice, which we discuss below, is much broader in its scope. Also, providing a minimum standard may not be the only thing that matters. The minimum standards approach implies that the wealth of the rich, or the more general pattern of inequality, are of no concern. We have seen that it is very difficult to say what we mean by minimum standards without some reference to the standards of living prevailing in the rest of society. Moreover, there may be valid reasons for worrying about the overall degree of inequality, as well as about the standards of living of those at the bottom.

Social justice

Very broadly, social justice embodies the concept of equality of opportunity. As discussed in Le Grand (1999), it can easily be illustrated by a clear example of when there is a social injustice. Suppose there are two people with different incomes. We learn that they are equally able, but that one grew up in a deprived area and went to a sink school, leaving with no qualifications and therefore only able to find low-paid employment; while the other grew up in an affluent area, went to a grammar school, and on to a well-paid career.

This outcome would be considered by most people to be unjust. And in understanding the reasons why people think it is unjust, we can understand what social justice means. First, the judgement about whether or not a particular outcome is 'fair' is heavily influenced by how people came to be in the circumstances in which they find themselves. If people are in poorly-paid jobs because they were lazy at school, the conclusion about whether this is a fair outcome is likely to be quite different. The key is that people are poor because of factors that are beyond their control. The minimum standards approach completely ignores the processes that generate individual cases of poverty. Second, the barriers to equal outcomes involved social – as opposed to genetic – factors. If the two people had different outcomes because of differing levels of ability (for example, one was David Beckham), then fewer people would be prepared to argue that this is unfair (although they may wish that they could bend a ball like Beckham). Social justice goes beyond the provision of minimum standards, and demands that all individuals have the chance to progress in society.

Assessing government progress towards delivering on social justice is therefore likely to involve measures of income mobility, rather than just poverty. This is not straightforward in practice. An assessment of long-term income mobility, such as between generations, will inevitably take several decades. Also, even if we can measure income mobility accurately, it is important to distinguish between natural and social barriers to mobility. Human capital includes naturally-occurring talents, some of which are likely to be passed down from parents to children. The children of more able parents may secure better-paid jobs in part because they have inherited their parents' ability, not just because their parents' relatively high incomes secured them a better education in a leafy suburb.

Equality

Social justice demands equality of opportunity, but not equality of outcomes. Many people who argue for social justice believe that unequal outcomes are fair so long as the process that generates such outcomes is fair. For others, however, an equitable outcome demands equality – in other words, that every member of society should have the same income – or at least that outcomes are not very unequally distributed.

If all individuals were identical in tastes and preferences, then full equality could be justified on utilitarian grounds. A utilitarian goal for society is that the sum of individuals' happiness or utilities should be as large as possible. Suppose that, as utilitarianism requires, we can compare peoples' levels of happiness or utility. Suppose further that diminishing marginal benefit of income (discussed in Chapter 4) implies that an extra £1's worth of income offers less utility to the rich than to the poor. Then taking money away from the rich and giving it to the poor will raise the sum of utilities, and as we continue to redistribute income from the rich to the poor, total utility in society will rise. It will be at its highest when all individuals have the same income.

However, this policy prescription can be challenged on several grounds. First, there are obvious difficulties in comparing people's levels of happiness or utility. Second, even if this can be done, it is not always obvious that an extra £1's worth of income is worth less to the rich than to the poor: as people's incomes rise they may develop more expensive tastes. More generally, we cannot assume that people have identical preferences and tastes. Third, taxing the rich and giving money to the poor may make both rich and poor work less hard, thus reducing total production and so total income, and hence the total amount of utility that can be achieved.

If total equality is an unreasonable goal, should we worry about equality of outcomes at all? One reason might be that equality of opportunity is impossible in a society in which there is great inequality of outcomes. This may be because those who are better off can use their financial resources to ensure that their children do well. They may also have the political power to manipulate the process to their advantage. If the government cannot achieve equality of opportunity by policies to promote education or employment, it may need to address the equality of outcomes directly. It has also been argued that there are ethical and practical reasons for caring directly about equality of outcomes (see Giddens, 1999) – ethical in that we are all part of the same community and should not therefore have living standards that are too diverse, and practical in that the consequences of a high level of equality are likely to be low levels of trust and high levels of crime.

The market system and poverty

It is extremely unlikely that a market system will produce a distribution of resources that is fair, defined against any of these objectives. At the very least, there are likely to be some people whose income does not meet a basic minimum standard, including those whose health prevents them from working. In principle, private markets can – and do – provide insurance against ill-health or unemployment. However, there are a number of reasons why markets for this type of insurance are unlikely to operate efficiently, necessitating some form of government intervention. In the past, some right-wing commentators have argued that, because the market operates via impersonal forces, rather than intentional actions, the resulting distribution of resources is neither just nor unjust – it just *is*. However, further examination of the mechanisms through which the market outcome is reached reveals some potential problems with the operation of the market, and some examples in which the market itself may be judged to work unfairly. Both of these are discussed below.

Insurance failure

Private insurance against disability, unemployment and old age was widespread prior to the 1930s in most European countries and in North America. Since the 1930s, provision for these events has come to be viewed as one of the primary functions of government. There are several reasons why private markets may fail to provide insurance for all who want to buy it, or may provide too low a level of cover.

Social risks

As was discussed in Chapter 4, there are some types of risk that affect all members of the (potential) insured population simultaneously, and that private insurers cannot insure against. These are known as *social risks*. Inflation is one such risk; a fall in aggregate demand, resulting in an increase in unemployment, is another. The private insurance market cannot pool these risk, because all their insured customers would face the same level of risk. Governments, on the other hand, can raise taxes on other parts of the population, or borrow from future generations.

Adverse selection

The problem of adverse selection has already been discussed in the chapters on education, health and housing. Here, it affects the private market for insurance against, for example, unemployment. Insurance companies find it difficult to distinguish between high-risk individuals who are going to experience many periods out of work, and low-risk individuals who are rarely, if ever, going to be unemployed. The insurers offer insurance at a single price, which is more attractive to the high-risk group, and as a result, the ratio of high to low risks among the insured – and the cost of premiums – will rise. Many people with only a low risk of unemployment or poor health may consider that private insurance offers a poor deal and will fail to take it out as a result.

Moral hazard

The problem of moral hazard arises when the fact that people are insured causes them to reduce their efforts to avoid the insured event (see Chapters 2 and 4 on health care and pensions). For example, if people take out insurance against unemployment, they may be less likely to look for another job when made unemployed. The effect of moral hazard is to increase the amount insurers have to pay out, which in turn increases premiums and makes private insurance less attractive. Note that, while moral hazard may justify government intervention, publicly-provided insurance will suffer from exactly the same problem.

Market mechanisms and the distribution of resources

How is the distribution of resources determined under a market system? Put simply, people derive an income from their stock of wealth by selling it in the market place. This could involve putting land or physical capital to profitable use, but for most people it will mean trading their human capital and deriving income through employment. The market outcome therefore depends on the initial allocation of resources and the price that people can get for their resources. People owning large quantities of 'high price' resources will have high incomes; and people with few resources or with 'low price' resources will have low incomes.

The market outcome will therefore reflect the initial distribution of resources. Some of this will be the distribution of natural talents, but it will also include inherited wealth. Some inherited wealth may reflect the historical distribution of natural talents, but may also include resources appropriated in the past by force or other unfair means. Whether we think that the market works fairly may depend on our view of whether the initial allocation was fair, and/or whether we think it is fair for the outcomes of one generation to be affected by the outcomes of a previous one.

The government will also affect the initial distribution of human capital through its provision of health and education. There may be disagreement about whether the government should provide equal provision to all, or additional help to those who are otherwise disadvantaged. At the very least, however, it seems unfair if the government provides more support to those who are otherwise advantaged (better schools in leafy suburbs, for example).

The market outcome also depends on prices. In principle, people are free to sell their financial and physical assets and human capital to the highest bidder, allowing everyone to get the best price. In general, these prices will reflect the productivity of an asset, as well as supply and demand conditions. Assets that are in limited supply, but for which there is a very high demand, will fetch a particularly high price. Market outcomes should therefore simply reflect the impersonal laws of supply and demand. However, there may be cases where market prices are not set fairly. Here are a few examples:

- Some occupations may limit supply artificially (and increase their price) by imposing restrictive practices. It has been argued, for example, that doctors' training is longer than is strictly necessary.

- Some individuals may enjoy market power and be able to influence the price their services command. Thus, concern about the remuneration of top executives ('fat cat pay') may reflect not just a belief that it is unfair that company chiefs are paid so much more than workers, but also that top directors may be exploiting their positions to serve their own interests.

- At the other extreme, there may be some people who are unable to exercise any power in the market and are likely to be exploited by employers, who can pay them less than their value. This argument applies to low-skilled workers and particularly to women, who may be limited in their employment choices because of child care responsibilities. It acted as an important rationale for the introduction of the National Minimum Wage (see below).

- There may be discrimination on the grounds of gender, age, race or disability.

In all these cases, the market itself may not work fairly, thus justifying some form of government intervention.

Government policies

In practice, governments intervene in a number of ways to try to affect the distribution of resources – through direct provision, through regulation, and through taxes and subsidies. We look at each of these in turn, focusing in particular on how the intervention addresses each of the possible objectives discussed above.

Provision

The government provides insurance directly against a number of circumstances that result in poverty (disability, unemployment and old age). As we have seen, private markets may not work effectively to provide such insurance. Since Beveridge, the UK government has provided a comprehensive system of social insurance.

Benefits paid to the unemployed, the disabled and the retired are known as *categorical benefits*, since all who fall within the relevant category are eligible, regardless of their income. While the circumstances in which people receive such benefits are often correlated with low income, even millionaires are potentially eligible. Thus such benefits contribute to providing minimum standards and reducing inequality, but they are not targeted directly at these problems.

Moreover, categorical benefits typically have eligibility criteria linked to previous employment. Some people who are currently poor will not satisfy the criteria, and will fail to qualify for the benefits. Thus contingent benefits alone are unlikely to achieve a minimum living standard for everyone, nor to reduce inequality completely. It goes without saying that these benefits do very little to promote social justice. They are designed as a form of income replacement. They may prevent some people from falling further behind, but are unlikely to help these people to progress.

This has led some people to propose a more radical form of *asset-based welfare*. Rather than simply providing income replacement, it has been argued that the government should provide people with financial assets. It is worth considering why there may be a case for giving people financial wealth. Financial assets perform a number of roles. First, as we saw in Chapter 4 on pensions, people save in order to finance spending in retirement (and spending in other periods when income is low, such as unemployment). Assets therefore play an important role in consumption-smoothing. The government also does this through its system of social insurance, so asset-based welfare would not do anything different to the existing benefits.

Assets also play another role in allowing people to finance consumption when spending needs are particularly high (repairing a damaged roof, for example). The government plays a much more limited role in providing support to meet unexpected spending needs, and many people on low incomes are unable to borrow money in the formal financial sector, leading many to borrow at extortionate rates from informal sources such as loan sharks. Giving people small amounts of financial assets might help them to avoid this.

Assets also play a third important role in providing the funds for investment in education or training, or in starting a business. Assets may provide people with opportunities that social insurance fails to do, and this thinking lay behind the introduction of the Child Trust Fund, which gives each child in the UK £250 at birth, accessible only when they reach the age of 18. Whether this will prove to be enough to change people's opportunity sets, or whether they will simply spend the money on consumer goods remains to be seen, but the underlying point, that it may take more than social insurance to achieve social justice, is an important one.

Regulation

The government also affects the distribution of outcomes by regulating prices. An obvious example of this is the National Minimum Wage, introduced in the UK in 1999.

Many economists have long been opposed to a minimum wage, arguing that it will result in unemployment among affected workers. If the wage currently reflects workers' productivity, then forcing employers to pay above this level will cause the demand for labour to fall, since it will not be profitable to pay people above the level of their productivity. However, as we have seen, there may be some workers who, with limited employment opportunities, are being paid at less than their productivity level. In this case, it is less clear that setting a minimum wage will affect their employment adversely – and indeed this proved to be the case in the UK (see Dickens *et al.* 1999; Stewart 2004).

Of course, setting a minimum wage will have distributional consequences. If there is little or no unemployment, the cost will be borne by shareholders in the form of lower profits, or consumers in the form of higher prices. It will, of course, benefit workers who would otherwise be paid less than the minimum wage. The introduction of the National Minimum Wage in the UK was estimated to raise the pay of well over one million low-paid workers by about 15 per cent overnight at the point of introduction. Some of these lived in low-income households, but many low-paid workers live in fairly well-off households – for example, women who are the secondary earners and have well-paid partners. A minimum wage is not well-targeted at reducing poverty and inequality, not least because many of those who are very poor are not in employment.

What about social justice? Underlying the introduction of the minimum wage is a strong belief in ensuring that people receive fair pay and, as we have seen, this may reflect the fact that, in a pure market system, some people at the bottom may be paid less than the level of their productivity. Also, increasing wages for people at the bottom will increase the rewards to working, and may encourage some people to enter the labour market. This has arguably become more important in recent years, since, in the increasingly global economy, the wages of low-skilled workers in developed countries have fallen relative to those of skilled workers. Thus the introduction of a minimum wage may indirectly have a positive effect on employment (and hence help people to progress), though there is very little evidence related to this.

Rapid growth in executive pay (compared to average wage growth) has also prompted calls for regulation of pay at the top as well as pay at the bottom. Such wage caps are used in some sports – for example, basketball and American football in the USA, and rugby in the UK – the rationale being that such caps are needed to stop the wealthy clubs from dominating competitions and to keep leagues competitive. In the case of top executives, the response has been to impose regulation on the process by which executive remuneration is determined, rather than on the levels of pay themselves.

Taxes and subsidies

Last, but by no means least, the government affects the distribution of resources through the tax and benefit system. The UK tax system is progressive in that the rich pay a higher proportion of their incomes in tax than do poorer households. Also, alongside the categorical benefits discussed above, there are a number of means-tested benefits targeted specifically at households with low incomes (and low financial wealth), including income support, housing benefit, council tax benefit and pension credit. Since the 1970s there has been a steady increase in the proportion of total benefits that are means-tested relative to categorical benefits.

Since they are targeted at people on low incomes, means-tested benefits are likely to reduce poverty more effectively than are categorical benefits. However, even they are imperfect, because take-up is less than 100 per cent. Around one in five people who are eligible for means-tested benefits do not apply for them. This may be because of a lack of knowledge, because of perceived stigma of claiming a means-tested benefit, because of the complexity of the administrative procedure, or because they do not expect their entitlement to be high – or, most probably, for a mixture of all these reasons.

The tax and benefit system also substantially reduces inequality. This can be shown by comparing the Gini coefficient calculated on the basis of pre-tax and benefit incomes, currently around 0.5, and on the basis of post-tax and benefit incomes, around 0.35.

The benefit system is likely to have far less of a positive effect in terms of promoting social justice. As with categorical benefits, the aim of means-tested benefits is to provide short-term income relief rather than any longer-term solution to the root causes of why some people are – and remain – poor. Indeed, means-tested benefits are seen by some as being part of the problem. It has been argued, particularly in the USA, but also in the UK, that the provision of such benefits creates a 'culture of dependency'. This argument, most closely associated with Murray (1984), states that the provision of benefits may in fact be a cause of poverty. This may work in a number of ways. First, there may be a cultural mechanism: once people start receiving benefits it becomes acceptable for them (and their friends and neighbours) to live off the state rather than to seek work. Second, there is an economic mechanism – the existence of means-tested benefits creates a powerful incentive against entering employment or increasing earnings because, as the benefits are withdrawn, individuals are left little better or no better off. In many developed countries, benefits are withdrawn pound for pound as earnings rise. In addition, individuals may lose access to in-kind benefits such as free dental services or subsidised housing, as well as facing additional costs associated with working, which may include child care provision. These costs are likely to be particularly important for the growing number of lone parents who make up an ever-increasing share of poor households, particularly poor households with children. The state of affairs in which individuals are unable to make themselves better-off as a result of the disincentives in the benefit system is known as *the poverty trap*.

Recognising that there are powerful economic reasons why people on benefits may not seek employment is important for a number of reasons. First, it changes the moral tone of the debate. The term 'culture of dependency' carries connotations of the poor being feckless and lazy scroungers, whereas, in fact, they may simply be acting as rational economic agents. Second, it leads us to look for solutions to the problem in the re-design of the benefits system in order to create economic incentives for people to work.

Recent reforms to the welfare state in the USA and the UK have focused on attempts to 'make work pay' by introducing in-work credits – the Earned Income Tax Credit (EITC) in the USA, and the Working Families Tax Credit (WFTC) in the UK. These are means-tested benefits, but receipt of them is conditional on people working. The way WFTC works is illustrated in Figure 9.2. Individuals are eligible to receive the maximum amount of credit once they satisfy the work criterion. In the UK, this is a minimum of 16 hours a week. Above a threshold level of earnings (denoted by T), however, the amount of credit paid is gradually tapered away with earnings until the individual is no longer eligible for any payment. For WFTC, the taper rate was set at 60 per cent. In other words, for each additional £1 of earnings above the threshold, the individual would lose 60 pence of credit. Eligibility for WFTC was also limited to households with children. This reflects both the additional needs of these households

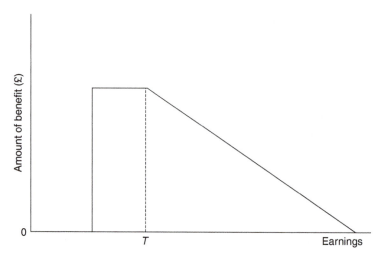

Figure 9.2   Hypothetical schedule of in-work tax credit.

(and hence the fact that they are likely to receive more generous benefits) and particular child care cost barriers to entering employment.

WFTC has had the biggest positive effect on the employment of lone parents. Most studies suggest that WFTC increased employment among this group by around 10 per cent, representing an additional 60,000–85,000 lone parents in work (see Brewer and Browne, 2006). This is not surprising. For lone parents, the employment effects of in-work benefits such as WFTC are unambiguously positive. Lone parents who are not working have an incentive to move into employment in order to become eligible for the benefit. Lone parents who are already working receive a boost to their incomes as a result of the benefit and, as a result, may decide that they can afford to reduce the number of hours they need to work in order to maintain the same level of (post-benefit) income. If their earnings place them on the taper, the high effective marginal tax rate of 60 per cent may also discourage them from working an extra hour. Both these effects may cause them to reduce their hours of employment, but they will not leave employment completely, because then they will lose eligibility.

Compare this with women in couples who are secondary earners. If their partner is working, they benefit from a higher income as a result of the reform without having to work. The increase in income may make them less likely to enter employment if they are currently not working. If they are in work, the effect of both the higher level of post-reform income and the higher effective marginal tax rate could cause them to reduce their hours and possibly to withdraw from the labour market altogether. Most studies that have analysed the effects of the reforms on women in couples found either no effect, or a small negative effect, on employment. Thus, while in-work benefits were designed to make employment more attractive, the fact that eligibility was conditional on the employment of just one household member may have inadvertently reduced employment among second earners. This highlights just how difficult it is to provide financial assistance to low income households at the same time as promoting employment.

SUMMARY

- Poverty, inequality and income mobility are different ways of trying to sum-marise elements of the distribution of resources in society that may matter to policy-makers. In order to derive summary measures, a number of assumptions must be made about the unit of measurement, the time period and so on.

- Governments are often motivated to intervene to affect the distribution of resources by equity concerns. But, to different people, this may mean ensuring minimum standards, trying to achieve greater equality of outcomes or promot-ing equality of opportunity, often termed social justice.

- Efficiency concerns are also important. Private markets are likely to fail to pro-vide insurance against shocks such as unemployment or disability, and against aggregate risks, thus requiring government intervention. The market may also work unfairly in determining the allocation of resources, such as the possibility that low-skilled workers might be exploited.

- Historically, the government has sought to redistribute resources through the tax and benefit system, providing both means-tested and categorical benefits. One of the problems with such benefits is that they may contribute to a 'culture of dependency' and hence do little to promote social justice. More recently, the UK government has used in-work tax credits to encourage employment and introduced a limited form of asset-based welfare.

FURTHER READING

Barr (2004b) and Stiglitz (2000) cover most of the material in this chapter.

For more detailed material on income poverty and inequality, see Goodman et al. (1997) and Atkinson (1983, 1989). On income mobility, see Dearden et al. (1997) and Johnson and Reed (1996). For discussions of relative deprivation, see McKay (2004) and Willitts (2006).

There is a useful website, funded by the Joseph Rowntree Foundation, which offers up-to-date statistics on poverty and social exclusion in the UK, see http://www.poverty.org.uk/. The Institute for Fiscal Studies (www.ifs.org.uk) also produces regular updates on poverty and inequality in the UK (see, for example, Brewer et al., 2007).

The chapters in Walker (1999) offer a number of interesting perspectives on the modern welfare state. Le Grand (2006), ch. 9, and Kelly and Lissauer (2000) discuss asset-based welfare.

There are a host of studies analysing the effect of the introduction of the National Minimum Wage – examples include Dickens et al. (1999) and Stewart (2004). On in-work tax credits, see Blundell (2000), Hotz and Scholz (2002), and Brewer and Browne (2006).

QUESTIONS FOR DISCUSSION

1. 'If there is income mobility, then income inequality doesn't matter.' Do you agree?

2. What value is there in the government's child poverty target?

3. Is it valid to define poverty as not having a mobile phone?

4. 'Since 1997, relative poverty has fallen, but inequality has risen.' How?

5. Does the fact that the National Minimum Wage has not led to an increase in unemployment among low-wage workers imply that it was set at too low a level?

6. Should the pay of top executives be subject to a salary cap?

7. 'Instead of giving people financial assets, the government could more effectively achieve its aims by subsidising higher education and providing business start-up loans.' Do you agree?

CHAPTER 10

The Market and the Government

In the first chapter we discussed a number of possible objectives society might have with respect to allocating scarce resources among its members. In subsequent chapters we saw how market and government systems can be used to allocate resources in various 'problem' areas, and discussed whether their use can meet the relevant objectives in the area concerned. Throughout, certain key issues emerged repeatedly. Many of the difficulties involved in allocating resources within these areas have strong links with one another; indeed, many are simply aspects of the same conceptual problem. It is the purpose of this final chapter to emphasise these links, and to draw out from the discussion some general lessons about different economic systems. More specifically, the chapter brings together material from previous chapters concerning the ability of markets and the government to achieve efficiency, equity and other objectives in the allocation of scarce resources. We begin with the market and efficiency, continue with the market and equity, and briefly discuss the ability of the market to achieve other ends, such as freedom and community. We then consider the ability to attain these objectives of the different forms of government intervention – namely, provision, tax and subsidy policies and regulation – and the mixtures of those forms, such as quasi-markets.

The market and efficiency

In Chapter 1 we saw that, under certain conditions, the market allocation of a commodity will provide a socially efficient quantity of that commodity. Let us restate the argument. Under conditions to be discussed shortly, the *market demand* curve will be identical to the *marginal social benefit* (*msb*) curve. Also, under similar conditions, market supply reflects social cost; that is, the *market supply* curve is identical to the *marginal social cost* (*msc*) curve. The socially efficient level of provision is the point where the marginal social cost equals the marginal social benefit; that is, where the *msb* and *msc* curves intersect. Under market allocation, the quantity of the commodity that is actually provided will be the point where demand equals supply; that is, where the demand and supply curves intersect. Since these curves are identical with the *msb* and *msc* curves, the points of intersection will be the same. Hence the quantity provided in the market will be the socially efficient quantity.

Demand

But what are the conditions required for this result to be achieved? We can now be more specific than was possible in Chapter 1. First, consider the identity of the *msb* and *market demand* curves. This requires the fulfilment of the following conditions:

(A) that individuals in their roles as consumers are well-informed; and that they are able to judge the quality of the commodities they consume, and are able to act on those judgments;

(B) that individuals are rational and the best judges of their own wants; and

(C) that the marginal private benefit equals the marginal social benefit.

If the first two conditions hold, then an individual's demand for a commodity will reflect accurately his/her marginal private benefit for that commodity. If the third condition holds, then the sum of the individual demands for a commodity (the market demand) will equal the marginal social benefit.

However, we have seen that, for many of the commodities discussed in this book, these conditions are not fulfilled. For example, in markets for health care, education, housing and pensions, there exists *imperfect information*. Prospective patients are in a poor position to evaluate different methods of medical treatment; parents may lack the essential information necessary to choose the right school for their children; the purchaser of a house may find it difficult to assess its faults before actually living in it; and people find it difficult to easily access and process information to enable them to make the right choice of pension. The lack of relevant information means that consumers may not be able to assess accurately what will benefit them. If this is so, their demand for the commodity concerned will not reflect the benefit they actually derive from its consumption, and condition (A) will not be fulfilled.

It should be noted that the existence of imperfect information does not necessarily imply that markets will fail. Market institutions may arise that will provide the necessary information: surveyors in the case of housing, for example, or financial advisers in the case of pensions. But, for this to work, the consumers concerned have to be aware that they lack relevant information and to be prepared to pay for it, if necessary. Also, the very fact that they lack information means that consumers find it difficult to assess the quality of the information they purchase – which may lead to the market in information itself being inefficient.

Even if there is no obvious consumer ignorance, it is possible to challenge the view that individuals are always the best judges of their own wants: condition (B). In some cases consumers may be *irrational*. An obvious example of this is people with a mental illness. However, a new branch of economics known as behavioural economics has used psychological experiments to demonstrate that even people with no history of mental illness may behave in ways that do not conform to some simple interpretations of rationality. So, for example, in Chapter 4 on pensions, we saw that automatic enrolment (that is, individuals had to choose to opt out of a pension scheme) boosted participation in company pension schemes compared to conscious enrolment (that is, individuals had to opt in), although the choices on offer (in or out of the pension scheme) were exactly the same in each case. Inertia in this case seemed to be over-riding simple rationality.

More generally, some people believe that individuals are subject to such extensive social and economic conditioning that they cannot make rational decisions concerning their consumption – that, for example, advertising and other pressures induce them to 'waste' their money on cigarettes or alcohol instead of buying proper food or housing.

Others would view these kinds of arguments as being unacceptably paternalistic. They would question simple notions of rationality and argue that individuals have a right to have their desires respected, regardless of the origin of those desires or whether they were 'rational' or 'irrational'. In this view, the ultimate authority as to what benefits individuals should be the individuals themselves; no one else is an appropriate judge.

The difference between these points of view is partly a philosophical one concerning the nature of individual rights, and partly an empirical one concerning the extent of individual irrationality. However, there would be general agreement that, if substantial consumer ignorance exists, then individuals may not be the best judges of their own interests; and that there may be cases where even well-informed individuals' demands for a commodity may not reflect accurately their own interests.

Condition (C) – that marginal private benefit equals marginal social benefit – is also unlikely to be met in many of the areas considered in this book, because this requires that the commodity concerned has no *external benefits* associated with it; and that individuals' consumption of the commodity benefits only themselves. But we have seen that health care, education, housing and police patrols all generate external benefits. For example, the existence of infectious diseases means that the marginal private benefit of some forms of health care is less than the marginal social benefit. Education is not only of direct benefit to those receiving the education concerned, but can also benefit those working with them and the community generally. House improvements can benefit not only the people who live in the house concerned, but also those who live in adjoining houses. If an individual purchases security from crime by paying for police protection for his/her house, s/he is likely to benefit his/her neighbours as well. All in all, therefore, in each of these areas, market allocation on its own is unlikely to result in an efficient level of provision.

Supply

Now let us look at the supply side. The following conditions are required to ensure that market supply accurately reflects social cost, or, more specifically, that the *market supply* curve is identical with the *msc* curve:

(D) that producers are well-informed;

(E) that marginal private costs are identical with marginal social costs; and

(F) that there are no monopolistic elements or barriers to competition in the relevant markets.

If conditions (D) and (E) are not met, then individual production and consumption decisions will not reflect accurately their social costs. If condition (F) is not met, then producers will be able to manipulate to their own advantage the prices their products receive.

Again, these conditions are often not fulfilled in the areas discussed. Examples of condition (D) not being met are the phenomena of *moral hazard* and *adverse selection* that can affect insurance markets. We encountered these in Chapter 2 with respect to health, in Chapter 4 with respect to pensions, and in Chapter 9 with respect to insurance against disability and unemployment. Insurers cannot always know how their insures are behaving (the problem of moral hazard) or their risk status (adverse selection); as a consequence, their premiums will often be higher than social efficiency would require. The production of many commodities generate *external costs*, driving a wedge between marginal private and marginal social costs, and hence violating condition (E). We saw in Chapter 5 how landlords or other house owners who let their property deteriorate impose external costs on their neighbours, and in Chapter 6 how private cars can create congestion: both are cases of costs being imposed on 'external individuals'. Much industrial activity, including the exploitation of energy resources, pollutes and despoils the natural environment. Indeed, the whole climate change issue discussed in Chapter 8 can be viewed as the quintessential case of market failure caused by external costs.

As far as condition (F) is concerned (the absence of monopoly), we have seen that monopolistic elements exist in many of the areas discussed, including schools, hospitals and the markets for professionals (such as doctors). Whether such monopolies are an inevitable part of market allocation, or whether they are an aberration, is debatable. On the one hand, some of these monopolies arise because they are protected by government actions of various kinds: the monopoly to practise granted to certain professions, for example. On the other hand, government licensed monopolies are often at least in part a reaction to a particular form of market failure: that of imperfect information. So, for example, most countries restrict the practice of medicine to qualified doctors, thus giving them a degree of monopoly power; but this is mainly to protect potential patients against quacks exploiting their ignorance of medicine.

Moreover, there are some circumstances in which the forces that drive a competitive market are likely to encourage the development of a monopoly. These are situations where there are substantial fixed costs, or more precisely where *economies of scale* or *sunk costs* exist, such that the larger the firm, the more able it is to lower its average cost of production. In these circumstances, bigger firms will drive their smaller competitors out of business, until eventually the market is monopolised by one large firm. Economies of scale are not a particularly prominent feature of production in all the areas we have discussed in the book, but they are present in some of them: hospitals, for example, often have substantial fixed costs. To the extent that they exist, it may prove impossible for an initially competitive market to avoid degenerating into a monopolistic one.

So, in the areas reviewed in this book, some or all of conditions (A) to (F) are unlikely to be met. Consequently, market allocations are unlikely to be efficient. Will they also fail to achieve other objectives, such as equity?

The market and equity

In the absence of any universally accepted definition of equity it is not easy to determine whether a particular method of resource allocation, such as the market system, achieves it. The best we can do is to concentrate on the interpretations of the term that have emerged in our previous discussions. Most of these reflect one of two basic philosophies. The first emphasises the desirability of equality in the areas considered. Examples include the equal treatment for equal need objective in health care, educational policies designed to promote equality of opportunity, and policies aimed at reducing inequality in the distribution of income. The second philosophy concentrates only on the attainment of minimum standards in each area. It is the philosophy underlying the concern that everyone should live in a 'decent home', and the perception of the poverty problem as being one of simply bringing incomes of the poor above a specified level.

Whichever of those interpretations is preferred, it is unlikely that market allocation will achieve it. In a market system, people's incomes – and hence their ability to purchase commodities – are determined by the resources they own and the prices they can obtain from selling those resources. Since the initial distribution of the ownership of resources is unequal, and since there are substantial barriers to competition in many resource markets (particularly that for labour), it would be remarkable if market processes produced an equal (or close to equal) distribution of income. Nor is there any reason to expect that minimum standards will necessarily be achieved; there will always be those with few resources, and hence with levels of consumption below any reasonable minimum.

The market and other objectives

Although we have concentrated on efficiency and equity as the principal objectives that a society will wish to pursue, we have seen that other objectives may also be important. There are two objectives. The first objective is freedom and the promotion of civil liberties. The second is fostering a sense of community. How does the market system perform in relation to these aims?

It is often argued that competitive markets promote one kind of freedom: that of choice. The existence of large numbers of small producers, each vying for the consumers' business, ensures that even the most idiosyncratic of consumers will be satisfied. Freedom of choice could also be enhanced by injecting market-type elements into areas where they do not currently exist. Under the education voucher scheme, for example, parents would be free to choose whatever education they wished for their children, and not be compelled to accept the particular version provided by the government.

However, we saw in Chapter 6 that we might want to restrict the operation of the market with respect to, for example, private bounty hunters, on the grounds that this might seriously infringe civil liberties. Also, as we have seen, many markets contain considerable elements of monopoly. These, as well as impeding efficiency in the manner already described, also operate to limit freedom of choice. If, because of economies of scale, there is only one hospital in town, then choice is non-existent; if entry into a profession is limited, then freedom of choice of supplier is restricted. Overall, therefore, while there is a strong presumption that markets encourage freedom or liberty, we cannot guarantee unequivocally that this will occur automatically in every situation.

Many people believe that markets are incompatible with another social objective mentioned – the promotion of altruism or a sense of community. They argue that the market fosters personal attributes, such as greed and a lack of concern for one's neighbour, that are incompatible with communal or co-operative behaviour. On the other hand, it could be claimed that, since markets are means by which mutually profitable transactions take place, then they promote everyone's satisfaction and thereby promote a sense of communal well-being. In support of this view, it could be pointed out that street markets are usually pleasant places to stroll around; and that 'market' towns, so-called because they provide the market-place for their local areas, are often thought of as attractive places to live, with a strong sense of community.

It could also be argued that markets promote respect for others. Recently, some anthropologists have investigated the market orientation of indigenous peoples in Latin America and East Africa. They found that the less market-oriented the society was, the less likely were participants in psychological experiments to behave in more generous (or more egalitarian) ways. Overall, the anthropologists suggest, experience of market transactions may make people fairer or less exploitative when dealing with strangers (Henrich et al. 2001).

In summary, we can say that market allocation without government intervention is unlikely to achieve completely either efficiency or equity, and may fail to meet certain other objectives as well. However, this does not necessarily imply that the government should therefore intervene, because it could be that such intervention might make things worse: it might create more inefficiency or more inequity than the market operating on its own. We need therefore to examine possible forms of government intervention and explore their ability to meet society's aims.

Government policy

In earlier chapters, we distinguished between three forms of government intervention: *direct provision; tax and subsidy* policies; and *regulation*. Under a *direct provision* system of government, the government owns and operates the institutions that provide the good or service concerned, and employs the people involved in providing it. Examples include government-provided hospitals and schools, the public road system, public or council housing and the police service.

The use of government *subsidy* is widespread in the areas we have explored. Health care, education, roads: all are provided free to the user or at subsidised prices. Much housing is also subsidised, either through direct subsidies to tenants, or through the tax system to owner-occupiers. *Taxation* or charging policies may be used as an instrument for the control of environmental and congestion externalities, as with the green taxes discussed in Chapter 8 and the congestion charge discussed in Chapter 7. Taxation, together with social security is, of course, also used as a major tool of income redistribution, as we saw in Chapter 9. However, as most of the arguments concerning taxation as an instrument of social policy are similar to those concerning government subsidy, in what follows we concentrate on the latter.

Government *regulation* can take a number of forms. One is *quantity* regulation, where the government regulates the amount of the good or service being produced. An example of this is the control of polluting activities through regulations concerning the levels at which they may be undertaken, as discussed in Chapter 8, or the scheme for controlling the cars entering Athens, discussed in Chapter 7. Another form of regulation concerns the *quality* of the good or service being produced: an example here is the qualification requirements necessary for practising medicine, mentioned in Chapter 2. A third is *price* regulation: examples are rent control, where the price of privately rented housing is regulated – discussed in Chapter 5; and the minimum wage, where the 'price' of labour is controlled – discussed in Chapter 9.

As should be clear from the examples given, while all these forms of government intervention often accompany one another, there is no necessity for them to do so. Thus it is perfectly possible to have government provision without subsidy, subsidy without provision or regulation, regulation without subsidy and so on. Moreover, one can substitute for the other. Indeed, many of the current debates in several of the areas explored in this book involve just such a substitution. In health care and education, for example, there are reforms at various stages of development that involve replacing the present systems of combined government provision and subsidy by some form of *quasi-market*. In quasi-market systems, government remains a subsidiser of services but ceases to provide them. Instead, by a variety of means, it finances independent suppliers to provide the service concerned, and, in order to ensure that its money is well-spent, expands its regulatory activities to monitor and regulate these suppliers. Quasi-markets are thus systems that combine government subsidy and regulation, while reducing, or in some cases even eliminating, the government's role as provider.

Government and efficiency

The arguments concerning the possible consequences of each kind of government intervention in terms of efficiency are rather different; it is important therefore to keep them distinct.

Direct provision

There are a number of reasons for supposing that government provision will diverge from the socially efficient level of production. First, government providers are usually monopolies; indeed, their monopoly status is on occasion guaranteed by the government. Hence their market is not 'contestable': that is, it is difficult, if not impossible, for potential competitors to enter the market. Also, the fact that the monopolies are government-owned means that, unlike private monopolies, there is no threat of bankruptcy; the management does not have to answer to shareholders; and managers are not under the threat of take-over if they are inefficient; hence all these incentives to efficiency are removed.

Now it could be argued that this ignores a key difference between those who work for government providers – or more generally those who work in the public sector – and those who work in the private sector. This concerns the motivation of the individuals concerned. There is a view that public-sector workers are primarily motivated not by the need to make profits or more generally to further their own interests, but more by the desire to provide a good service to the people they are supposed to be helping: what may be termed the public service ethos. In terms of a metaphor employed elsewhere by one of the present authors, they may be 'knights' (public spirited altruists) rather than 'knaves' (self-interested egoists). So doctors working in a publicly-owned health facility might have as their principal concern not the profit to be earned by the facility or their own incomes, but the welfare of their patients; and teachers in state schools are concerned with the welfare of their pupils, not the schools' profits.

If this is correct, then it has certain advantages from the point of view of social efficiency. As we have seen in most of the areas with which we are concerned, users of the services have poor information about both the quality and the quantity of the service they are receiving. Patients generally have little medical knowledge and find it difficult to judge whether they are receiving good or bad care, or even too much or too little care; and, perhaps to a lesser extent, parents and pupils do not always find it easy to assess the quality of education that a school is providing. This asymmetry of information gives those providers who are only concerned with their own concerns – the knaves – an opportunity to exploit their users' ignorance by providing a service not at the socially efficient level. Knavish doctors, for example, who are paid according to the number of operations they perform, may operate on patients more frequently than necessary; or, if instead they are paid a salary, then they may prefer leisure to work, and hence may operate too infrequently.

More generally, professionals are often self-employed, with their income therefore being directly related to the amount of the service they provide. In that case, they may try to increase their income and status by recommending that potential consumers use more services than they really need. On the other hand, if they are employees, so that their incomes are not directly related to the level of service provided, they may try to reduce their work-loads by under-providing the service.

Nor is the problem of motivation in government confined to professionals. There are also issues concerning public-sector managers and bureaucrats.

Knavish bureaucrats, for example, who work in the public sector may be so-called 'budget-maximisers': that is, they may be more interested in promoting their incomes and status by expanding their number of employees, and hence their budget, than in providing the public service.

Public-sector worker who are knights, on the other hand, would be concerned primarily with their users' welfare, and hence with the quality of the service being provided; therefore they would not sacrifice the service for their own interests in the same way. Knightly doctors, for example, would provide exactly the care they think their patients need, regardless of how they are paid. However, there is a problem here in that they may not be motivated to think very hard about the cost of the care they are providing (except in the unlikely event that they themselves have to bear that cost). So they may provide care that is indeed of benefit to the patient but that, from a social point of view, costs more than it benefits. In other words, knights might not be motivated to be socially efficient.

So the absence of competition, either actual or threatened, the lack of any danger of take-over, and the presence of knightly motivations among public-sector workers all reduce incentives to keep costs to a minimum, while the presence of knavish motivations might lower quality relative to cost. Hence, in any of these circumstances, the marginal cost of government production would generally be higher than the marginal social cost of production.

However, government providers do not always have to be monopolies. Following the quasi-market changes in the British education system, for example, government schools have to compete for pupils. Similarly, the implementation of National Health Service reforms results in government-owned hospitals having to compete for patients with private or voluntary hospitals.

The consequences of this competition for the efficiency of government providers will depend in part on the organisations with which they are competing. If the latter all have the objective of maximising their profits, as is likely to be the case if they were all private, then, unless the government provider concerned is subsidised, it will go out of business if it does not also minimise its costs. If, on the other hand, its potential competitors are not profit-maximisers – if they are all voluntary organisations, for example – then it only has to match their behaviour to survive. In that case, the marginal cost of provision (by all the organisations involved) might be higher than the actual social cost.

So there are two sets of circumstances where it is possible that government provision will be inefficient (where costs are not minimised): where the government provider is a monopoly, or where it is competing against other organisations whose principal concern is not the maximisation of profits. If the commodity concerned was being sold to consumers at a price that had to cover costs (that is, if there was no government subsidy), then the consequence of the cost of provision being above the marginal social cost would result in the price being too high for social efficiency. Demand would fall, and less would be consumed or provided than would be socially efficient.

However, government-provided commodities are often not sold to consumers at cost-price, but are offered free or at a price below the cost of provision.

In other words, government *provision* is often accompanied by government *subsidy*. What are the efficiency implications of the latter?

Taxes and subsidies

If a commodity is provided free at the point of use to consumers, with its provision being subsidised from taxation (and if there is no other cost to consumers such as time or travel) then the only cost to the consumer of consuming the commodity concerned is the perceived extra cost in terms of any extra tax s/he might have to pay as a result of its consumption. Since this is likely to be very small indeed, the amount demanded will be greater than the socially efficient level of demand. If the *msb* curve is the same as the market demand curve, and if the extra tax cost is assumed to be as near zero as makes no difference, the amount demanded will be given by the point at which the *msb* curve intersects the horizontal axis.

More generally, if a commodity is sold at a price below cost, there will be 'excess' demand (compared with the level of demand that would prevail if the price was equal to cost). Faced with this excess demand, the government has two choices. It can either meet all the demand, thus ensuring that more of the commodity is provided and consumed than is socially efficient. Or, if it knows the amount that is socially efficient (we shall discuss this assumption below) it can simply provide this amount and use some other rationing device to decide who gets what. Such devices include queuing or waiting lists, or the delegating of the decision to the judgement of bureaucrats, managers or professionals such as doctors and teachers.

The problem with queuing or waiting lists is that the people at the front of the queue or at the top of the waiting list may have got there by luck, by having plenty of free time or by having the right contacts. In such cases there is no guarantee that they are the people who really need the commodity the most. The problem with delegating the relevant decisions to professionals or bureaucrats is that, in making those decisions, as we saw earlier, the latter may pursue their own interests – and these may not coincide with those of either consumers or the government. That is, they may be knaves rather than knights.

There is a yet more serious difficulty if the government, through its taxation and subsidy policies, forsakes the use of market prices as a means of allocating resources: that of *information*. As we saw in Chapter 1, movements in market prices provide information to producers. If there is a change in consumer preferences for a commodity such that there is an increase in the demand for it, its price will rise, thus conveying this information to producers; they will see that production of the commodity has become more profitable, and, if they are profit-maximisers they will increase supply to meet the increased demand. If they over-react by increasing supply too much, then this information will be conveyed to them again by a movement in prices – this time, a fall.

Now it should be noted that, at times, prices will convey the wrong information. As we saw in Chapter 8, because of the absence of the relevant property rights, the price of many natural resources, including air and water, is zero. This conveys to consumers and producers the (incorrect) information that the supply of the resource is infinite: that there is no scarcity. Hence the resource is over-used, relative to the socially efficient level. In such cases, government tax or subsidy policies can be used to create a price where none existed, and thus promote efficiency: the pollution charge discussed in Chapter 8 is an obvious example.

However, these cases aside, the effect of a government tax or subsidy policy can be to drive a wedge between prices, demand and supply, such that the role of prices as conveyors of information is reduced or even eliminated. In the absence of market signals, such as movements of prices, the government will find it very difficult to assess the overall efficient level of production of the commodity con-cerned. Because, without a price mechanism, it has only very limited ways of assessing the social benefit of the commodity and relating that to its social cost.

The problem is particularly acute with respect to the assessment of social benefit. Essentially there are two mechanisms available to governments for this purpose: voting procedures and, again, delegation to bureaucrats or profession-als. Now there are reasons for supposing that voting procedures might give a better indication of the 'true' social benefit of the production of a good than relying on market signals, such as the movement of prices. First, the mechanism of voting allows everyone who is affected by the consumption and production of a good to have a say in its level of provision. Hence, if there are external ben-efits or costs associated with its production or consumption, then, in theory at least, the political process will take these into account. Second, voting gives everyone an equal say, in the sense that each person has only one vote; hence this overcomes the disadvantage of market demand which gives a greater weight to those who are better off.

However, these advantages have to be set against a powerful set of disadvan-tages. First, under certain conditions it can be shown that majority voting gives greater weight to the preferences of some groups over others. In particular, it can favour the 'median voter'. For example, suppose there is a vote over how much of a commodity should be subsidised. Some voters will want a large sub-sidy; some will opt for a small one; and some for none at all. If all voters' pref-erences are ranked along a scale, there will be one voter who is the 'median': that is, half the electorate would vote for a subsidy larger than the one this median voter wants, and half would vote for a subsidy smaller than the one this voter wants. If there are only two political parties, the one that offers a level of subsidy that is the one favoured by the median voter will win the election; because, if it offers any other level of subsidy, by definition it will attract the votes of less than half of the electorate. Hence both parties will compete for the median voter, whose preferences will therefore be given a disproportionate weight.

A second disadvantage of simple majority voting procedures derives from the very fact that everyone has only one vote. This means that it is impossible to gauge the depth of someone's preferences: how much s/he really wants the commodity concerned relative to other possibilities. If s/he had many votes, s/he could 'rank' alternatives according to how many votes s/he gave them; with only one vote, s/he can only vote for or against. There are more complex voting systems that do give some weight to preferences; but they can be cumbersome and difficult for the electorate to understand.

A third problem is that elections or referenda are expensive to arrange and organise. In consequence, in practice people do not have frequent votes over levels of subsidy or provision of particular goods and services; rather, they vote infrequently over broad packages offered by different political parties. This does not allow for 'fine-tuning' in the allocation of resources.

Fourth, when people vote they are rarely properly informed about either the benefits or the costs of the various proposals with which they are confronted. Economists are divided as to whether they are likely to be better informed about the benefits or about the costs. Some argue that the activities of pressure groups favouring particular kinds of government expenditures will lead people to exaggerate the benefits from those expenditures, and to underestimate the costs; if this is correct, they will vote for a level of provision that is higher than the socially efficient level. Others argue that the benefits from government spending are often very diffuse, while the costs, in terms of increased taxation, are very obvious; hence people will be tempted to vote for too little government spending. In either case it is unlikely that the amount they vote for will coincide with the socially efficient level.

Finally, there is an additional source of potential inefficiency that arises from government subsidy. This is the disincentives for work and savings created by the taxation necessary to finance the subsidy. The actual size of the losses in each case is a matter of empirical investigation.

Regulation

In theory, a perfectly informed government with suitably motivated civil servants could achieve an efficient allocation of a good or a service by using them to regulate its production. Thus, if it knew the exact position of the *msb* and *msc* curves, and hence the point of intersection, it could compel the organisation concerned to produce (and price) at the appropriate level, in terms of both quantity and quality. However, in practice, it will face two problems. First, it will find it very difficult to obtain the relevant information. We have already seen the difficulties involved in obtaining information concerning social *benefits* in the absence of a properly functioning market. But, in addition, in this case the government will need to obtain information from the organisations concerned on their costs – information that the latter will have little incentive to supply.

The second, and related, problem is that of 'regulator capture'. The regulators of the production of a commodity usually have to meet frequently with the representatives of the producers. Inevitably, there will be a tendency for them to develop personal relationships of various kinds which will perhaps lead them to be sympathetic to the interests of the producers. The eventual level of regulation might therefore correspond more to those interests than to those of the society as a whole (as represented by the socially efficient level).

Both of these phenomena create problems for each kind of regulation. The absence of perfect information means that quantity regulation can result in either too much or too little of the good being produced. Poor information and regulator capture can result in quality regulation being used to protect those being regulated from competition, and thereby create inefficiency. And both can result in regulated prices being set either too high, thus creating excess demand and necessitating rationing as discussed above, or too low, thus creating over-production or excess supply.

There may also be consequences of government regulation for efficiency over time. Regulation that is too heavy may stifle incentives for invention and innovation. It may also discourage potential suppliers from entering the market, or encourage those already in it to leave (as with private landlords and rent control). Price regulation, in particular, impedes the information role of price movements discussed above.

In short, all forms of government intervention may create inefficiency – inefficiency that may be less, equal to, or greater than the inefficiencies in the market that the interventions are intended to correct.

Government and equity

What of government's ability to achieve other objectives, such as equity? Again, it will be useful to divide our discussion into the likely effects on equity of each of the three forms of government intervention: provision; tax or subsidy policies; and regulation. There seems to be no particular reason for supposing that government *direct provision* will be either equitable or inequitable *on its own* (that is, if it is not accompanied by subsidy or regulation) so far as the distribution of the good or service itself is concerned. However, there may be consequences for the distribution of income. For example, the replacement of a monopoly private supplier by a monopoly government one may create a more equal distribution of income because (a) the latter would have less incentive to exploit its monopoly position; and (b) the profits would accrue to taxpayers rather than to its shareholders (who, on average, are likely to be richer).

Government *subsidy* may achieve equity, if the latter is defined in terms of minimum standards, because subsidising a good or service will make it easier for poorer people to consume it and thereby help to ensure that everyone has a minimum quantity. Here it is useful to distinguish between the effects of universal and means-tested subsidies. If the subsidy is means-tested – that is, if it is confined only to people on low incomes – then it may also promote equity in the sense of greater equality of consumption: it will encourage poor people's consumption relative to that of the rich. However, this assumes that the means test does not discourage poor people from consuming the good or service. Chapter 9 discussed some of the reasons why, in the case of cash benefits, means tests might deter take-up of the benefit concerned, including administrative complexity and possible social stigma. These problems also confront the use of means tests in other areas, such as means-tested charges for health care.

A further problem with means tests, again discussed in Chapter 9, is their effect on the marginal tax rate faced by individuals, and hence on their incentive to work. Those in receipt of a means-tested service may lose their entitlement if they increase their income, and hence may be discouraged from trying to earn more by working harder. Given these difficulties, it has been argued that universal subsidies are preferable to means-tested ones. However, such subsidies have problems of their own. They encourage demand for the good or service by both rich and poor; hence, while this may result in everyone having at least a *minimum standard* of consumption, it will do little to promote greater *equality* of consumption. Indeed, in some cases it might make matters worse. As was discussed earlier, subsidies create excess demand, necessitating the use of non-price rationing devices, devices that may on occasion favour the better-off.

Finally, government *regulation*. Regulation that is designed to control prices, such as minimum wages or rent control, often has the explicit intention of promoting equity. However, again there may be perverse consequences. Minimum wages, for example, may reduce employment, making it more difficult for workers to get jobs; they may also push up costs and prices, thereby affecting consumers. Rent control may reduce the overall supply of rented housing, thus adversely affecting those who cannot afford to buy a house. Government regulation designed to promote quality may also have undesirable consequences for equity. Qualification requirements for professionals, for example, can be used to restrict entry into the profession and hence raise incomes in the profession concerned. Similarly, quality controls on products can be used to restrict competition to supply those products, thus increasing the profits of existing suppliers.

Of course, none of these are *necessary* consequences of regulation. If the regulators are perfectly informed and truly impartial, then some of them may be avoided. But, as we have seen in the discussion of the consequences of government regulation for efficiency, the same market failures that provided the motivation for the government intervention in the first place militate against impartiality and perfect information.

Government and other objectives

Perhaps the major criticism of government intervention with respect to objectives other than efficiency and equity is that it erodes individual liberty; perhaps its major justification is that it promotes a sense of community. These arguments raise issues that take us well beyond the confines of this book, and indeed beyond the normal province of economic analysis. However, a few brief comments are in order.

It would be hard to deny that societies with the most extensive government intervention – the old communist economies of Eastern Europe – were also illiberal, oppressive regimes. On the other hand, tyranny has also coexisted with capitalism (in Nazi Germany, for example) and some highly interventionist societies have extensive political freedoms (Sweden, for example). The connection between government intervention and the erosion of individual liberties is thus far from automatic.

As the constitutional embodiment of the community, it might be expected that government intervention would promote a spirit of community. If a combination of government provision and subsidy, for example, can ensure that everyone uses a particular service, such as the government education system or the National Health Service, then fellow-feeling and a common sense of citizenship may be enhanced. However, again, the experience of Eastern Europe is instructive, where arguably the only communal response to governments' heavy-handed interventions was to unite their citizens against them.

Quasi-markets

Quasi-markets are mechanisms for resource allocation that use government tax and subsidy policy to distribute purchasing power between individuals, but rely upon competition between independent providers (either publicly or privately owned) to deliver the service concerned. Examples include the voucher system in education and the health reforms in the English and Welsh NHS, where independent hospitals and other medical providers compete to provide services to government-funded commissioners or purchasers.

In essence, quasi-markets are an attempt to combine the benefits of markets – in particular, the positive incentives they offer for efficiency and consumer responsiveness – with the equity advantages of government tax and subsidy policies. So, for example, in the case of an education voucher, parents come to the quasi-market not with their own resources, as in a normal market, but with a government-funded voucher, the value of which is determined by an equity principle. The parents then decide on which school to spend the voucher. Schools thus have incentive to be responsive to the needs and wants of parents, and efficient in their use of resources.

Quasi-markets do suffer from some of the problems of normal markets, notably that of imperfect information, and measures have to be put in place to deal with these (such as choice advisers to help parents decide which school to choose). But they offer an interesting way of providing services that may help to avoid some of the difficulties associated with pure market or pure government provision.

Conclusion

Both market and non-market systems of resource allocation thus have advantages and disadvantages with respect to their ability to achieve social objectives. Which system one ultimately finds superior will depend on two factors: one's values concerning the relative weights that should be put upon society's various objectives, such as efficiency and equity; and the extent to which the final allocation under each system meets these objectives. The first is a matter of value judgements about which economists – in their role as economists – have little to say. The second, however, is an empirical question to which economists have a great deal to contribute. What is needed is more empirical investigation – by economists and others – to substantiate the competing claims of the different systems. If this book has succeeded in inducing any of its readers to pursue such investigations, one of its main objectives will have been achieved.

SUMMARY

■ There are a number of conditions necessary for the market allocation of a commodity to be *efficient*. Both consumers and producers are *perfectly informed*; consumers are *rational* and the best judge of their own needs; neither the consumption nor the production of the commodity generates *external benefits* or *external costs*; and there are no monopolistic elements or *barriers to competition* in the relevant markets.

■ For each of the problem areas investigated in this book, most of these conditions are violated. Moreover, market allocation will generally not be *equitable* and, while it may promote *liberty* in the sense of freedom of choice, it is also likely to encourage self-interested behaviour, and perhaps thereby affect the spirit of *community*.

■ Government intervention can also fail. Government *provision* may be inefficient, especially if the government provider is a monopoly. Although on occasion government *tax or subsidy* policy can be used to correct market failures, especially with respect to externalities, they can also drive a wedge between prices, demand and costs, thus damaging the role of prices as conveyors of information. Alternative methods of deriving information, such as voting mechanisms or reliance on the judgement of bureaucrats or professionals, all have deficiencies of their own. Government *regulation* also suffers from information difficulties, and from the associated problem of regulator capture.

■ Government provision has no necessary consequences with respect to *equity*. Means-tested government subsidy can help to attain a minimum standard of consumption of a commodity, so long as the means test itself does not discourage consumption by the poor. Universal subsidy avoids the discouraging effects of means tests, but does little to promote equality of consumption. Government regulation may have perverse consequences for equity, especially if those who are adversely affected by the regulations are poorer than those who benefit from them. Finally, government intervention may restrict individual *liberty*, but promote a sense of *community*.

■ Quasi-markets, where government finances but does not provide a service, are an attempt to combine the benefits of markets – in particular, the positive incentives they offer for efficiency and consumer responsiveness – with the equity advantages of government tax and subsidy policies.

FURTHER READING

An excellent analysis of the reasons for market failure can be found in Barr (2004b), though in places some knowledge of economics is required. Recent developments in the exciting new field of behavioural economics can be found in Kahneman and Tversky (2000). Many of the ideas of government failure, particularly with respect to efficiency, derive from the theory of 'public choice': the classic, though in places technical, review of the relevant literature is Mueller (2003). Motivational issues are discussed in Le Grand (2006); and the potential of quasi-markets in public services are discussed in Le Grand and Bartlett (1993) and Le Grand (2007).

QUESTIONS FOR DISCUSSION

1. 'It is a happy coincidence that the form of economic organisation most likely to promote efficiency – perfect competition – is also that which involves the greatest decentralisation of power. The market is thus the cornerstone of liberty.' Do you agree?

2. Discuss the problems that imperfect information (on both the demand and supply sides) creates for market allocations.

3. Is the appropriate government response to externalities *always* to tax or subsidise the activity concerned?

4. 'There are shortages of doctors, nurses, policeman, etc., but none of food, shirts, cars, etc., because the market is used in the second case but not in the first.' Discuss.

5. Some argue that, while the pursuit of self-interest in the market generally promotes social welfare, its pursuit in government is invariably disastrous. Do you agree?

6. 'Quasi-markets are the least worst way of providing public services.' Do you agree?

References

Atkinson, A. B. (1983) *The Economics of Inequality*, 2nd edn (Oxford: Oxford University Press).

Atkinson, A. B. (1989) *Poverty and Social Security* (London: Harvester Wheatsheaf).

Banks, J., Blundell, R. and Tanner, S. (1998) 'Is there a retirement-savings puzzle?', *American Economic Review*, 88 (4): 769–88.

Banks, J. and Smith, S. (2006) 'Retirement in the UK', *Oxford Review of Economic Policy*, 22 (1): 40–56.

Barr, N. (2000) 'Reforming pensions – myths, truths and policy choices', World Bank Working paper. Available at: www.imf.org/external/pubs/ft/wp/2000/wp00139.pdf.

Barr, N. (2004a) 'Higher education funding', *Oxford Review of Economic Policy*, 20 (2): 264–83.

Barr, N. (2004b) *Economics of the Welfare State*, 4th edn (Oxford: Oxford University Press).

Barr, N. and Diamond, P. (2006) 'The economics of pensions', *Oxford Review of Economic Policy*, 22 (1): 1–21.

Becker, G. (1968) 'Crime and punishment: An economic approach', *The Journal of Political Economy*, 76: 169–217.

Becker, G. and Stigler, G. (1974) 'Law enforcement, malfeasance, and compensation of enforcers', *Journal of Legal Studies*, 3: 1–18.

Begg, D., Fischer, S. and Dornbusch, R. (2005) *Economics*, 8th edn (Maidenhead: McGraw-Hill).

Belfield, C. (2002) *Economic Principles for Education: Theory and Evidence* (Cheltenham: Edward Elgar).

Blanden, J. and Gregg, P. (2004) 'Family income and educational attainment: A review of approaches and evidence for Britain', *Oxford Review of Economic Policy*, 20 (2): 245–63.

Blundell, R. (2000) 'Work incentives and in-work benefits reform: A review', *Oxford Review of Economic Policy*, 16 (1): 27–44.

Blow, L., Leicester, A. and Oldfield, Z. (2003) 'London's congestion charge', Institute for Fiscal Studies Briefing Note. Available at: http://www.ifs.org.uk/bns/bn31.pdf.

Brand, S. and Price, R. (2000) 'The economic and social costs of crime', Home Office Research Study 217. Available at: www.homeoffice.gov.uk/rds/pdfs/hors217.pdf.

Brewer, M. and Browne, J. (2006) 'The effect of the working families' tax credit on labour market participation', Institute for Fiscal Studies Briefing Note No. 69. Available at: http://www.ifs.org.uk/bns/bn69.pdf

Brewer, M., Goodman, A., Muriel, A. and Sibieta, L. (2007) 'Poverty and inequality in the UK: 2007', Institute for Fiscal Studies Briefing Note No. 73. Available at: www.ifs.org.uk/ bns/bn73.pdf.

Choi, J., Laibson, D. and Madrian, B. (2004a) 'Plan design and 401(K) savings outcomes', *National Tax Journal*, 57: 275–98.

Choi, J., Laibson, D., Madrian, B. and Metrick, A. (2004b) 'For better or for worse: Default effects and 401(k) savings behavior,' in David Wise (ed.), *Perspectives in the Economics of Aging* (Chicago, Ill.: University of Chicago Press), 81–121.

Coase, R. H. (1960) 'The problem of social cost', *Journal of Law and Economics*, 3:1–44.

Cropper, M. and Oates, W. (1992) 'Environmental economics: A survey', *Journal of Economic Literature*, 30 (2): 675–740.

Culter, David (2002) 'Equality, efficiency and market fundamentals: The dynamics of international medical care reform', *Journal of Economic Literature*, Vol. XL: 881–906.

Culyer, A. J. and Newhouse, J. (eds) (2000) *Handbook of Health Economics* (Vols 1A and 1B) (Amsterdam: Elsevier).

Dasgupta, P. (2006) 'Comments on the Stern Review's economics of climate change', Mimeo. Available at: www.econ.cam.ac.uk/faculty/dasgupta/STERN.pdf.

Dearden, L., Machin, S. and Reed, H. (1997) 'Intergenerational mobility in Britain', *Economic Journal*, 107: 47–64.

Department of Transport (2004) 'Feasibility study of road pricing in the UK'. Available at: http://www.dft.gov.uk/pgr/roads/roadpricing/feasibilitystudy/studyreport/.

Diamond, P. (1977) 'A framework for social security analysis', *Journal of Public Economics*, 8: 275–9.

Diamond, P. (2004) 'Social security', *American Economic Review*, 94 (1): 1–24.

Diamond, P. and Hausman, J. (1994) 'Contingent valuation – is some number better than no number?', *Journal of Economic Perspectives*, 8 (4): 45–64.

Dickens, R., Machin, S. and Manning, A. (1999) 'The effects of minimum wages on employment: Theory and evidence from Britain', *Journal of Labor Economics*, 17 (1): 1–23.

Dietz, R. (2002) 'The estimation of neighbourhood effects in the social sciences: An interdisciplinary approach', *Social Science Research*, 31: 539–75.

DiIulio, J. (1996) 'Help wanted: Economists, crime and public policy', *Journal of Economic Perspectives*, 10 (1): 3–24.

Dolan, P. and Olsen, J. A. (2002) *Distributing Health Care: Economic and Ethical Issues* (Oxford: Oxford University Press).

Dominey, N. and Kempson, E. (2006) 'Understanding older people's experiences of poverty and material deprivation', Department for Work and Pensions Research Report No. 363. Available at: http://www.dwp.gov.uk/asd/asd5/rrs2006.asp#material.

Drummond, M., Sculpher, M., Torrance, G., O'Brien, B. and Stoddart, G. (2005) *Methods for the Economic Evaluation of Health Care Programmes*, 3rd edn (Oxford: Oxford University Press).

Durlauf, S. (2004) 'Neighbourhood Effects', in J. Henderson and J.-F. Thisse , *Handbook of Regional and Urban Economics*, Vol. 4 (Amsterdam, North-Holland).

Ehrlich, I. (1996) 'Crime, punishment and the market for offences', *Journal of Economic Perspectives*, 10 (1): 43–67.

Ekins, P. and Barker, M. (2001) 'Carbon taxes and car`bon emissions trading', *Journal of Economic Surveys*, 15 (3): 325–76.

Ellis, R. (1998) 'Creaming, skimping and dumping: Provider care on the intensive and extensive margins', *Journal of Health Economics*, 17: 537–55.

Feinstein, L. (2004) 'Mobility in pupils' cognitive attainment during school life', *Oxford Review of Economic Policy*, 20 (2): 213–39.

Feldstein, M. (2004) 'Rethinking social insurance', *American Economic Review*, 95 (1): 1–24.

Folland, S., Goodman, A. and Stano, M. (2001) *The Economics of Health and Health Care*, 3rd edn (Upper Saddle River, NJ: Prentice-Hall).

Freeman, R. (1996) 'Why do so many young American men commit crimes and what might we do about it?', *Journal of Economic Perspectives*, vol 10 (1): 25–42.

Freeman, R. (1999) 'The economics of crime' in O. Ashenfelter, R. Layard and and D. Card (eds), *The Handbook of Labor Economics*, Vol. III (Amsterdam: Elsevier Science).

Frey, B. (1997) 'On the relationship between intrinsic and extrinsic work motivation', *International Journal of Industrial Organisation*.15, 5: 427–40.

Friedman, D. (2001) 'Crime', *Concise Encyclopedia of Economics*. Available at: http://www.econlib.org/LIBRARY/Enc/Crime.html.

Frank, R. H. (2005) *Microeconomics and Behavior*, 6th edn (New York: McGraw-Hill).

Fullerton, D. Leicester, A. and Smith, S. (2007) 'Environmental taxes', Paper written for Mirrlees Review 'Reforming the tax system for the 21st century' (London: Institute for Fiscal Studies).

Galster, G. (2002) 'Neighbourhood dynamics and housing markets', in T. O'Sullivan and K. Gibb (eds), *Real Estate Issues – Housing Economics and Public Policy* (Oxford: Blackwell Science).

Gibbons, S. (2004) 'The costs of urban property crime', *Economic Journal*, 114:F441–F463.

Gibbons, S. and Machin, S. (2003) 'Valuing English primary schools', *Journal of Urban Economics*, 53 (2): 197–219.

Giddens, A. (1999) 'Notes on social justice and the welfare state', in R. Walker (ed.), *Ending Child Poverty: Popular Welfare for the 21st Century* (Bristol: Policy Press).

Giles, C., Johnson, P., McCrae, J. and Taylor, J. (1996) *Living with the State: The Incomes and Work Incentives of Tenantsin the Social Rented Sector* (London: Institute for Fiscal Studies).

Glaeser, E., Sacerdote, B. and Scheinkman, J. (1996) 'Crime and social interactions', *Quarterly Journal of Economics*, 111(2): 507–48.

Glennerster, H. (1991) 'Quasi-market for education?', *The Economics Journal*, 101: 1268–76.

Glennerster, H. (2002) 'United Kingdom education 1997–2001', *Oxford Review of Economic Policy*, 18: 120–36.

Grogger, J. (1998) 'Market wages and youth crime', *Journal of Labor Economics*, 16 (4): 756–91.

Goodman, A., Johnson, P. and Webb, S. (1997) *Inequality in the UK* (Oxford: Oxford University Press).

Hanushek, E. (2002) 'Publicly-provided education', in A. Auerbach and M. Feldstein (eds), *Handbook of Public Economics*, vol. 4 (Amsterdam, North-Holland).

Henrich, J., Boyd, R., Bowles, S., Camerer, C., Fehr, E., Gintis, H. and McElreath, R. (2001) 'In search of Homo economicus: Behavioural experiments in 15 small-scale societies', *American Economic Review*, 91: 73_8.

Hill, M. (2007) *Pensions* (Bristol: Policy Press.

Hills, J. (2006) 'A new pension settlement for the twenty-first century? The UK Pensions Commission's analysis and proposals', *Oxford Review of Economic Policy*, 22 (1): 113–32.

Hills, J. (2007) *Ends and Means: The Future Roles of Social Housing in England*, CASE Report No. 34 (London: Centre for Analysis and Social Exclusion, London School of Economics). HM Treasury (2004) *The Barker Review of Housing Supply*. Available at: http://www.hm-treasury.gov.uk/consultations_and_legislation/barker/consult_barker_index.cfm.

HM Treasury (2006) *The Stern Review of the Economics of Climate Change*. Available at: http://www.hm-treasury.gov.uk/independent_reviews/stern_review_economics_climate_change/stern_review_report.cfm.

Hotz, V. and Scholz, J. (2002) 'The earned income tax credit', Mimeo. Available at: http://papers.ssrn.com/sol3/papers.cfm?abstract_id = 256085.

Hoxby, C. (2003a) 'School choice and school competition: Evidence from the United States', *Swedish Economic Policy Review*, 10: 11–67.

Hoxby, C. (2003b) *The Economics of School Choice* (Chicago, Ill.: University of Chicago Press).

Johnson, P. and Reed, H. (1996) 'Intergenerational mobility among the rich and poor: Results from the National Child Development Survey', *Oxford Review of Economic Policy*, 12 (1): 127–42.

Jones, A. (ed.) (2006) *The Elgar Companion to Health Economics* (Aldershot: Edward Elgar).

Kahneman, D. and Tversky, A. (eds) (2000) *Choices, Values, and Frames* (Cambridge: Cambridge University Press).

Kane, T. and Staiger, D. (2002) 'The promise and pitfalls of using imprecise school accountability measures', *Journal of Economic Perspectives*, 16 (4): 91–114.

Katz, L., Kling, J. and J. Liebman (2001) 'Moving to opportunity in Boston: Early results of a randomized mobility experiment', *Quarterly Journal of Economics*, 116 (2): 607–54.

Kelly, G. and Lissauer, R. (2000) *Ownership for All* (London: Institute for Public Policy Research).

Ladd, H. (2002) 'School vouchers: A critical view', *Journal of Economic Perspectives*, 16 (4): 3–24.

Ladd, H. (2003) 'Comment on Caroline Hoxby: School choice and competition: evidence from the United States', *Swedish Economic Policy Review*, 10: 67–76.

Landes, W. and Posner, R. (1974) 'The private enforcement of law', *Journal of Legal Studies*, 4: 1–46.

Leape, J. (2006) 'The London Congestion Charge', *Journal of Economic Perspectives*, 20 (4): 157–76.

Le Grand, J. (1999) 'Conceptions of social justice', in R. Walker (ed.), *Ending Child Poverty: Popular Welfare for the 21st Century* (Bristol: Policy Press).

Le Grand, J. (2006) *Motivation, Agency and Public Policy: Of Knights and Knaves, Pawns and Queens*, Revd paperback edn (Oxford: Oxford University Press).

Le Grand, J. (2007) *The Other Invisible Hand: Delivering Public Services through Choice and Competition* (Oxford: Princeton University Press).

Le Grand, J. and Bartlett, W. (1993) *Quasi-Markets and Social Policy* (London: Macmillan).

Levitt, S. (2004) 'Understanding why crime fell in the 1990s: Four factors that explain the decline and six that do not', *Journal of Economic Perspectives*, 18 (1): 163–90.

Lipsey, R. and Chrystal, A. (2003) *Economics* (Oxford: Oxford University Press).

Loewry, E. (1980) 'Cost should not be a factor in medical care', *New England Journal of Medicine*, 302: 697.

Lomberg, B. (2007) *Solutions for the World's Biggest Problems* (Cambridge: Cambridge University Press).

McKay, S. (2004) 'Poverty of preference: what do consensual deprivation indicators really measure?', *Fiscal Studies*, 25 (2): 201–24.

McPake, B., Kumaranayake, L. and Normand, C. (2002) *Health Economics – An International Perspective* (London: Routledge).

Machin, S. and Meghir, C. (2004) 'Crime and economic incentives', *Journal of Human Resources*, 39 (4): 958–79.

Machin, S. and Stevens, M. (2004) 'The assessment: Education', *Oxford Review of Economic Policy*, 20 (2): 157–72

Mackie, P. (2005) 'The London Congestion Charge: A tentative economic appraisal. A comment on the paper by Prud'homme and Bocajero', *Transport Policy*, 12 (3): 288–90.

Mankiw, N. G. (2007) *Principles of Economics*, 4th edn (Mason, Ohio: Thompson/South Western).

Marshall, M., Shekelle, P., Davies, H. and Smith, P. C. (2003) 'Public reporting on quality in the United States and the United Kingdom', *Health Affairs*, 22(3): 134–48.

Mueller, D. C. (2003) *Public Choice III*, 3rd edn (Cambridge: Cambridge University Press).

Murray, C. (1984) *Losing Ground: American Social Policy 1950–1980* (New York: Basic Books).

The MVA Consultancy, Institute for Transport Studies at Leeds University and the Transport Studies Unit at Oxford University (2003) 'Time savings: Research into the value of time', inR. Layard and S. Glaister (eds), *Cost–Benefit Analysis* (Cambridge: Cambridge University Press).

Newbery, D. (1990) 'Pricing and congestion: Economic principles relevant to pricing roads', *Oxford Review of Economic Policy*, 6 (2): 22–38; reprinted in R. Layard and S. Glaister (eds), *Cost–Benefit Analysis* (Cambridge: Cambridge University Press).

Nordaus, W. (2007) 'Critical assumptions in the Stern Review on climate change', *Science*, 317: 201–2.

Nordaus, W. (2008) 'The Stern Review on the economics of climate change', *Journal of Economic Literature*, forthcoming.

Nussbaum, M. (1999) *Sex and Social Justice* (Oxford: Oxford University Press).

OECD (2007a) *Health at a Glance* (Paris: Organisation for Economic Co-operation and Development).

OECD (2007b) *Education at a Glance*(Paris: Organisation for Economic Co-operation and Development).

Oliver, A. (2005) 'The English National Health Service: 1979–2005', *Health Economics*, 14: S75–S99.

O'Sullivan, A. and Gibb, K. (2002) *Housing Economics and Public Policy* (Oxford: Blackwell).

Oxley, M. (2004) *Economics, Planning and Housing* (Basingstoke: Palgrave Macmillan).

Pearce, D. (2003) 'The social cost of carbon and its policy implications', *Oxford Review of Economic Policy*, 19 (3): 362–84.

Portner, P. (1994) 'The contingent valuation debate: Why economists should care', *Journal of Economic Perspectives*, 8 (4): 3–17.

Plant, R. (1999) 'Social justice', in R. Walker (ed.), *Ending Child Poverty: Popular Welfare for the 21st Century* (Bristol: Policy Press).

Propper, C. and Wilson, D. (2003) 'The use and usefulness of performance measures in the public sector', *Oxford Review of Economic Policy*, 19 (2): 250–68.

Propper, C. and Wilson, D. (2006) 'The use of performance measures in health care systems', in A, Jones (ed.), *The Elgar Companion to Health Economics* (London: Edward Elgar).

Propper, C., Wilson, D. and Burgess, S. (forthcoming) 'Extending Choice in English Health Care: The implications of the economic evidence', *Journal of Social Policy*.

Prud'homme, R. and Bocajero, J. (2005) 'The London Congestion Charge: A tentative economic appraisal', *Transport Policy*, 12 (3): 279–87.

Royal Society (2002) 'Economic instruments for the reduction of carbon dioxide emissions', Royal Society Policy document 26/02. Available at: http://royalsociety.org/document.asp?tip = 1&id = 1385Sen, A. (1985) *Commodities and Capabilities* (Amsterdam: North-Holland).

Sen, A. (1999) *Development as Freedom* (Oxford: Oxford University Press).

Smeeding, T. (2006) 'Poor people in rich nations: The United States in comparative perspective', *Journal of Economic Perspectives*, 20 (1): 69–90.

Smith, P. (1995) 'On the unintended consequences of publishing performance data in the public sector', *International Journal of Public Administration*, 18, pp. 277–310.

Smith, S. (2006) 'The retirement-consumption puzzle and involuntary early retirement: Evidence from the British Household Panel Survey', *Economic Journal,* 116, C130–C148.

Stewart, M. (2004) 'The employment effects of the national minimum wage', *Economic Journal,* 114: C110–C116.

Stiglitz, Joseph (2000) *The Economics of the Public Sector,* 3rd edn (New York/London: W. W. Norton).

Thaler, R. and Benartzi, S. (2004) 'Save more tomorrow: Using behavioural economics to increase employee saving', *Journal of Political Economy,* 112: S164–S187.

Thaler, R. and Benartzi, S. (2007) 'Heuristics and biases in retirement savings behaviour', *Journal of Economic Perspectives,* 21 (3): 81–104.

Titmuss, R. (1970) *The Gift Relationship* (London: Allen & Unwin).

Townsend, P. (1979) *Poverty in the United Kingdom* (Harmondsworth: Penguin). (London: Transport for London) (not referred to)Walker, R. (1999) *Ending Child Poverty: Popular Welfare for the 21st Century* (Bristol: Policy Press)

Whiteford, P. and Whitehouse, E. (2007) 'Pension challenges and pension reforms in OECD countries', *Oxford Review of Economic Policy,* 22 (1): 78–94.

Whitehead, C. (2002) 'The economics of social housing', in T. O'Sullivan and K. Gibb (eds), *Real Estate Issues – Housing Economics and Public Policy* (Oxford: Blackwell Science).

Whitehead, C. and Scanlon, K. (2007) *Social Housing in Europe* (London: London School of Economics).

Willitts, M. (2006) 'Measuring child poverty using material deprivation: Possible approaches', Department for Work and Pensions Research Report No. 28, Department of Work and Pensions, London. Wilson, D., Burgess, S. and Propper, C. (2007) 'The impact of school choice in England: implications from the economic evidence', *Policy Studies,* 28 (2), pp.129–43.

Index